FUNDAMENTALS
OF
ENVIRONMENTAL
BIOTECHNOLOGY

FUNDAMENTALS OF ENVIRONMENTAL BIOTECHNOLOGY

Banwari Lal

CYBER TECH PUBLICATIONS
4264/3, Ansari Road, Daryaganj, New Delhi-110002
Ph.: 011-23244078, 011-43559448 Fax: 011-23280028
E-Mail: cyberpublicationsdelhi@yahoo.com
E.mail: cybertechpublications@g.mail.com
website: www.cybertechpublications.com

Fundamentals of Environmental Biotechnology
Banwari Lal

First Edition 2011

Published by G.S. Rawat
For Cyber Tech Publications
4264/3, Ansari Road, Daryaganj, New Delhi-110002
Ph.: 011-23244078, 011-43559448 Fax: 011-23280028
E-Mail: cyberpublicationsdelhi@yahoo.com
E.mail: cybertechpublications@g.mail.com
website: www.cybertechpublications.com

Printed at: Asian Offset Printers, Delhi-53

CONTENTS

Preface

Biological degradation of recent biomass and of organic chemicals during solid waste or wastewater treatment proceeds either in the presence of molecular oxygen by respiration, under anoxic conditions by denitrification, or under anaerobic conditions by methanogenesis or sulfidogenesis. Respiration of soluble organic compounds or of extracellularly solubilized biopolymers such as carbohydrates, proteins, fats, or lipids in activated sludge systems leads to the formation of carbon dioxide, water, and a significant amount of surplus sludge. Some ammonia and H_2S may be formed during degradation of sulfur-containing amino acids or heterocyclic compounds. Oxygen must either be supplied by aeration or by injection of pure oxygen. The two process variant for oxygen supply differ mainly in their capacity for oxygen transfer and the stripping efficiency for carbon dioxide from respiration. Stripping of carbon dioxide is necessary to prevent a drop in pH and to remove heat energy. Respiration in the denitrification process with chemically bound oxygen supplied in the form of nitrate or nitrite abundantly yields dinitrogen. However, some nitrate escapes the reduction to dinitrogen in wastewater treatment plants and contributes about 2% of the total N_2O emissions in Germany (Schön et al., 1994).

Denitrifiers are aerobic organisms that switch their respiratory metabolism to the utilization of nitrate or nitrite as terminal electron acceptors, if grown under anoxic conditions. Only if the nitrate in the bulk mass has been used completely does the redox potential become low enough for growth of strictly anaerobic organisms, such as methanogens or sulfate reducers. If anaerobic zones are allowed to form in sludge flocs of an activated sludge system, e.g., by limitation of the oxygen supply, methanogens and sulfate reducers may develop in the center of sludge flocs and form traces of methane and hydrogen sulfide, found in the off-gas.

Under strictly anaerobic conditions, soluble carbon compounds of wastes and wastewater are degraded stepwise to methane, CO_2, NH_3, and H_2S via a syntrophic interaction of fermentative and acetogenic bacteria with methanogens or sulfate reducers. The complete methanogenic degradation of biopolymers or monomers via hydrolysis/fermentation, acetogenesis, and methanogenesis can proceed only at a low H_2 partial pressure, which is maintained mainly by interspecies hydrogen transfer.

Interspecies hydrogen transfer is facilitated when acetogens and hydrogenolytic methanogenic bacteria are arranged in proximity in flocs or in a biofilm within short diffusion distances. The reducing equivalents for carbon dioxide reduction to methane or sulfate reduction to sulfide are derived from the fermentative metabolism, e.g., of clostridia or *Eubacterium* sp., from â oxidation of fatty acids, or the oxidation of alcohols. Methane and CO_2 are the main products in anaerobic environments where sulfate is absent, but sulfide and CO_2 are the main products if sulfate is present.

– Author

1

Bacterial Metabolism in Wastewater Treatment Systems

INTRODUCTION

Water that has been used by people and is disposed into a receiving water body with altered physical and/or chemical parameters is defined as wastewater. If only the physical parameters of the water were changed, e.g., resulting in an elevated temperature after use as a coolant, treatment before final disposal into a surface water may require only cooling close to its initial temperature. If the water, however, has been contaminated with soluble or insoluble organic or inorganic material, a combination of mechanical, chemical, and/or biological purification procedures may be required to protect the environment from periodic or permanent pollution or damage. For this reason, legislation in industrialized and in many developing countries has reinforced environmental laws that regulate the maximum allowed residual concentrations of carbon, nitrogen, and phosphorous compounds in purified waste-water, before it is disposed into a river or into any other receiving water body However, enforcement of these laws is not always very strict. Enforcement seems to be related to the economy of the country and thus differs significantly between wealthy industrialized and poor developing countries. In this chapter basic processes for biological treatment of waste or wastewater to eliminate organic and inorganic pollutants are summarized.

DECOMPOSITION OF ORGANIC CARBON COMPOUNDS IN NATURAL AND MANMADE ECOSYSTEMS

Catabolic processes of microorganisms, algae, yeasts, and lower fungi are the main pathways for total or at least partial mineralization/decomposition of bioorganic and organic compounds in natural or manmade environments. Most of this material is derived directly or indirectly from recent plant or animal biomass. It originates from carbon dioxide fixation via photosynthesis ('! plant biomass), from plants that served as animal feed ('! detritus, feces, urine, etc.), or from fossil fuels or biologically or geochemically transformed biomass ('! peat, coal, oil, natural gas). Even the carbon portion of some xenobiotics can be tracked back to a biological origin, i.e., if these substances were produced from oil, natural gas, or coal. Only because the mineralization of carbonaceous material from decaying plant and animal biomass in nature under anaerobic conditions with a shortage of water was incomplete, did the formation of fossil oil, natural gas, and coal deposits from biomass occur through biological and/or geochemical transformations. The fossil carbon of natural gas, coal, and oil enters the atmospheric CO_2 cycle again as soon as these compounds are incinerated as fuels or used for energy generation in industry or private households.

Biological degradation of recent biomass and of organic chemicals during solid waste or wastewater treatment proceeds either in the presence of molecular oxygen by respiration, under anoxic conditions by denitrification, or under anaerobic conditions by methanogenesis or sulfidogenesis. Respiration of soluble organic compounds or of extracellularly solubilized biopolymers such as carbohydrates, proteins, fats, or lipids in activated sludge systems leads to the formation of carbon dioxide, water, and a significant amount of surplus sludge. Some ammonia and H_2S may be formed during degradation of sulfur-containing amino acids or heterocyclic compounds. Oxygen must either be supplied by aeration or by injection of pure oxygen. The two process variant for oxygen supply differ mainly in their capacity for oxygen transfer and the stripping efficiency for carbon dioxide from respiration. Stripping of carbon dioxide is necessary to prevent a drop in pH and to remove heat energy. Respiration in the denitrification process with chemically bound oxygen supplied in the form of nitrate or nitrite abundantly yields dinitrogen. However, some nitrate escapes the reduction to dinitrogen in wastewater treatment plants and contributes about 2% of the total N_2O emissions in Germany (Schön et al., 1994). Denitrifiers are aerobic organisms that switch their respiratory metabolism to the utilization of nitrate or nitrite as terminal electron acceptors, if grown under anoxic conditions. Only if the nitrate in the bulk mass has been used completely does the redox potential become low enough for growth of strictly anaerobic organisms, such as methanogens or sulfate reducers. If anaerobic zones are allowed to form in sludge flocs of an activated sludge system, e.g., by limitation of the oxygen supply, methanogens and sulfate reducers may develop in the center of sludge flocs and form traces of methane and hydrogen sulfide, found in the off-gas.

Under strictly anaerobic conditions, soluble carbon compounds of wastes and wastewater are degraded stepwise to methane, CO_2, NH_3, and H_2S via a syntrophic interaction of fermentative and acetogenic bacteria with methanogens or sulfate reducers. The complete methanogenic degradation of biopolymers or monomers via hydrolysis/fermentation, acetogenesis, and methanogenesis can proceed only at a low H_2 partial pressure, which is maintained mainly by interspecies hydrogen transfer. Interspecies hydrogen transfer is facilitated when acetogens and hydrogenolytic methanogenic bacteria are arranged in proximity in flocs or in a biofilm within short diffusion distances. The reducing equivalents for carbon dioxide reduction to methane or sulfate reduction to sulfide are derived from the fermentative metabolism, e.g., of clostridia or *Eubacterium* sp., from â oxidation of fatty acids, or the oxidation of alcohols. Methane and CO_2 are the main products in anaerobic environments where sulfate is absent, but sulfide and CO_2 are the main products if sulfate is present.

BASIC BIOLOGY, MASS, AND ENERGY BALANCE OF AEROBIC BIOPOLYMER DEGRADATION

To make soluble and insoluble biopolymers – mainly carbohydrates, proteins, and lipids – accessible for respiration by bacteria, the macromolecules must be hydrolyzed by exoenzymes, which often are produced and excreted only after contact with respective inductors. The exoenzymes adsorb to the biopolymers and hydrolyze them to monomers or at least to oligomers. Only soluble, low molecular weight compounds (e.g., sugars, disaccharides, amino acids, oligopeptides, glycerol, fatty acids) can be taken up by microorganisms and be metabolized for energy production and cell multiplication.

Once taken up, degradation via glycolysis (sugars, disaccharides, glycerol), hydrolysis and deamination (amino acids, oligopeptides), or hydrolysis and â oxidation (phospholipids, long-chain fatty acids) proceeds in the cells. Metabolism of almost all organic compounds leads to the formation of acetyl-CoA as the central intermediate, which is used for biosyntheses, excreted as acetate, or oxidized to CO_2 and reducing equivalents in the tricarboxylic acid (TCA) cycle. The reducing equivalents are respired with molecular oxygen in the respiration chain. The energy of a maximum of only 2 mol of anhydridic phosphate bonds of ATP is conserved during gly-colysis of 1 mol of glucose through substrate chain phosphorylation. An additional 2 mol of ATP are formed during oxidation of 2 mol of acetate in the TCA cycle, whereas 34 mol ATP are formed by electron transport chain phosphorylation with oxygen as the terminal electron acceptor. During oxygen respiration, reducing equivalents react with molecular oxygen in a controlled combustion reaction.

When carbohydrates are respired by aerobic bacteria, about one third of the initial energy content is lost as heat, and two thirds are conserved biochemically in 38 phosphoanhydride bonds of ATP. In activated sludge reactors or in wastewater treatment ponds that are not loaded with highly concentrated wastewater, wall irradiation and heat losses with the off-gas stream of aeration into the atmosphere prevent self-heating. In activated sludge reactors for treatment of highly concentrated wastewater, however, self-heating up to thermophilic temperatures may occur if the wastewater is warm in the beginning, the hydraulic retention time for biological treatment is short (short aeration time), and the air or oxygen stream for aeration is restricted so as to supply just sufficient oxygen for complete oxidation of the pollutants (small aeration volume).

The conserved energy in the terminal phosphoanhydride bond of ATP, formed during substrate chain and oxidative phosphorylation by proliferating bacteria is partially used for maintenance metabolism and partially for cell multiplication. Partitioning between both is not constant, but depends on the nutritional state. In highly loaded activated sludge reactors with a surplus or at least a non-growth-limiting substrate supply, approximately 50% of the substrate is respired in the energy metabolism of the cells and 50% serves as a carbon source for cell growth (Table 1.1). The biochemically conserved energy must be dissipated to be used for the maintenance metabolism of existing cells and cell growth.

If the substrate supply is growth-limiting, e.g., in a low-loaded aerobic treatment system, a higher proportion of ATP is consumed for maintenance, representing the energy proportion that bacteria must spend for non-growth–associated cell survival metabolism, and less energy is available for growth. Overall, more of the substrate carbon is respired, and the ratio of respiration products to surplus sludge formed is higher, e.g., around 70% : 30% (Table 1.1). In a trickling filter system, an even higher proportion of the substrate seems to be respired. This might be due to protozoa grazing off part of the biofilm.

For comparison, Table 1.1 also summarizes carbon dissipation in anaerobic me-thanogenic degradation. Only about 5% of the fermentable substrate is used for cell growth (surplus sludge formation) in anaerobic reactors, whereas 95% is converted to methane and CO_2, and most of the energy of the substrates is conserved in the fermentation products.

MASS AND ENERGY BALANCE FOR AEROBIC GLUCOSE RESPIRATION AND SEWAGE SLUDGE STABILIZATION

In most textbooks of microbiology, respiration of organic matter is explained by Eq. 1, with glucose used as a model substance. Except for an exact reaction stoichi-ometry of the oxidative metabolism, mass and energy dissipation, if mentioned at all, are not quantified. Both parameters are, however, very important for activated sludge treatment plants. The surplus sludge formed during wastewater stabilization requires further treatment, causes disposal costs, and – in the long run – may be an environmental risk, and heat evolution during unevenly high-loaded aerobic treatment may shift the population toward more thermotolerant or thermophilic species and thus, at least for some time, may decrease the process efficiency.

1 mol $C_6H_{12}O_6$ + 6 mol O_2 '! 6 mol CO_2 + 6 mol H_2O + heat energy (1)

Table 1.1 Carbon flow during (A) aerobic degradation in an activated sludge system under (a) saturating and (b) limiting substrate supply[a] and during (B) anaerobic degradation.

(A) Aerobic degradation:

(a) Saturating substrate supply = high-load conditions

1 unit substrate carbon '! 0.5 units CO_2 carbon + 0.5 units cell carbon

(b) Limiting substrate supply = low-load conditions

1 unit substrate carbon '! 0.7 units CO_2 carbon + 0.3 units cell carbon

(B) Anaerobic degradation:

1 unit substrate carbon '! 0.95 units (CO_2 + CH_4) carbon + 0.05 units cell carbon

[a] Estimated from surplus sludge formation in different wastewater treatment plants.

If 1 mol of glucose (MW=180 g) is degraded in an activated sludge system at a high BOD loading rate (e.g., >0.6 kg m^{-3} d^{-1} BOD), approximately 0.5 mol (90 g) is respired to CO_2 and water, with consumption of 3 mol of O_2 (96 g), releasing 19 mol of ATP (Fig. 1.1). The other 0.5 mol of glucose (90 g) is converted to pyruvate by one of three glycolytic pathways, accompanied by the formation of 0.5–1 mol ATP. Pyru-vate or its subsequent metabolic products, e.g., acetate or dicarboxylic acids, are directly used as carbon substrates for cell multiplication and surplus biomass formation. A maximum amount of 20 mol ATP is thus available for growth and maintenance (Fig. 1.1). At a pH of 7, about 44 kJ of energy is available for growth per mol of ATP hydrolyzed to ADP and inorganic phosphate (Thauer et al., 1977). For an average molar growth yield of aerobes of 4.75 g per mol ATP (Lui, 1998), 90 g biomass can be generated from 180 g glucose. If the combustion energy per g of cell dry mass is 22 kJ, about 890 kJ (2870–980 kJ) is lost as heat during respiration (Fig. 1.1). The energy loss is the sum of heat losses during respiration and cell growth.

At a low BOD loadir~ rate, the proportion of glucose respired in relation to the proportion of glucose fixed as surplus biomass can shift. Up to 0.7 mol (126 g) of glucose can be oxidized to CO_2, requiring 4.2 mol of oxygen (134.4 g O_2). Thus, for respiration of 1 mol of glucose, different amounts of oxygen may be consumed, depending on the loading rate of the wastewater treatment system and the different amounts of carbon dioxide and of surplus sludge formed (Fig. 1.1, Table 1.1).

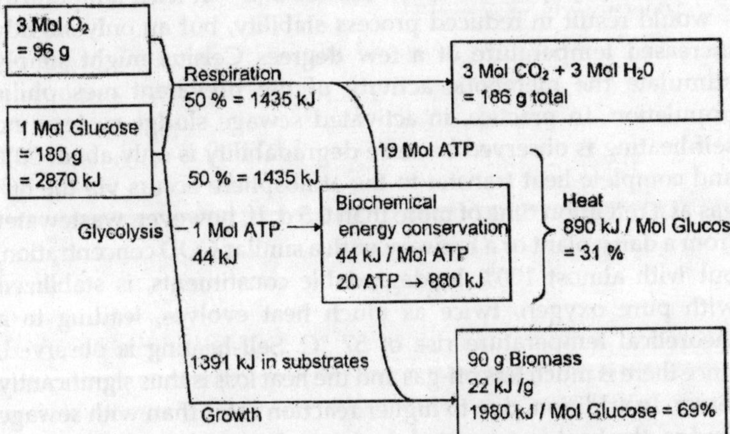

Fig. 1.1 Mass and energy dissipation during glucose respiration at pH 7.

The energy and carbon balance deduced above can be analogously applied to aerobic stabilization of raw sewage sludge. If the initial dry matter content is around 36g L^{-1} (average organic dry matter content of sewage sludge) and if a biodegradability of 50% within the residence time in the sludge reactor is obtained, about 9 g L^{-1} of new biomass is formed, and thus 27 g L^{-1} (36 - 18 + 9) remains in the effluent.

The released heat energy is approximately 89 kJ L^{-1} of reactor content. To estimate the theoretical temperature rise, this amount of heat energy must be divided by 4.185 kJ (specific energy requirement for heating 1 L of H_2O from 14.5–15.5 °C). Thus, by respiration of 18 g L^{-1} organic dry matter, the reactor temperature increases by 21.3°C within the residence time required for degradation (d"16 h), provided that no heat energy is lost. A great proportion of the heat energy is, however, transferred via the liquid phase to the aeration gas and stripped out, whereas a smaller proportion is lost through irradiation from the reactor walls. Since air, containing almost 80% nitrogen, is normally used as an oxygen source in aeration ponds or activated sludge reactors, the heat transfer capacity of the off-gas is high enough to prevent a significant increase in the wastewater temperature. Thus, ambient or at least mesophilic temperatures can be maintained. An increasing temperature of several degrees Celsius would lead to a shift in the population in the reactor and – at least temporarily – would result in reduced process stability, but an only slightly increased temperature of a few degrees Celsius might simply stimulate the metabolic activity of the prevalent mesophilic population. In practice, in activated sewage sludge systems no self-heating is observed because degradability is only about 50% and complete heat transfer to the atmosphere occurs via the off-gas at a retention time of more than 0.5 d. If, however, wastewater from a dairy plant or a brewery with a similar COD concentration, but with almost 100% biodegradable constituents, is stabilized with pure oxygen, twice as much heat evolves, leading to a theoretical temperature rise of 57 °C. Self-heating is observed, since there is much less off-gas and the heat loss is thus significantly lower. In addition, due to higher reaction rates than with sewage sludge, the heat is generated during a shorter time span (shorter retention time).

MASS AND ENERGY BALANCE FOR ANAEROBIC GLUCOSE DEGRADATION AND SEWAGE SLUDGE STABILIZATION

For anaerobic wastewater or sludge treatment, oxygen must be excluded to maintain the low redox potential that is required for survival and metabolic activity of the acet-ogenic, sulfidogenic, and methanogenic populations. Hydrolysis of polymers, uptake of soluble or solubilized carbon sources, and the primary metabolic reactions of glycolysis up to pyruvate and acetate formation seem to proceed identically or at least analogously in aerobic and anaerobic bacteria. Whereas aerobes oxidize acetate in the TCA cycle and respire the reducing equivalents with oxygen, anaerobes, such as *Ruminococcus* sp., *Clostridium* sp., or *Eubacterium* sp., either release molecular hydrogen or transform pyruvate or acetate to highly reduced metabolites, such as lac-tate, succinate, ethanol, propionate, or *n*-butyrate. For further degradation within the anaerobic food chain, these reduced metabolites must be oxidized anaerobically by acetogenic bacteria. Since the anaerobic oxidation of propionate or *n*-butyrate by acetogenic bacteria is obligately accompanied by hydrogen production but is only slightly exergonic under conditions of a low H_2 partial pressure (Bryant, 1979), acetogens can grow only when hydrogen is consumed by hydrogen-scavenging organisms such as methanogens or sulfate reducers.

During anaerobic degradation of 1 mol glucose, approximately 95% of the glucose carbon is used for biogas formation (171 g = 127.7 L CH_4 + CO_2), and only about 5% of the substrate carbon (9 g) converted to biomass (Table 1.1). Much less heat energy is released during anaerobic metabolism than during aerobic respiration (131 kJ mol^{-1} versus 890 kJ mol^{-1}, respectively), and the biogas contains almost 90% of the energy of the fermented substrate (Fig. 1.2). Due to the heat energy requirement to warm the wastewater and due to heat losses via irradiation from pipes and reactor walls, heat generation is not nearly sufficient to maintain a constant mesophilic fermentation temperature. For this reason, anaerobic digesters must be heated.

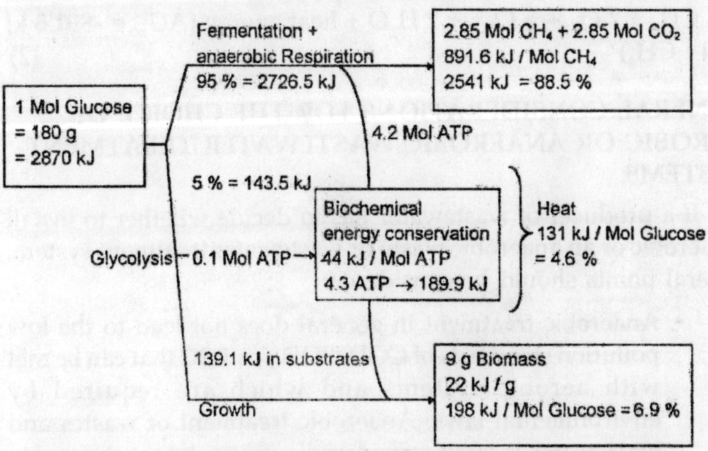

Fig. 1.2 ***Mass and energy dissipation during anaerobic glucose fermentation at pH 7.***

In sewage sludge with 36 g L^{-1} organic dry matter content and 50% biodegradabil-ity, 0.9 g surplus sludge and 17.1 g biogas (equivalent to 12.75 L) are formed during anaerobic stabilization. Only 13.1 kJ of heat energy per mol of glucose is released, leading to a self-heating potential of 3.1 °C. Since the heat energy is released only during the hydraulic residence time of the wastewater in the reactor, which is usually more than 10 d (except for high-rate industrial wastewater treatment, where in special situations the HRT may be shorter than one day), much more heat energy is lost by irradiation via the reactor walls than is required to maintain the temperature. If highly concentrated wastewater streams of the food and beverage industry are stabilized anaerobically at hydraulic retention times of <1 d (high space loading), more heat energy is generated within a much shorter time. But even then, process energy from external sources has to be supplied to maintain a temperature of 30–37 °C. Proper insulation of anaerobic reactors can minimize but not replace external heating of the reactor. The methane in the biogas, generated during anaerobic sludge or wastewater stabilization processes, contains about 90% of the energy of the fermented substrate. Since methane is a climate-relevant gas it may not be emitted into the atmosphere but must be combusted to CO_2. Methane from anaerobic reac-

tors can be used as a fuel for gas engines to generate electricity and/or heat energy (Eq. 2):

$$CH_4 + 2\,O_2 \rightarrow CO_2 + 2\,H_2O + \text{heat energy } (\ddot{A}G^{o\prime} = -891.6 \text{ kJ mol}^{-1}\ CH_4) \quad (2)$$

GENERAL CONSIDERATIONS FOR THE CHOICE OF AEROBIC OR ANAEROBIC WASTEWATER TREATMENT SYSTEMS

If a producer of wastewater has to decide whether to install an aerobic or an anaerobic waste or wastewater treatment system, several points should be considered:

- Anaerobic treatment in general does not lead to the low pollution standards of COD, BOD_5, or TOC that can be met with aerobic systems and which are required by environmental laws. Anaerobic treatment of wastes and wastewater is often considered a pretreatment process to minimize the oxygen demand and surplus sludge formation in a subsequent aerobic post-treatment stage. Only after a final aerobic treatment can the COD, BOD_5, or TOC concentration limits stated in the environmental laws be met. If limiting concentrations for nitrogen and phosphate also have to be achieved, further treatment steps such as nitrification, denit-rification, and biological or chemical phosphate removal, must be considered.
- Highly concentrated wastewater should in general be treated anaerobically, because of the possibility of energy recovery in biogas and the much lower amounts of surplus sludge to be disposed of. For aerobic treatment, a high aeration rate is necessary and much surplus sludge is

generated. Aeration causes aerosol formation and eventually requires off-gas purification.

- The efficiency of COD degradation for the bulk mass in concentrated wastewater or sludges (degradability of organic pollutants) generally seems to be about similar in aerobic or anaerobic bacteria. However, the degradation rates may be faster in aerobic treatment procedures than in anaerobic treatment procedures.
- Wastewater with a low concentration of organic pollutants should be treated aero-bically due to its higher process stability at low pollutant concentrations, although aerobic treatment is more expensive and more sludge remains for disposal. If mineralized sludge is required, aerobic treatment at a low loading or at prolonged hydraulic retention times is necessary to reinforce respiration of all endogenous reserve material.
- Anaerobic treatment systems are more expensive to construct but less expensive to operate than aerobic treatment systems.

AEROBIC OR ANAEROBIC HYDROLYSIS OF BIOPOLYMERS: KINETIC ASPECTS

Hydrolysis of biopolymers and fermentation or respiration of monomers can be catalyzed by strictly anaerobic, facultative anaerobic, and aerobic microorganisms. With some exceptions (e.g., small protein molecules, dextran), biopolymers are insoluble and form fibers (cellulose), grains (starch) or globules (casein after enzymatic precipitation) or can be melted or emulsified (fat). Henze et al. (1997) reported hydrolysis constants k_h for dissolved organic polymers of 3–20 d^{-1} under aerobic conditions and of 2–20 d^{-1} under anaerobic conditions, whereas for suspended solids the hydrolysis constants k_h were 0.6 to 1.4 d^{-1} under aerobic conditions and 0.3 to 0.7 d^{-1} under anaerobic conditions. For a kinetic description of hydrolysis and fermentation, a substrate-limited first-order reaction was assumed by Buchauer (1997), who deduced that the temperature-dependent reaction rate for hydrolysis is a little lower than the reaction rate for fermentation of the hydrolysis products. The rate-limiting step is therefore hydrolysis of particles and not fermentation of solubilized material (Buchauer, 1997).

Since hydrolysis is catalyzed not only by freely soluble exoenzymes, diluted in the bulk mass of liquid, but to a much higher extent by enzymes that are excreted in the neighborhood of bacterial colonies growing attached to the surface of the particles, the above description of complex fermentation processes is not always valid. Cellulases can be arranged in cellulosomes, which attach to the particles, which in turn serve as carriers until they themselves are solubilized. For this reason, Vavilin et al. (1997) included biomass in their description of the hydrolysis of cellulose, cattle manure, and sludge. Shin and Song (1995) determined the maximum rates of acidification and methanation for several substrates. For hydrolysis of particulate organic matter, the ratio of surface area to particle size is important. They found that for glucose, starch, carboxymethyl cellulose, casein, and food residues from a restaurant, hydrolysis proceeded faster than methanogenesis, whereas for newspaper and leaves hydrolysis was the rate-limiting step.

HYDROLYSIS OF CELLULOSE BY AEROBIC AND ANAEROBIC MICROORGANISMS: BIOLOGICAL ASPECTS

Cellulose and lignin are the main structural compounds of plants. Both substances are the most abundant biopolymers on earth. Cellulose fibers are formed of linear chains of 100–1400 glucose units linked together by â-1,4-glycosidic bonds. Inter-and intramolecular hydrogen bonds and van der Waals interactions arrange the highly organized fibrous regions (crystalline region), which alternate with less organized amorphous regions in the cellulose fibers.

The fibers are embedded in a matrix of hemicelluloses, pectin, or lignin. The hemicelluloses consist mainly of xylans or glucomannans, which have sidechains of acetyl, gluconuryl, or arabinofuranosyl units. To make cellulose fibers accessible to microorganisms, the hemicellulose, pectin, or lignin matrix must be degraded microbiologically or solubilized chemically. Cellulose degradation in the presence of oxygen in soil or in the absence of oxygen in the rumen of ruminants, in swamps, or in anaerobic digesters is the most important step in mineralization of decaying plant material. Cellulolytic organisms are found among aerobic soil fungi, e.g., within the genera *Trichoderma* and *Phanaerochaete* and in anaerobic rumen fungi, e.g. *Neocallimastix* and *Piromyces*, and among bacteria, e.g., within the genera *Cellulomonas*, *Pseudomonas*, and *Thermomonospora* (aerobic cellulose degraders) and *Clostridium*, *Fibrobacter*, *Bacteroides*, and *Ruminococcus* (anaerobic cellulose degraders). For more details on cellulolytic bacteria and the mechanism of cellulose cleavage, please see Coughlan and Mayer (1991).

Glycosyl hydrolases are involved in cellulose and hemicellulose degradation by cleaving glycosidic bonds between different carbohydrates and between carbohydrates and noncarbohydrates. Endo- and exocellulases - in some organisms organized in cellulosomes - must be excreted into the medium. Cellulases are complex biocatalysts and contain a catalytic site and a substrate-binding site.

The presence of a noncatalytic substrate binding site permits tight attachment to the different forms of cellulose substrate and keeps the enzyme close to its cleaving sites. Substrate binding is reversible, which allows the enzyme to 'hike' along the fibers and obtain total solubilization. Many aerobic fungi and some bacteria excrete endoglucanases that hydrolyze the amorphous region of cellulose (degradation within the chain), whereas exoglucanases hydrolyze cellulose from the ends of the glucose chains. Cellobiose is cleaved off by cellobiohydrolases from the nonreducing ends in the amorphous region, and finally the crystalline region is also hydrolyzed.

Cleavage of cellobiose to glucose units by â-glucosidases is necessary to prevent cellobiose accumulation, which inhibits cellobiohydrolases (Be'guin and Aubert, 1994).

Anaerobic bacteria such as *Clostridium thermocellum* form a stable enzyme complex, the cellulosome, at the cell surface (Lamed and Bayer, 1988). Cellulosomes are active in degrading crystalline cellulose. The catalytic subunits of a cellulosome, en-doglucanases and xylanases, cleave the cellulose fiber into fragments, which are simultaneously degraded further by â-glucosidases. Cellulosome-like proteins are found also in *Ruminococcus* sp. and *Fibrobacter* sp. cultures. The cell-bound enzymes are associated with the capsule or the outer membrane. Other specific adhesions or ligand formations with the cellulose can be facilitated by fimbrial connections, glycosylated epitopes of carbohydrate binding proteins, or the glycocalyx and carbohydrate binding modules (Krause et al., 2003). Some bacteria have not developed a mechanism to adhere to cellulose fibers, but excrete cellulases into the medium. Adsorption of bacteria onto cellulose fibers via cellulosomes offers the advantage of close contact with the substrate, which is hydrolyzed mainly to glucose, which is then taken up and metabolized. Small amounts of cellobiose must be present initially to induce cellulase expression. The contact of bacteria with the solid substrate surface keeps them close to cellobiose and thus keeps cellulase activities high. However, accumulation of hydrolysis products such as glucose repress cellulase activity.

In nature most cellulose is degraded aerobically. Only about 5%–10% is thought to be degraded anaerobically, which may be an underestimate. Since most ecosystems are rich in carbonaceous substances but deficient in nitrogen compounds, many cellulolytic bacteria can also fix dinitrogen. This is advantageous to them and to syntrophic or symbiotic organisms (Leschine, 1995). Other examples of mutual interactions between organisms of an ecosystem are interspecies hydrogen transfer between anaerobes (anaerobic food chain), transfer of growth factors (mycorhizzae, Kefir), and production of fermentable substrates for the partner organisms (bacterial interactions in the rumen).

Hydrolysis of biological structural components such as cellulose, lignin, and other structural or storage polymers (Table 1.2) is difficult. The limiting step of hydrolysis seems to be liberation of the cleavage products. In contrast to the slow hydrolysis of celluloses, mainly due to lignin encrustation of naturally occurring celluloses, starch can be easily hydrolyzed. The branching and helical structure of starch facilitates hydrolysis (Warren, 1996). Whereas cellulose forms fibers with a large surface covered with lignin, starch forms grains with an unfavorable surface-to-volume ratio for enzymatic cleavage. Thus, although amylases may be present in high concentrations, the hydrolysis rate is limited by the limited access of the enzymes to the substrate.

Whereas celiulose and starch are biodegradable, other carbohydrate-derived cellular compounds are not biodegradable and – after reaction with proteins – form humic acid-like residues by the Maillard reaction.

Table 1.2 Polysaccharides and derivatives occurring in nature.

Compound	Bond	Unit	Occurrence
Cellulose	â-1,4-	glucose	plant cell wall
Chitin	â-1,4-	*N*-acetyl glucosamine	fungal cell and insect wall exoskeleton
Murein	â-1,4-	*N*-acetyl-glucosamine *N*-acetyl-muramic acid	bacterial cell wall
Chitosan	â-1,4-	*N*-glucosamine, substituted with acetyl residues	fungal and insect materials
Mannans	â-1,4-	mannose	plant material
Xylans	â-1,4-	xylopyranose, substituted with acetyl-arabinofuranoside residues	plant material
Starch	a-1,4-	glucose	storage material in plant
		amylose (contains few a-1,6-branches)	
		amylopectin (contains many a-1,6-branches)	
Glycogen	a-1,4-	highly branched a-1,6 bonds	glucose with storage material in bacteria
Dextran	a-1,2-	glucose	storage material in yeasts
	a-1,3-	glucose	exopolymer of bacteria
	a-1,4-	glucose	
	a-1,6-	glucose	
Laminarin	â-1,3-	glucose	reserve material in algae

Biomass Degradation in the Presence of Inorganic Electron Acceptors and by an Anaerobic Food Chain

In ecosystems in which molecular oxygen is available, plant and animal biomass is degraded to CO_2 and H_2O, catalyzed by either single species of aerobic microorganisms or the whole population of the ecosystem, in competition for the substrates. A single organism may be able to hydrolyze the polymers and oxidize the monomers to CO_2 and H_2O with oxygen. In ecosystems where molecular oxygen is deficient - such as swamps, wet soil, the rumen of animals, the digestive tract of humans, or in river and lake sediments - oxidation of dead biomass proceeds anoxically by reduction of electron acceptors such as nitrate and nitrite or anaerobically by reduction of sulfate, Fe^{3+}, Mn^{4+}, or CO_2. The oxidation of the carbon source is either complete or incomplete with acetate excretion. In the absence of inorganic electron acceptors, oxidized metabolites such as pyruvate or acetate are reduced to lactate or ethanol or biotransformed to, e.g., *n*-butyrate or *n*-butanol. In permanently anaerobic ecosystems with seasonal overfeeding, periodic accumulation of such metabolites can occur, e.g., in autumn after the non-evergreen plants drop their leaves or decay completely. The biopolymers of the leaves or the plants themselves decompose by extracellular enzymatic hydrolysis. The monomers are fermented, and the fermentation products may be degraded further to biogas by acetogenic and methanogenic bacteria. Whereas single cultures of aerobes can catalyze the whole mineralization process to finally form CO_2 and H_2O, single cultures of strictly anaerobic bacteria are not capable of degrading biopolymers to CH_4 and CO_2. Under anaerobic conditions biopolymers must be degraded by a food chain via depolymerization (hydrolysis), fermentation (acidogenesis), oxidation of fatty acids (acetogenesis), and biogas formation (methanogenesis) as the last step (McInerney, 1988). In an initial exoen-zyme-catalyzed reaction the biopolymers are hydrolyzed to soluble mono-, di-, or ol-igomers. These are taken up by the bacteria and fermented to CO_2, H_2, formate, acetate, propionate, butyrate, lactate, etc. If fatty acid isomers are produced, they are mainly derived from degradation of amino acids after proteolysis. Fatty acids are further oxidized by acetogenic bacteria, before the cleavage products CO_2, H_2, and acetate can be taken up by methanogens and be converted to methane and CO_2. Lac-tate is oxidized to pyruvate, which is decarboxylated to yield acetate, CO_2, and H_2. If ethanol is present, it is oxidized to acetate and hydrogen, and the hydrogen is used for CO_2 reduction.

Table 1.3 summarizes the reactions that can be catalyzed by methanogens and that can contribute to methane emission in various ecosystems. In sewage digesters about two thirds of the methane is derived from acetate cleavage and one third from CO_2 reduction with H_2. If hexoses are the substrates and glycolysis is the main degradation pathway, then the 2 mol of pyruvate can be decarboxylated by pyruvate: fer-redoxin oxidoreductase to yield 2 mol acetate and 2 mol CO_2. The hydrogens of the 2 mol $NADH_2$ from glycolysis and the 2 mol FdH_2 from pyruvate decarboxylation are then released as molecular hydrogen at low H_2 partial pressure (Eq. 3). Two moles of CH_4 are then formed from acetate and 1 mol of CH_4 by CO_2 reduction (reactions 1 and 2 of Table 1.3).

1 mol glucose '! 2 mol acetate + 2 mol CO_2 + 4 mol H_2 (at low pH_2) (3)

Table 1.3 Reactions catalyzed by methanogens and standard changes in free energy.

Reaction				**ÄG°' (kJ per mol of methane)**
Substrates (mol)			***Products (mol)***	
Acetate		->	$CH_4 + CO_2$	-31.0
$4\ H_2 + CO_2$		->	$CH_4 + 2\ H_2O$	-135.6
4 HCOOH		->	$CH_4 + 3\ CO_2 + 2$	-130.1
4 CO + 2		->	$CH_4 + 3\ CO_2$	-211.0
4 Methanol		->	$3\ CH_4 + CO_2 + 2$	-104.9
Methanol +		->	$CH_4 + H_2O$	-112.5
2 Ethanola +		->	CH_4 + 2 acetate	-116.3
4 2-	2	->	CH_4 + 4 acetone + 2	-36.5
4 Methylamine + 2		->	$3\ CH_4 + CO_2 + 4$	-75.0
2	2	->	$3\ CH_4 + CO_2 + 2$	-73.2
4	6	->	$9\ CH_4 + 3\ CO_2 + 4$	-74.3
2	2	->	$3\ CH_4 + CO_2 + 2$	-73.8
Dimethylsul fide +	H_2O		H_2S	

b Other primary alcohols that are used as hydrogen donors for CO_2 reduction are 1-propanol and 1-butanol (in a few species).

Other secondary alcohols used as hydrogen donors for CO_2 reduction are 2-butanol, 1,3-butanediol,

cyclopentanol, and cyclohexanol (in a few species).

Compiled from Whitman et al. (1992) and Winter (1984).

In complex ecosystems formate is formed if high concentrations of hydrogen accumulate. Syntrophic interactions are usually associated with interspecies hydrogen transfer, but evidence for interspecies formate transfer was also reported (Thiele et al., 1988). The feasibility of the electron carrier depends on its solubility, which is much less for hydrogen than for formate, and on its diffusion coefficient in water, which favors hydrogen 30 times over formate. The efficiency of the appropriate electron transfer depends mainly on the distance between the producing and consuming bacteria. It can be expected, that formate transfer is favored when the distance between communicating bacteria is high and hydrogen transfer when the distance is small (de Bok et al., 2004). Interspecies formate transfer is thought to play a major role in degradation of syntrophic butyrate (Boone et al., 1989) and propionate (Stams, 1994; Schink, 1997). However, at an increased H_2 partial pressure formate is also produced by methanogens, either in pure cultures or in a sewage sludge population (Bleicher and Winter, 1994), and this may also contribute to increasing formate concentrations. Other substrates for methanogenic bacteria (Table 1.3), such as methanol (derived, e.g., from methoxy groups of lignin monomers) or methylamines and dimethylsulfide (e.g., from methylsulfonopropionate in algae; Fritsche, 1998) are relevant only in ecosystems where these substances are produced during microbial decay. A few methanogens can also use reduced products such as primary, secondary, and cyclic alcohols as a source of electrons for CO_2 reduction (Widdel, 1986; Zellner and Winter, 1987a; Bleicher et al., 1989; Zellner et al., 1989).

ROLES OF MOLECULAR HYDROGEN AND ACETATE DURING ANAEROBIC BIOPOLYMER DEGRADATION

Molecular hydrogen is produced during different stages of anaerobic degradation. In the fermentative stage, organisms such as *Clostridium* sp. and *Eubacterium* sp. produce fatty acids, CO_2, and hydrogen from carbohydrates. In the acetogenic stage, acetogens such as *Syntrophobacter wolinii* and *Syntrophomonas wolfei* produce acetate, CO_2, and hydrogen or acetate and hydrogen by anaerobic oxidation of propion-ate and *n*-butyrate (McInerney, 1988). Fermentative bacteria release molecular hydrogen even at a high H_2 partial pressure and simultaneously excrete reduced products (e.g., clostridia, *Ruminococcus, Eubacterium* sp.). However, the release of molecular hydrogen during acetogenesis of fatty acids or of other reduced metabolites may occur only when hydrogen does not accumulate, for thermodynamic reasons. Molecular hydrogen is consumed by methanogens (Table 1.4, reaction 1) or, alternatively, by sulfate reducers (Table 1.4, reaction 2) via interspecies hydrogen transfer.

In the rumen and in sewage sludge digesters, the hydrogen concentration can be decreased by acetate formation from CO_2 and H_2 (Table 1.4, reaction 3) by bacteria such as *Acetobacterium woodii* and *Clostridium thermoaceticum.* Some additional reactions consuming hydrogen to decrease its concentration are also listed in Table 1.4 (reactions 4–6).

Table 1.4 Hydrogen-consuming reactions in anaerobic ecosystems (Schink, 1997).

Substrates (mol)				*Products (mol)*	ÄG°' (kJ per
(1) $4 H_2 + CO_2$			->	$CH_4 + 2 H_2O$	-131.0
(2) $4 H_2 + SO_4^{2}$			->	$S^{2-} + 4 H_2O$	-151.0
(3) $4 H_2 + 2$			->	$CH_3COO^- +$ 2 H_2O	-0.9
(4) H_2 + S0			->	H_2S	-0.9
(5)	+ H_2		->	$CH_3COO^- +$	0.0
(6) COOH-CH-CH-COOH		+ H_2	->	COOH-CH_2-CH_2-COOH	0.0

To maintain a low H_2 partial pressure, a syntrophism of acetogenic, hydrogen-producing and methanogenic, hydrogen-utilizing bacteria is essential (Ianotti et al., 1973). Complete anaerobic degradation of fatty acids with hydrogen formation by obligate proton-reducing acetogenic bacteria is possible only at H_2 partial pressures $<10^{-4}$ atm (*n*-butyrate) or 10^{-5} atm (propionate), which cannot be maintained by methanogens or sulfate reducers. However, by reversed electron transport electrons can be shifted to a lower redox potential suitable for proton reduction (Schink, 1997). If hydrogen accumulates beyond this threshold concentration, the anaerobic oxidation of fatty acids becomes endergonic and does not proceed (for details, see Chapter 8, this volume). Whereas hydrogen prevents â oxidation of fatty acids by ac-etogens even at very low H_2 partial pressure, much higher concentrations of acetate (in the millimolar range) are required for the same effect. The fermentative metabolism of acidogenic bacteria is exergonic even at H_2 partial pressures $>10^{-4}$ atm. Whereas acetogenic bacteria apparently depend mainly on ATP generation by chemiosmotic phosphorylation, fermentative bacteria produce most of their ATP by substrate chain phosphorylation. This may be why fermentative bacteria do not depend on a syntrophic interaction with electron-consuming bacteria, such as methanogens or sulfate reducers.

In addition to the possibility of anaerobic oxidation of organic compounds via syn-throphic interactions between acetogenic bacteria and acetoclastic + hydrogeno-trophic methanogens (see also Section 1.2.5), other synthrophic associations between acetate-oxidizing bacteria and H_2/CO_2-utilizing methanogens under thermophilic (Lee and Zinder 1988) and mesophilic (Schnuerer et al. 1996) growth conditions have been observed. Thermodynamic analysis of mesophilic synthrophic acetate oxidation revealed a hydrogen partial pressure of < 0.1–2.6 Pa, which is in the range found in methanogenic ecosystems (Dolfing, 2001). In thermophilic methan-ogenic reactors, acetate is degraded either by synthrophic acetate oxidizers (dominant process at low acetate concentrations) and acetate-degrading methanogens (acetate concentration above the threshold concentration) or by acetate-utilizing meth-anogens of the genera *Methanosaeta* or *Methanosarcina* (Ahring, 2003). Synthrophic acetate oxidation and methane formation from the cleavage products may explain the lack of acetoclastic methanogens (*Methanosarcina* sp. or *Methanosaeta* sp.) in anaerobic reactors.

ANAEROBIC CONVERSION OF BIOPOLYMERS TO METHANE AND CO_2

The principle of the anaerobic metabolism of biopolymers was outlined by the pioneering work of Wolin (1976) and Bryant (1979). There is an essential requirement for syntrophic interaction between different metabolic groups for complete anaerobic degradation (Wolin, 1976, 1982). The most sensitive switch of the carbon flow of substrates to biogas is the H_2 partial pressure. The substrate supply for biomethana-tion processes must be limited so that the most slowly growing group in the food chain, the obligate proton-reducing acetogens, can still excrete hydrogen at a maximum rate, but at the same time hydrogen accumulation $>10^{-5}$ atm is prevented by active methanogenesis or sulfate reduction (Bryant, 1979).

Whereas hydrogen seemed to be the most sensitive regulator of anaerobic degradation, formate (Bleich-er and Winter, 1994), acetate, or other fatty acids accumulated to much higher concentrations (McInerney, 1988) but did not repress anaerobic degradation. If hydrogen accumulated due to an oversupply or to inhibition of methanogens, anaerobic biodegradation was disturbed successively in different stages. Initially, in the aceto-genic stage â oxidation of fatty acids and alcohols failed, leading to an accumulation of these acid metabolites. Later, the spectrum of metabolites of the fermentative flora changed toward more reduced products like ethanol, lactate, propionate, and *n*-butyrate, leading to an even higher concentration of volatile fatty acids and a further decrease in pH. At pH values below 6.5, methanogenic reactions were almost completely prevented. At this stage acidification with a rich spectrum of reduced products still proceeded.

Anaerobic Degradation of Carbohydrates in Wastewater

Carbohydrates are homo- or heteropolymers of hexoses, pentoses, or sugar derivatives, which occur in soluble form or as particles, forming grains or fibers of various sizes. In some plants, starch forms grains up to 1 mm in diameter, which is 1000 times the diameter of bacteria. Starch metabolism by bacteria requires hydrolytic cleavage by amylases to form soluble monomers or dimers, since only soluble substrates can be taken up and metabolized.

The anaerobic degradation of biopolymers in general and of cellulose in particular can be divided into hydrolytic, fermentative, acetogenic, and methanogenic phases (Fig. 1.3). Hydrolysis and fermentation of the hydrolysis products can be catalyzed by the same trophic group of microorganisms. The distinction of the two phases is of more theoretical than practical relevance. Concerning reaction rates in a methane fermenter that is fed with a particulate substrate, the rate-limiting step is hydrolysis rather than the subsequent fermentation of the monomers, if acetogenesis and me-thanogenesis proceed faster. The hydrolysis rates of polymers can be very different. Hemicellulose and pectin are hydrolyzed ten times faster than lignin-encrusted cellulose (Buchholz et al., 1986, 1988). In the acidification reactor of a two-stage anaerobic process, hydrolysis of polymers to monomers is normally slower than fermentation of monomers to fatty acids and other fermentation products. For this reason, no sugar monomers can be detected during steady-state operation. In the methane reactor, â oxidation of fatty acids, especially of propionate or *n*-butyrate, is the rate-limiting step (Buchholz et al., 1986). Fatty acid degradation is the slowest reaction overall in a two-stage methane reactor fed with carbohydrate-containing wastewater from sugar production. Thus, the methane reactor has to be larger than the acidification reactor to permit longer hydraulic retention times.

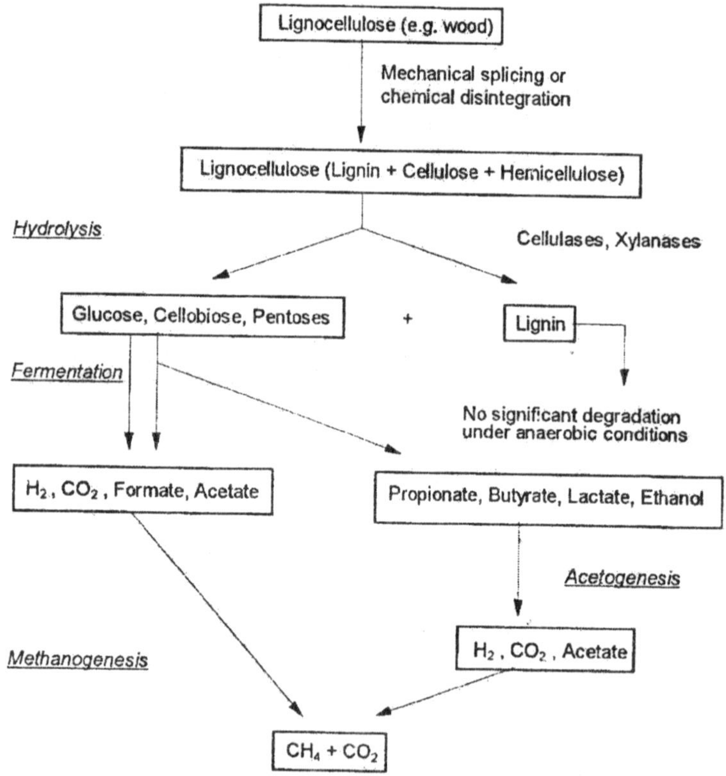

g. 1.3 *Anaerobic degradation of lignocellulose and cellulose to methane and CO_2 (according to ATV, 1994).*

The rate of cellulose degradation depends strongly on the state of the cellulose in the wastewater. If cellulose is lignin-encrusted, lignin prevents access of cellulases to the cellulose fibers. If cellulose is mainly in a crystalline form, cellulases can easily attach to it, and then hydrolysis can be a relatively fast process. At increasing loading in an anaerobic reactor fed with crystalline cellulose, acetogenesis became the rate-limiting process, leading to propionate and butyrate formation (Winter and Cooney, 1980). In decaying plant material, cellulose is very often lignin-encrusted. Due to the highly restricted access to these complexes by cellulases, hydrolysis of cellulose is the rate-limiting step in its degradation to methane and CO_2.

Whether microorganisms are capable of degrading lignin under anaerobic conditions is still under discussion. In a natural environment without time limitation, lig-nin was reported to be degraded anaerobically (Colberg and Young, 1985; Colberg, 1988). However, since these results were based on long-term experiments performed in situ and anaerobiosis was not controlled, it remains doubtful, whether the small amount of lignin that disappeared was really degraded under strictly anaerobic conditions. The occurrence of coal and fossil oil suggests that lignin compounds are highly resistant to microbial attack.

During anaerobic degradation of starch, hydrolysis by amylases proceeds with high velocity if good contact between starch grains and amylases is maintained. Whereas in an anaerobic reactor at low loading, starch degradation can proceed in the absence of acetogenic bacteria, as indicated in Figure 1.4 (route a), at high loading, volatile fatty acids are formed and acetogens are essential for total degradation (Fig. 1.4, route b). Figure 1.4 illustrates how the rate-limiting acetogenic reactions may be avoided by adjusting the conditions so that hydrolysis and fermentation occur no faster than methanogenesis. The rationale behind this is that many fermentative bacteria produce only acetate, formate, CO_2, and hydrogen when H_2-scaveng-ing methanogens or sulfate reducers are able to maintain a sufficiently low H_2 partial pressure, but a wide spectrum of fermentation products, typical for the metabolism of the respective bacterial species in pure culture, is produced at higher H_2 partial pressure (Winter, 1983, 1984). Methanogenesis in continuous syntrophic methanogenic cultures can be disturbed by spike concentrations of sugars or – at low concentrations of sugars – by the presence of inhibitory substances like NH_3, H_2S, antibiotics (Hammes et al., 1979; Hilpert et al., 1981), or xenobiotics. In consequence, the H_2 partial pressure increases and volatile fatty acids are generated (Winter, 1984; Winter et al., 1989; Wildenauer and Winter, 1985; Zellner and Winter, 1987b). Once propionate or *n*-butyrate are produced, anaerobic degradation requires acetogens for â oxidation (Fig. 1.4, route b).

Anaerobic Degradation of Protein

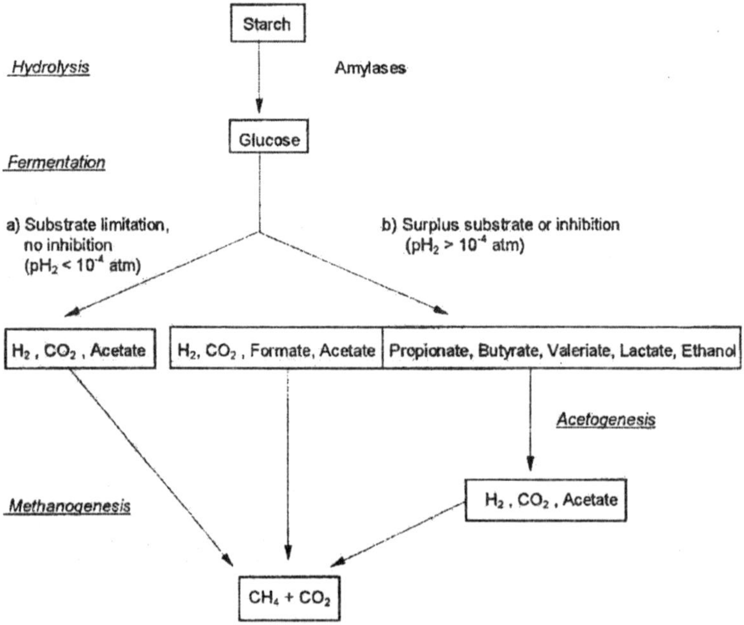

Fig. 1.4 Anaerobic degradation of starch under low- and high-loading conditions.

Proteins are biological macromolecules, either soluble or solid (e.g., feathers, hair, nails). Outside the cell at an acid pH or in the presence of enzymes, soluble proteins precipitate, e.g., precipitation of casein by addition of rennet enzyme. The reaction sequences necessary for protein degradation in a methanogenic ecosystem are outlined in Figure 1.5. Hydrolysis of precipitated or soluble protein is catalyzed by several types of proteases that cleave membrane-permeable amino acids, dipeptides, or oligopeptides. In contrast to the hydrolysis of carbohydrates, which proceeds favorably at a slightly acid pH, optimal hydrolysis of proteins requires a neutral or weakly alkaline pH (McInerney, 1988). In contrast to the fermentation of carbohydrates, which lowers the pH due to volatile fatty acid formation, fermentation of amino acids in wastewater reactors does not lead to a significant pH change, due to acid and ammonia formation. Acidification of protein-containing wastewater proceeds optimally at pH values of 7 or higher (Winterberg and Sahm, 1992), and ammonium ions together with the CO_2–bicarbonate–carbonate buffer system stabilize the pH.

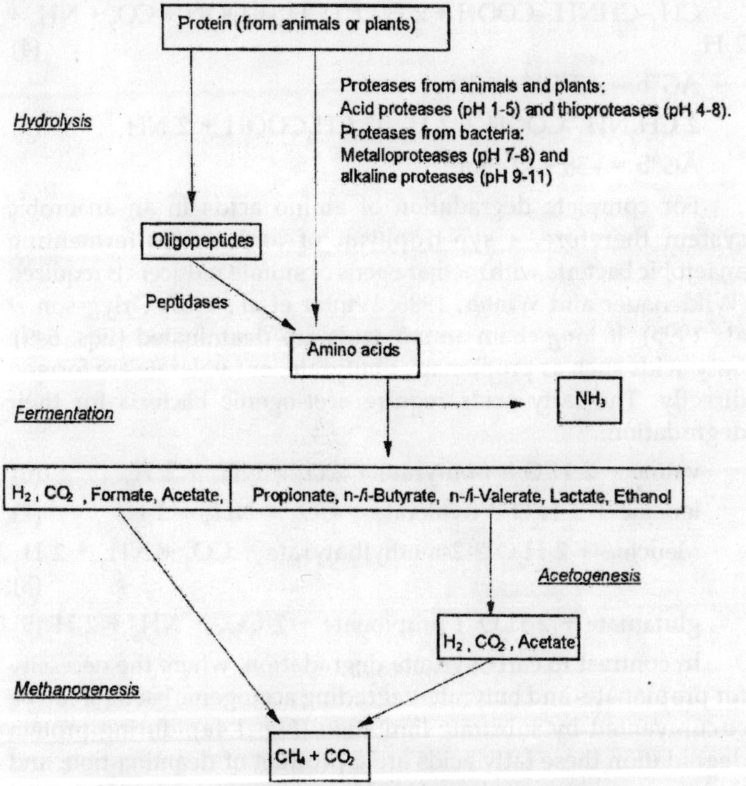

Fig. 1.5 Anaerobic degradation of proteins.

Acetogenesis of fatty acids from deamination of amino acids requires a low H_2 partial pressure for the same reasons as for carbohydrate degradation. This can be maintained by a syntrophic interaction of fermentative, protein-degrading bacteria and acetogenic and methanogenic or sulfate-reducing bacteria. Except for syntroph-ic interaction of amino acid-degrading bacteria with methanogens for maintenance of a low H_2 partial pressure, clostridia and presumably also some other sludge bacteria may couple oxidative and reductive amino acid conversion via the Stickland reaction. One amino acid, e.g., alanine (Eq. 4) is oxidatively decarboxylated and the hydrogen or reducing equivalents produced during this reaction are used to reductively convert another amino acid, e.g., glycine, to acetate and ammonia (Eq. 5).

CH_3-$CHNH_2$-COOH + 2 H_2O '! CH_3-COOH + CO_2 + NH_3 + 2 H_2 (4)

ÄG°b = +7.5 kJ mol^{-1}

2 CH_2NH_2-COOH + 2 H_2 '!2 CH_3COOH + 2 NH_3 (5)

ÄG°b = –38.9 kJ mol^{-1}

For complete degradation of amino acids in an anaerobic system therefore, a syn-trophism of amino acid-fermenting anaerobic bacteria with methanogens or sulfate reducers is required (Wildenauer and Winter, 1986; Winter et al., 1987; Örlygsson et al., 1995). If long-chain amino acids are deaminated (Eqs. 6–9), fatty acids such as propionate, *i*-butyrate, or *i*-valerate are formed directly. The fatty acids require acet-ogenic bacteria for their degradation.

valine + 2 H_2O '! *i*-butyrate + CO_2 + NH_3 + 2 H_2 (6)

leucine + 2 H_2O '! *i*-valerate + CO_2 + NH_3 + 2 H_2 (7)

i-leucine + 2 H_2O '! 2-methylbutyrate + CO_2 + NH_3 + 2 H_2 (8)

glutamate + 2 H_2O '! propionate + 2 CO_2 + NH_3 + 2 H_2 (9)

In contrast to carbohydrate degradation, where the necessity for propionate- and butyrate-degrading acetogenic bacteria can be circumvented by substrate limitation (Fig. 1.4a), during protein degradation these fatty acids are a product of deamina-tion, and their formation cannot be avoided by maintaining a low H_2 partial pressure. In the methanogenic phase there is no difference in methanogenic activity whether carbohydrates or proteins are fermented, except that the methanogens in a reactor fed with protein need to be more tolerant to ammonia and higher pH.

Anaerobic Degradation of Neutral Fats and Lipids

Fats and lipids are another group of biopolymers that contribute significantly to the COD in sewage sludge, cattle and swine manures, and wastewater from the food industry, e.g., slaughterhouses or potato chip factories (Winter et al., 1992; Broughton et al., 1998). To provide a maximum surface for hydrolytic cleavage by lipases or phospholipases, solid fats, lipids, or oils must be emulsified. Glycerol and saturated and unsaturated fatty acids (palmitic acid, linolic acid, linolenic acid, stearic acid, etc.) are formed from neutral fats. Lipolysis of phospholipids generates fatty acids, glycerol, alcohols (serine, ethanolamine, choline, inositol), and phosphate. Lipolysis of sphingolipids generates fatty acids and amino alcohols (e.g., sphingosine), and li-polysis of glycolipids generates fatty acids, amino alcohols, and hexoses (glucose, ga-lactose). A scheme for anaerobic degradation of fats is shown in Figure 1.6. Sugar moieties and glycerol can be degraded to methane and CO_2 by interaction between fermentative and methanogenic bacteria in low-loaded systems or by cooperation between fermentative, acetogenic, and methanogenic bacteria in high-loaded systems. The long-chain fatty acids are degraded by acetogenic bacteria by â oxidation to acetate and molecular hydrogen. If acetate and molecular hydrogen accumulate, the anaerobic digestion process is inhibited (Hanaki et al., 1981). Odd-numbered fatty acids are degraded to acetate, propionate, and hydrogen, and even-numbered fatty acids to acetate and hydrogen (Bryant, 1979). Only at a very low H_2 partial pressure, which can be maintained by hydrogen-utilizing methanogens or sulfate reducers, is â oxidation of at least *n*-butyrate or propionate exergonic. Meth-anol, ethanol, and ammonia are formed from choline (Fig. 1.6). After hydrolysis, fermentation, and acetogenesis of the fat components in the methanogenic phase acetate, CO_2, and hydrogen are converted to biogas. All subsequent intracellular reactions can be influenced by syntrophic interaction via interspecies hydrogen transfer, except for the extracellular initial lipase reaction.

Carbohydrates, proteins, fats, and biogenic oils can also be degraded anaerobical-ly under thermophilic conditions. The overall degradation scheme is the same, but the microorganism populations are different (e.g., Winter and Zellner, 1990). Ther-mophilic fat degradation is becoming more important in practice, since waste fat from fat separators and fat flotates of the food industry are often cofermented in agricultural biogas plants. Since, for hygienic reasons, the input material must be au-toclaved, a thermophilic process should be used, keeping the fat in a melted, soluble form for more effective metabolism. Biogas plants with cofermentation of waste fat residues are considered waste treatment systems

(Chapter 11, this volume) and must be designed to meet the hygienic demands relevant to treatment of the respective waste.

COMPETITION OF SULFATE REDUCERS WITH METHANOGENS IN METHANE REACTORS

Municipal wastewater or wastewater from sugar production, slaughterhouses, breweries, etc., normally contains less than 200 mg L^{-1} of sulfate. If sulfuric acid is used, e.g., to clean stainless steel containers and pipes in the dairy industry or to maintain an acid pH in bioreactors for bakers' yeast or citric acid production, or if ammonium sulfate is used to inhibit metabolic routes in bakers' yeast for the production of biochemicals, the wastewater contains large amounts of sulfate. Sulfite-containing wastewater is also generated by the starch and cellulose industry during bleaching of the raw products.

If these wastewaters are subjected to anaerobic treatment, the methanogenic bacteria must compete with sulfate reducers for the hydrogen equivalents from COD degradation (Omil et al., 1998). In anaerobic digesters sulfate reduction is the favored reaction, due to the higher affinity of sulfate reducers for reducing equivalents or hydrogen, leading to sulfide production at the expense of reduced biogas formation. Sulfide subsequently forms heavy metal precipitates and, if still present in larger amounts, remains in solution and may be toxic to acetogens and methanogens. Some hydrogen sulfide leaves the reactor with the biogas, which may contain up to a few percent of H_2S. Then gas purification is necessary before the gas can be used as fuel for gas engines. Hydrogen sulfide in biogas causes not only odor problems but also corrosion of fermenters and pipes. Methanogenesis of dissolved and partic-ulate organic material in sulfate-rich wastewater is possible, if acidogenesis and sul-fate reduction (stripping of H_2S together with CO_2) is separated from methanogen-esis in a phased or a staged process (Lens et al., 2002). The higher affinity of sulfate reducers than methanogens for reducing equivalents can also be used for sulfate and heavy metal ion removal from wastewater in the first stage of a two-stage anaerobic process (Elferink et al., 1994).

In comparison to methanogens, which have a rather restricted substrate spectrum (Table 1.3), sulfate reducers are metabolically more versatile. Sulfate reducers can utilize polymers such as starch, monomers such as sugars, fatty acids, formate, aliphatic and aromatic compounds, as well as molecular hydrogen (Widdel, 1988) to generate reducing equivalents for sulfate reduction (Eq. 10):

$$8\ (H) + 2\ H^+ + SO_4^{2-}\ '!H_2S + 4\ H_2O \qquad (10)$$

Undissociated hydrogen sulfide is toxic to both methanogens and sulfate reducers. A 50% inhibition of methanogenesis was observed at a total sulfide concentration of 270 mg L^{-1} (Oleszkiewicz et al., 1989), whereas 85 mg L^{-1} sulfide inhibited sulfate reducers (McCartney and Oleszkiewicz, 1991). For stable methanogenesis, no more than 150 mg L^{-1} sulfide should be accumulated (Speece et al., 1986). H_2S toxicity can be avoided by intensive flushing with biogas to strip the H_2S for adsorption onto $Fe_2(OH)_3$. If large amounts of H_2S are formed during anaerobic treatment, essential heavy metal ions for methanogens (Fe, Ni, Mo, Co, etc.) may be precipitated as sulfides, which may lead to deficiencies in heavy metal bioavailability for the wastewater population.

The metabolites of the fermentative and acetogenic phase of anaerobic wastewa-ter treatment systems, mainly acetate and CO_2 + H_2, are substrates for methano-gens and for sulfate reducers. If wastewater with a high sulfate concentration is treated in a methane reactor, the population may gradually shift from hydrogeno-trophic methanogens toward hydrogenotrophic sulfate reducers, due to a more favorable K_s value for hydrogen of the sulfate reducers. For pure cultures of *Desulfo-vibrio* sp. the K_s value for hydrogen is 1 ìM, but for hydrogenotrophic methanogens it is only 6 ìM (Kristjansson et al., 1982). For acetate, such a dramatic disadvantage of methanogens was not observed. The affinities of sulfate reducers and of methan-ogenic bacteria (valid at least for *Methanosaeta* sp.) for hydrogen are in the same range, 0.2–0.4 ìM (Elferink et al., 1994).

AMOUNT AND COMPOSITION OF BIOGAS DURING FERMENTATION OF CARBOHYDRATES, PROTEINS, AND FATS

From an economic point of view, the specific biogas amounts and the biogas quality from anaerobic treatment of wastewater and sludge are important process parameters. Therefore, a basis for prediction of amount and composition of biogas was elaborated as early as the 1930s (Buswell and Neave, 1930; Buswell and Sollo

1948; Buswell and Mueller, 1952). If the elemental composition of a wastewater is known, the theoretical amount and composition of the biogas can be predicted with the Bus-well equation (Eq. 11). The actual biogas amount is lower and can be calculated by including a correction factor for the degree of degradability, the pH (which influences CO_2 absorption), and a 5%–10% discount for biomass formation.

$C_cH_hO_oN_nS_s + 1/4(4c-h-2o+3n+2s)H_2O$ '! $1/8(4c-h+2o+3n+2s)CO_2$ (11) $+ 1/8\,(4c + h - 2o - 3n - 2s)CH_4 + nNH_3 + sH_2S$

According to the Buswell equation (Eq. 11), for the anaerobic treatment of a wastewater with carbohydrates as pollutants, the gas composition should theoretically be 50% methane and 50% CO_2 (Eq. 12):

1 mol $C_6H_{12}O_6$ '! 3 mol CH_4 + 3 mol CO_2 (12)

Since CO_2 is increasingly soluble in water with decreasing temperature and increasing pH, CO_2 reacts to form bicarbonate/ carbonate, and the biogas may contain more than 80% methane. The total amount of gas is then diminished by the amount of CO_2 that is absorbed and solubilized in the liquid. From a fat- and protein-containing wastewater, theoretically more than 50% methane can be generated (Table 1.5).

NITROGEN REMOVAL DURING WASTEWATER TREATMENT

Nitrogen-containing substances in wastewater are inorganic or organic. Together with phosphates, they represent the main source for eutrophication of surface water. For this reason they must be eliminated together with the organic carbon during wastewater treatment. Whereas phosphates form insoluble precipitates with many heavy metal ions and the precipitates can be separated by sedimentation or flotation, all nitrogen compounds, except for magnesium ammonium phosphate, are easily soluble in water and thus cannot be removed chemically by precipitation. For biological removal of amino nitrogen and of heterocyclic nitrogen compounds, their conversion to ammonia in an aerobic or anaerobic treatment process is the first step. Then ammonia must be nitrified, and the nitrate denitrified to yield nitrogen. Thus, depending on the kind of nitrogen compounds present in wastewater, nitrogen removal requires up to three processes in sequence: ammonification, nitrification, and denitrification.

The major portion of nitrogen compounds in municipal wastewater are reduced nitrogen compounds such as ammonia, urea, amines, amino acids, and proteins. Oxidized nitrogen compounds such as nitrate and nitrite normally are not present at all or not in relevant amounts. Nitrate and nitrite may, however, represent the main nitrogen load in wastewater of certain food or metal industry branches (Gen-sicke et al., 1998; Zayed and Winter, 1998).

***Table 1.5** Amount of biogas, biogas composition, and energy content.*

Substrate	*Amount*	*Compositio*		*Energy*
	(cm³ g⁷j	*% CH_4*	*% co₂*	ffcVCdxra *)*
Carbohydr atose	746.7	50	50	4.95
Fats[b]	1434	71	29	7.02
Proteins[c]	636	60	40	5.93

Calculated for hexoses.

Calculated for triglycerides containing glycerol plus 3 mol palmitic acid. Calculated for polyalanine and reaction of ammonia to $(NH_4)_2CO_3$. at standard conditions

The ammonia in raw municipal wastewater is mainly derived from urine and is formed in the sewer system by enzymatic cleavage of urea by ureases (Eq. 13):

$$NH_2CONH_2 + H_2O \rightarrow CO_2 + 2NH_3 \quad (13)$$

The residence time of the wastewater in the sewer system normally is not long enough for a significant contribution of ammonia from other sources, e.g., proteo-lysis and deamination of amino acids.

AMMONIFICATION

The main organic nitrogen compounds in municipal wastewater are heterocyclic compounds (e.g., nucleic acids) and proteins. Proteolysis and degradation of amino acids leads to liberation of ammonia by the various mechanisms of ammonification (Rheinheimer et al., 1988), including hydrolytic, oxidative, reductive, and desatura-tive deamination (Eqs. 14–17, respectively)

$$R\text{-}NH_2 + H_2O \text{ '! } R\text{-}OH + NH_3 \quad (14)$$

$$R\text{-}CHNH_2COOH + H_2O \text{ '! } R\text{-}CO\text{-}COOH + 2\ (H) + NH_3 \quad (15)$$

$$R\text{-}CHNH_2\text{-}COOH + 2\ (H) \text{ '! } R\text{-}CH_2\text{-}COOH + NH_3 \quad (16)$$

$$R\text{-}CH_2\text{-}CHNH_2\text{-}COOH \text{ '! } R\text{-}CH{=}CH\text{-}COOH + NH_3 \quad (17)$$

A significant amount of ammonia from urea cleavage or from ammonification of amino acids is assimilated in aerobic treatment processes for growth of bacteria (surplus sludge formation). It can be estimated that bacteria consist of roughly 50% protein and that the nitrogen content of protein is about 16%. Thus, for synthesis of 1 g of bacterial biomass, about 0.08 g of ammonia-N is required. To eliminate ammonia that is not used for cell growth during wastewater treatment, it must first be nitrified and then denitrified to molecular nitrogen or anaerobically oxidized with nitrite.

NITRIFICATION OF AMMONIA

Autotrophic Nitrification

Autotrophic nitrifiers are aerobic microorganisms oxidizing ammonia via nitrite (Eq. 18) to nitrate (Eq. 19). Organisms catalyzing nitrification (Eq. 18) belong to the genera *Nitrosomonas, Nitrosococcus, Nitrosolobus, Nitrosospira,* and *Nitrosovibrio,* organisms catalyzing nitration (Eq. 19) include, e.g., members of the genera *Nitrobact-er, Nitrococcus,* and *Nitrospira.*

$$NH_4^+ + 1.5\ O_2 \text{ '! } NO_2^- + 2\ H^+ + H_2O \quad (18)$$

$$NO_2^- + 0.5\ O_2 \text{ '! } NO_3^- \quad (19)$$

Ammonia oxidation to nitrite or nitrite oxidation to nitrate are energy-yielding processes for the autotrophic growth of the nitrifying bacteria. CO_2 is assimilated via the Calvin cycle. Since the positive redox potential of the oxidizable nitrogen compounds is not low enough to form $NADH_2$ for CO_2 reduction, $NADH_2$ must be formed by an energy-consuming reverse electron transport. For this reason, the growth yield of nitrifying bacteria is low. *Nitrosomonas* sp., e.g., must oxidize 30 g NH_3 to form 1 g of cell dry mass (Schlegel, 1992).

The oxidation of ammonia by nitrifiers is initiated by an energy-neutral monooxy-genase reaction that yields hydroxylamine (Eq. 20):

$NH_3 + XH_2 + O_2$ '! $NH_2OH + X + H_2O$ (20)

Then hydroxylamine is further oxidized, presumably via nitroxyl (Eq. 21) to nitrite (Eq. 22), which is the energy-yielding reaction during nitrification. For microbial oxidation of 1 mg NH_4^+-nitrogen to nitrite, 3.42 mg O_2 is required, and for the oxidation of 1 mg NO_2^--nitrogen to nitrate (Eq.. 19), 1.14 mg O_2.

$NH_2OH + X$ '! $XH_2 + (NOH)$ (21)

$(NOH) + 0.5\ O_2$ '! HNO_2 + energy (22)

Due to their slow growth autotrophic nitrifiers cannot successfully compete with heterotrophic bacteria for oxygen. In a highly loaded activated sludge system, the au-totrophic nitrifiers are overgrown by the heterotrophic sludge flora, which consume the oxygen. Ammonia oxidation starts only if the BOD_5 concentration in the waste-water is <110 mg L^{-1} (Wild et al., 1971). During nitrification of ammonia the alkalinity of the wastewater increases slightly, due to CO_2 consumption for autotrophic growth (pH increase), but in a counter reaction it drastically decreases due to nitric acid formation from ammonia (pH decrease from above neutral to acidic). If the buffer capacity of the wastewater is weak, the pH drops far below 7 and thus prevents further nitrification by autotrophic nitrifiers (Rheinheimer et al., 1988).

Heterotrophic Nitrification

Some bacteria of the genera *Arthrobacter*, *Flavobacterium*, and *Thiosphaera* are able to catalyze heterotrophic nitrification of nitrogen-containing organic substances (Eq. 23):

$R\text{-}NH_2$ '! R-NHOH '! R-NO '! NO_3^- (23)

Heterotrophic nitrifiers oxidize reduced nitrogen compounds, such as hydroxyla-mine and aliphatic and aromatic nitrogen-containing compounds, but in contrast to autotrophic nitrification, no energy is gained by nitrate formation. For this reason an organic substrate must be respired to satisfy the energy metabolism (Schlegel, 1992).

Some heterotrophic nitrifiers can denitrify nitrate or nitrite under aerobic growth conditions. The nitrogen metabolism of *Thiosphaera pantotropha* and *Paracoccus de-nitrificans* are well documented examples (Stouthamer et al., 1997). These organisms express a membrane-bound nitrate reductase under anoxic growth conditions, which works only in the absence of molecular oxygen. Under aerobic growth conditions a periplasmic nitrate reductase is expressed, which catalyzes nitrate reduction at least to the state of nitrous oxide.

DENITRIFICATION: NITRATE REMOVAL FROM WASTEWATER

Many aerobic bacteria seem to be able to switch their oxidative metabolism to nitrate respiration. Similar to oxygen respiration, the nitrate respiration of heterotrophic bacteria requires a complex carbon source as an electron source for denitrification (e.g., Eqs. 24 and 25). Denitrification (Eq. 26) starts with the reduction of nitrate to nitrite by membrane-bound nitrate reductase A (a). Then a membrane-bound nitrite reductase (b) catalyzes NO formation. Finally, NO reductase (c) and N_2O reductase (d) form N_2. The theoretical stoichiometry of denitrification with methanol or acetate as a carbon source is shown in Eqs. 27 and 28. For practical application a surplus of carbon source must be supplied, since the wastewater is not free of oxygen, and part of the carbon source is respired until anoxic conditions are achieved.

To evaluate the stoichiometry of nitrate to organic compounds for denitrification with a complex carbon source, the oxidation-reduction state of the carbon substrates and the oxygen concentration in the wastewater should be known. In waste-water treatment plants more than 2.85g COD is required for reduction of 1 g NO_3^- -N (Bernet et al., 1996).

$$CH_3OH + H_2O \rightarrow CO_2 + 6\ H^+ + 6\ e^- \qquad (24)$$

$$CH_3COOH + 2\ H_2O \rightarrow 2\ CO_2 + 8\ H^+ + 8\ e^- \qquad (25)$$

$$NO_3^- \xrightarrow{2e^-} NO_2^- \xrightarrow{e^-} NO \xrightarrow{e^-} 0.5\ N_2O \xrightarrow{e^-} 0.5\ N_2 \qquad (26)$$

a0 b0 c0 d0

$$5\ CH_3OH + 6\ HNO_3 \rightarrow 5\ CO_2 + 3\ N_2 + 13\ H_2O \qquad (27)$$

$$5\ CH_3\text{-}COOH + 8\ HNO_3 \rightarrow 10\ CO_2 + 4\ N_2 + 14\ H_2O \qquad (28)$$

Instead of nitrate, many denitrifying bacteria can use NO_2^-, NO, or N_2O as terminal electron acceptors. Alternatively, they may release these intermediates during denitrification of nitrate under unfavorable conditions, as was observed in soil (Conrad,

1996). If, e.g., surplus nitrate is supplied and hydrogen donors are not sufficiently available, NO and N_2O can be formed (Schön et al., 1994). Another condition for N_2O formation is a pH below 7.3, at which nitrogen oxidoreductase is inhibited (Knowles, 1982).

Except for dissimilatory nitrate reduction, many aerobic and anaerobic bacteria are capable of assimilatory nitrate reduction to supply the cells with ammonia for growth (Eqs. 29 and 30). However, the enzymes for nitrate assimilation are expressed only at concentrations of ammonia <1 mM.

$$NO_3^- \xrightarrow[a]{2e^-} NO_2^- \xrightarrow[b]{2e^-} HNO \xrightarrow[b]{2e^-} NH_2OH \xrightarrow[b]{2e^-} NH_3 \qquad (29)$$

$$HNO_3 + 8\,(H) \rightarrow NH_4^+OH^- + 2\,H_2O \qquad (30)$$

Here, nitrate reductase B (enzyme *a* in Eq. 29) reduces nitrate to nitrite, which is then reduced to ammonia by the nitrite reductase complex (enzyme b in Eq. 29). Whereas nitrate reduction by the oxygen-sensitive, membrane-bound enzyme nitrate reductase A conserves energy, no energy conservation is possible in the reaction catalyzed by the soluble enzyme nitrate reductase B, which is not repressed by oxygen. For details on the cell biology and the molecular basis of denitrification, please refer to Zumft (1997).

COMBINED NITRIFICATION AND DENITRIFICATION

A strict separation of the reactions participating in aerobic, autotrophic nitrification and in anoxic, heterotrophic denitrification is not required, as concluded from N^{15}-tracer experiments (Kuenen and Robertson, 1994). Autotrophic ammonia oxidizers seem to be able to produce NO, N_2O, or N_2 from nitrite if oxygen is limited, and ammonia as well as nitrite oxidizers can be isolated from anaerobic reactors (Kuenen and Robertson, 1994). *Nitrosomonas europaea* can use nitrite as an electron acceptor and pyruvate as an energy source under anoxic, denitrifying growth conditions (Ab-eliovich and Vonshak, 1992). In addition, several strains of *Nitrobacter* sp. were reported to denitrify during anoxic, heterotrophic growth (Bock et al., 1986).

Aerobic denitrification by *Thiosphaera pantotropha* was first described by Robertson and Kuenen (1984). *T. pantotropha* respires molecular oxygen and denitrifies nitrate simultaneously, provided that suitable electron acceptors are available. The conversion rate of acetate as electron donor with nitrate as electron acceptor was twice as high when the concentration of molecular oxygen was <30% of air saturation compared to 30%–80% air saturation (Robertson et al., 1988). Respiration, simultaneous nitrification, and denitrification were observed in the presence of oxygen and ammonia. During heterotrophic denitrification by *T. pantotropha*, ammonia is first oxidized to hydroxylamine by an ammonia monooxygenase, with ubiqui-none serving as electron donor. Hydroxylamine is subsequently oxidized to nitrite by a hydroxylamine oxidoreductase. During coupled nitrification–denitrification, 3 of the 4 electrons from the oxidation of hydroxylamine are used for reduction of nitrite to nitrogen and are not available to the electron transport reaction catalyzed by cytochrome oxidase. Regeneration of ubiquinone is mediated by electrons that are generated during oxidation of an organic substrate (heterotrophic nitrification).

Conversion rates of ammonia by heterotrophic nitrifiers such as *T. pantotropha* (Kuenen and Robertson, 1994) are smaller than those of autotrophic nitrifiers (35.4 for *T. pantotropha* versus 130–1550 nmol NH_3 min^{-1} mg^{-1} dry weight for *Nitrosomo-nas* sp.). If, however, the higher population density of heterotrophic nitrifiers, resulting from higher growth rates, is taken into consideration, the specific conversion rates are in a similar range. Heterotrophic nitrifiers can, in addition to their nitrifying capability, denitrify nitrite or nitrate to molecular nitrogen. In many waste-water treatment plants autotrophic nitrifiers may exist, producing nitrite from ammonia under moderately aerobic conditions; the ammonia is then converted to nitrate and/or reduced to nitrogen by heterotrophic nitrifiers in the presence of a suitable carbon source. In practice, the only disadvantage of heterotrophic nitrification is more surplus sludge generation for final disposal.

ANAEROBIC AMMONIA OXIDATION (ANAMMOX®)

To date, two anaerobic ammonia-oxidizing bacteria species have been isolated and preliminarily classified in the order Planctomycetales as candidatus *Brocardia anammoxidans* and candidatus *Kuenenia stuttgartiensis*. Under anaerobic conditions ammonia is oxidized to nitrite in membrane-bound intracytoplasmic anammoxo-soms (Schmidt et al., 2003).

In the Anammox process ammonia is oxidized to nitrogen, with nitrite serving as electron acceptor (Van de Graaf et al., 1995).

Use of N^{15} isotopes indicated that nitrite is reduced to hydroxylamine (Eq. 31), which then reacts with ammonia to yield hydrazine (N_2H_4, Eq. 32). By oxidation of hydrazine to molecular nitrogen (Eq. 33), four reducing equivalents are generated, which are required for nitrite reduction to hydroxylamine (Van de Graaf et al., 1997).

$2\ HNO_2 + 4\ XH_2$ '!$2\ NH_2OH + 2\ H_2O + 4\ X$ (31)

$2\ NH_2OH + 2\ NH_3$ '!$2\ N_2H_4 + 2\ H_2O$ (32)

$2\ N_2H_4 + 4\ X$ '! $2\ N_2 + 4\ XH_2$ (33)

Since the redox state is balanced in the above reactions, reducing equivalents for CO_2 reduction by the autotrophic microorganisms must be generated by oxidation of nitrite to nitrate (Eq. 34):

$HNO_2 + H_2O + NAD$ '! $HNO_3 + NADH_2$ (34)

Per mol of ammonia, 0.2 mol nitrate is generated and 20 mg biomass is produced (Van de Graaf et al., 1996). The Anammox process seems to be suitable for nitrogen removal in ammonia-rich effluents of anaerobic reactors that are fed with wastewa-ter rich in TKN compounds. Nitrogenous compounds can be eliminated from this wastewater by a combination of nitrification for nitrite supply and anaerobic ammonia oxidation (Strous et al., 1997). The process is sensitive to high, toxic nitrite concentrations of 70–180 mg N L^{-1} (depending on the kind of biomass). Furthermore, due to the low growth rate of the anammox bacteria, a startup time of 100–150 days with activated sludge as inoculum seems to be necessary (Schmidt et al., 2003).

In oxygen-limited environments (e.g. oxic–anoxic interfaces of biofilms or sludge flocs) aerobic and anaerobic ammonia oxidizers are natural partners. The ammonia is oxidized to nitrite and concomitantly the oxygen level is decreased. The anammox bacteria disproportionate the nitrite and the remaining ammonia to N_2. When ammonia is limited, the affinities of aerobic and anaerobic ammonia oxidizers may lead the natural partners to change to competitors (Schmidt et al., 2002). Other examples of 'uncontrolled' anammox activities were observed in different wastewater treatment plants with uncharacterized high ammonium losses.

NEW N-REMOVAL PROCESSES

The metabolic versatility of nitrogen-converting bacteria offers new concepts for nitrogen removal processes to treat wastewater. A *partial* nitrification of ammonia to nitrite (nitritation) would have the advantage of saving a significant amount of oxygen for the nitrification process, as compared to nitratation of ammonia. However, nitrite is toxic and must be kept below toxic concentrations. In a subsequent denit-rification process, fewer reducing equivalents from the degradation of different carbon sources, which often are a limiting factor in wastewater treatment plants, are then required.

In the SHARON process, which is a single reactor system for rapid ammonia oxidation to nitrite and subsequent denitrification of the nitrite with methanol, nitrite oxidizers that would generate nitrate are outcompeted by the slowly metabilizing ammonia oxidizers after a temperature shift toward higher temperatures, due to the higher temperature tolerance of the ammonia oxidizers, and by no sludge retention or sludge return in the reactor (Hellinga et al., 1998). Aeration was switched off periodically and denitrification of nitrite was initiated by adding meth-anol as a carbon source. The SHARON process in full scale was used to treat sludge liquor at the Rotterdam wastewater treatment plant (Mulder et al., 2001). The partial nitrification of ammonia to nitrite led to an ammonia/nitrite ratio that was suitable for a subsequent Anammox process in which nitrite was denitrified to N_2 with ammonia instead of methanol as the electron donor. This process was finally established in full-scale at the Rotterdam wastewater treatment plant (Schmidt, 2003).

Partial ammonia oxidation to nitrite and anaerobic oxidation of ammonia in one aerated reactor is the concept behind the CANON process (completely autotrophic nitrogen removal over nitrite) (Van Lossdrecht and Jetten, 1997). Aerobic and anaerobic ammonia-oxidizing bacteria cooperate as long as the nitrifying bacteria consume oxygen and create anoxic conditions for the anaerobic ammonia-oxidizing bacteria.

Another possibility for removing ammonia in one single step without using an organic carbon source is the OLAND process (oxygen-limited nitrification and denit-rification) (Kuai and Verstraete, 1998). Conversion of ammonia to N_2 is catalyzed by aerobic nitrifiers and anaerobic granular sludge as a source of *Planctomycetes* including anaerobic ammonia-oxidizing bacteria (Pynaert et al., 2004).

Other nitrogen-removal processes also exist, such as the NO_x process (simultaneous nitrification and denitrification of *Nitrosomonas*-like microorganisms under fully oxic conditions) and aerobic deammonification (conversion of ammonia to N_2 and nitrate), which allow ammonia removal without COD. An overview of these new concepts was presented by Schmidt et al., 2003.

Enhanced Biological Phosphate Removal

Based on an early observation that microorganisms take up more phosphate than required for cell growth, it was found that single cells accumulate polyphosphate in granules containing a few to several thousand phosphate units (Egli and Zehnder, 1994). Phosphate constitutes up to 12% of the cell weight of polyphosphate-accumulating bacteria, whereas bacteria that do not accumulate polyphosphate contain only 1%–3% phosphate (van Loosdrecht et al., 1997b). The accumulated polyphosphate is assumed to be an energy source for substrate assimilation during anaerobic growth conditions and poly-p-hydroxyalkanoate (PHA) synthesis. Evidence suggests that degradation of polyphosphate may be used to regulate intracellular pH under alkaline conditions (Seviour et al., 2003). For biological phosphate removal by 'luxury phosphate uptake', the polyphosphate-accumulating bacteria in wastewater have to be subjected in sequence to an anaerobic and an aerobic environment. All previous attempts to isolate polyphosphate-accumulating bacteria (culture-dependent approach) led to recovery of *Acinetobacter* sp. which belongs to the y-Proteobacteria and is the model organism for explanation of the polyphosphate accumulation mechanism found in textbooks. However, pure cultures of the polyphosphate-accumulating *Acinetobacter* sp. and wastewater communities seem to behave differently (van Loosdrecht et al., 1997a). A major discrepancy is that *Acinetobacter* sp. do not play a dominant role in activated sludge systems, as deduced from a survey using specific gene probes (Wagner et al, 1994). The culture-independent approach led to a mixed population for enhanced biological phosphorous removal (EBPR). The phosphorous-removing members (>10% of the total population) were assigned to the p-Proteobacteria (Rhodocylus group e.g. candidatus *Accumulibacter phosphatis)*, a-Proteobacteria and Actinobacteria *(Microlunatus phosphoruvorus)* and to members of the Cytophaga-Flexibacter-Bacteroides division (Seviour et al, 2003).

In *Acinetobacter* sp. polyphosphate accumulation is closely interconnected with poly-p-hydroxybutyrate (PHB) and glycogen metabolism (van Loosdrecht et al, 1997b). Under anaerobic conditions in the absence of nitrate, acetate is taken up by *Acinetobacter* cells, metabolized to p-hydroxybutyrate, polymerized to PHB, and stored intracellularly in inclusion bodies. Reducing equivalents for PHB formation from acetate are made available by glycolysis of glucose units from stored glycogen or are alternatively formed by other microorganisms for EBPR in an anaerobically operating TCA cycle.

The energy for polymerization comes from hydrolysis of the anhydride bonds of ATP and polyphosphate. To supply both the maintenance metabolism and the storage metabolism of *Acinetobacter* with sufficient energy under anaerobic conditions, anhydride bonds in polyphosphate are hydrolyzed, and inorganic phosphate is excreted (phosphate resolubilization) (Smolders et al, 1994). Stored glycogen in microorganisms for EBPR may also provide ATP for PHA synthesis.

For storage of 1 mg fatty acids, about 0.6 mg orthophosphate is released (Danesh and Oleszkiewicz, 1997). Under aerobic conditions two situations may be prevalent. In wastewater that does not contain a suitable carbon source for respiration, *Acinetobacter* sp. hydrolyze PHB, which is stored in the granules, and respire the â-hydroxybutyrate to gain energy for growth, maintenance, formation of glyco-gen, and polymerization of phosphate, which is taken up from the wastewater. In the presence of oxygen much more P_i is taken up by *Acinetobacter* sp. from the activated sludge flora than is released under anaerobic conditions ('luxury uptake'). Danesh and Oleszkiewicz (1997) reported that approximately 6 to 9 mg volatile fatty acids are required for biological removal of 1 mg phosphorous.

In wastewater that contains suitable carbon sources for *Acinetobacter* sp., these carbon sources are partially oxidized by the TCA cycle and are partially used for PHB formation (Kuba et al., 1994). Since reducing equivalents are needed for PHB formation, less ATP is formed by oxidative phosphorylation. The lower ATP yield is compensated by the energy from hydrolysis of polyphosphate to P_i, which the cells use to form ADP from AMP. Two moles of ADP are disproportionated to AMP and ATP by adenylate kinase, and little P_i is released into the medium.

Except for obligately aerobic bacteria of the genus *Acinetobacter*, nitrate-reducing bacteria compete with microorganisms for EBPR for organic substrates, e.g., volatile fatty acids such as acetate. Nitrate-reducing bacteria also can eliminate phosphate from the aqueous environment (Kerrn-Jespersen and Henze, 1993). The simultaneous presence of obligately aerobic bacteria and nitrate-reducing bacteria in activated sludge may explain why, in the presence of nitrate in the anaerobic phosphate resolubilization phase (oxygen absent), P_i does not accumulate in the medium. The denitrifying, polyphosphate-accumulating bacteria apparently do not inhibit P_i excretion by *Acinetobacter*, but they take up phosphate and accumulate it as polyphosphate. This may explain why resolubilization of phosphate by degradation of stored polyphosphate is not always observed in wastewater treatment plants for biological phosphate removal. Another possibility may be the inhibitory effect of nitric oxide (Section 1.3) on adenylate kinase, which is involved in polyphosphate degradation in *Acinetobacter* sp. .

For biological phosphate accumulation, the ability of cells to store reserve material plays an essential role. Polymerization of substrates and storage in intracellular granules may offer the advantage that, at times of substrate shortage or in an environment with low concentrations of substrates (at low k_m values), such organisms can survive much better than other heterotrophic bacteria that do not have effective strategies for substrate storage.

Biological phosphate elimination is a highly effective process leading to final concentrations in the wastewater of <0.1 mg L^{-1} phosphate. For optimal biological phosphate removal, the COD/P ratio in the wastewater should be about 20 g COD g^{-1} phosphate to permit good growth of the polyphosphate-accumulating bacteria. If biological phosphate elimination is used in combination with chemical precipitation, the minimum COD/P ratio should be 2 g COD g^{-1} phosphate (Smolders et al., 1996) in processes with or without separation of primary sludge. If most of the par-ticulate COD is separated in a primary sedimentation pond, ferrous ions should be added to supplement the biological phosphate removal with chemical precipitation. If no presedimentation of sludge is available or the sedimentation efficiency is low, no ferrous ions have to be added (van Loosdrecht et al., 1997b). A detailed description of the state of the art concerning biological phosphate elimination was given by Schön (1999). Problems with the stability of the EBPR process in wastewater treatment plants were periodically reported. The reason for this may be the occurrence of microorganisms known as glycogen nonpolyphosphate-accumulating organisms (GAOs).

These bacteria are selected under EBPR operation conditions (alternating anaerobic–aerobic phases during treatment) and compete with microorganisms for EBPR for the available volatile fatty acids (Blackall et al., 2002). Filipe et al. (2001) suggested an important role of pH during anaerobic and aerobic operation of reactors: growth of GAOs is favored at low pH, but at a pH of 7–7.5 the microorganisms for EBPR outcompete the GAOs. Further research is required to elucidate conditions under which GAOs are inhibited and growth of EBPR biomass is promoted.

BIOLOGICAL REMOVAL, BIOTRANSFORMATION, AND BIOSORPTION OF METAL IONS FROM CONTAMINATED WASTEWATER

Whereas solid organic and inorganic material in wastewater or sludge can be removed by sedimentation, soluble organic pollutants and xenobiotics should be eliminated from the aqueous environment by microbial mineralization or anaerobic degradation to gaseous products, with a varying portion (5%–50%) being used as substrates for bacterial growth.

Most of the inorganic components present in waste-water are soluble and are ionized. Trace amounts of many cations (e.g., Na^+, K^+, Ca^{2+}, Fe^{2+}, Ni^{2+}, Co^{2+}, Mn^{2+}, Zn^{2+}, etc.) and anions (e.g., PO_4^{3-}, Cl^-, S^{2-}) are essential micronutrients for bacterial growth. Other cations such as ammonia may also be required for bacterial growth, but the surplus amount must be oxidized to nitrate, and the nitrate denitrified to gaseous nitrogen, for N elimination from wastewater. Under anaerobic conditions sulfate is reduced to sulfide, low amounts of which are required for growth of bacteria. The sulfide not required for growth is toxic for bacteria if present as H_2S in high concentrations.

In anaerobic reactors at a slightly alkaline pH, most of the sulfide is precipitated as heavy metal sulfides; then it is harmless to microorganisms and their environment. To support detoxification, heavy metal ions may also be precipitated chemically.

Metal ion contaminants in wastewater can be removed by microorganisms by either a direct or indirect influence on the redox state of the metal ions or through bio-sorption of metal ions on the cell surface (Lovley and Coates, 1997). Some microorganisms have also developed resistance mechanisms against toxic metals by changing the oxidation state without supporting anaerobic growth. Certain bacteria, yeasts, fungi, and algae can actively accumulate intracellular metal ions against a gradient. The process of bioaccumulation of metal ions depends on living, metabo-lically active cells, whereas biosorption is a passive, energy-independent process that can be mediated also by inactive cell material. Biosorption of metal ions includes mechanisms such as ion exchange, chelation, matrix entrapment, and surface sorption (Unz and Shuttleworth, 1996). After biosorption or active removal of metal ions from wastewater or contaminated soil, the heavy metal-containing biomass must be separated and incinerated or regenerated by desorption or remobilization of the metals. As an example of successful biosorption, wastewater from the galvanizing industry that contained 29 mg L^{-1} Zn and 10.5 mg L^{-1} Fe was purified in a three-stage stirred-reactor cascade. With 15 g biomass, 7.5 L of wastewater was decontaminated (Brauckmann, 1997). The removal of metal ions by biologically catalyzed changes in the redox state is an alternative. The altered speciation (valence status) of metals can lead to precipitation, solubilization, or volatilization of the metal ions.

Many bacteria use metal ions as electron acceptors for anaerobic respiration. Examples are the reduction of Fe^{3+}, Cr^{6+}, Mn^{4+}, Se^{6+}, As^{5+}, Hg^{2+}, Pb^{2+}, or U^{6+} (Table 1.6). The dissimilatory metal-reducing bacteria can use H_2 or organic pollutants (e.g., xenobiotics) as electron donors and are capable of simultaneously removing organic and inorganic contaminants. Metal ions are reduced and precipitated by sul-fide that is generated by sulfate-reducing bacteria.

Solubilization of most heavy metal precipitates is favored at acid pH, which is the favorable pH for soil or sludge decontamination, whereas an alkaline pH is favorable for precipitation of heavy metal ions to decontaminate wastewater.

An example of the formation of precipitates or soluble compounds at different re-dox states occur in ferrous and manganese compounds. Under aerobic conditions Fe(III) (ferric iron) and Mn(IV) ions form insoluble Fe(III) and Mn(IV) oxides or hydroxides, but under anaerobic conditions they form soluble Fe(II) compounds (ferrous iron) or Mn(II) compounds. Most organisms that grow with energy conserved during reduction of Fe(III) or Mn(IV) are members of the *Geobacteriaceae*.

Table 1.6 Metals as electron acceptors for anaerobic respiration.

Reaction	*Microorganism*	*Reference*
$2 Fe^{3+} + H_2$ "! $2 Fe^{2+} + 2 H^+$	*Geobacter metallireducens*	Lovley and Lonergan (1990)
	Pelobacter carbinolicus	Lovley et al. (1995)
$Mn^{4+} + H_2$ "! $Mn^{2+} + 2 H^+$	*Geobacter metallireducens*	Lovley (1991)
	mixed culture	Langenhoff et al. (1997)
$2 Cr^{6+} + 3 H_2$ "! $2 Cr^{3+} + 6 H^+$	*Desulfovibrio vulgaris*	Lovley and Phillips (1994)
	Bacillus strain QC1-2	Campos et al. (1995)
$Se^{6+} + H_2$ "! $Se^{4+} + 2 H^+$	*Thauera selenatis*	Macy et al. (1993)
		strains SES-1; SES-3
$Se^{6+} + 3 H_2$ "! $Se^0 + 6 H^+$	Oremland et al. (1989)	
$Te^{4+} + 2 H_2$ "! $Te^0 + 4 H^+$	*Schizosaccharomyces pombe*	Smith (1974)
$Pb^{2+} + H_2$ "! $Pb^0 + 2 H^+$	*Pseudomonas maltophila*	Lovley (1995)
$As^{5+} + H_2$ "! $As^{3+} + 2 H^+$	*Geospirillum arsenophilus*	Ahmann et al. (1994)
$Hg^{2+} + H_2$ "! $Hg^0 + 2 H^+$	*Escherichia coli*	Robinson and Tuovinen (1984)
	Thiobacillus ferrooxidans	
$U^{6+} + H_2$ "! $U^{4+} + 2 H^+$	*Shewanella putrefaciens*	Lovley et al. (1991)

Transfer of electrons from the terminal reductase, localized in the outer membrane or at the cell surface, to the insoluble Fe(III) or Mn(IV) oxides outside the cells can proceed either in a direct way (contact between the oxides and the cells) or by 'soluble electron shuttles' (e.g., by humic substances) between the metal-reducing microorganism and the mineral (Lloyd, 2003). Since Fe is an essential element for microorganisms, aerobic bacteria must excrete siderophores, which bind Fe^{3+} to their phenolate or hydroxamate moiety and supply the cells with soluble Fe^{2+}. To accelerate Fe^{3+} reduction in biotechnological processes, the chelator nitrilotriacetic acid can be added. In addition to their use in synthesis of cell components (e.g., cytochromes, ferredox-in, etc.), Fe^{2+} salts can be electron donors for nitrate reduction (Straub et al., 1996).

The reduction of Hg^{2+} to metallic Hg by *Escherichia coli* or *Thiobacillus ferrooxi-dans* facilitates Hg separation and prevents methylation reactions under aerobic or sulfate-reducing conditions. The mechanism includes nonenzymatic transfer of methyl groups from methylcobalamin to Hg^{2+} to form methyl mercury or dimethyl mercury, which are both neurotoxins and become enriched in the food chain. Selenium and arsenic can be transformed microbiologically by methylation to dimethyl selenide or to di- or trimethyl arsine in a volatile form. Methylated arsenic compounds are less toxic than nonmethylated arsenic compounds (White et al., 1997).

Changing the redox state of natural and anthropogenic radionuclides by metal-reducing microorganisms offers a possibility to control their solubility and mobility by converting, e.g., U^{6+} to U^{4+}, Pu^{5+} to Pu^{4+}, or Np^{5+} to Np^{4+}. The tetravalent metals can be removed by chelators (e.g., EDTA) or by immobilization onto biomass from the contaminated environment (Lloyd, 2003).

In contrast to bacteria, fungi are capable of leaching soluble as well as insoluble metal salts, because they excrete organic acids such as citric acid, fumaric acid, lactic acid, gluconic acid, oxalic acid, or malic acid, which dissolve metal salts and form complexes with the metal ions. The leaching efficiency depends on the soil micro-flora. Some soil microorganisms seem to be able to degrade the carbon skeleton of the metal–organic complex and thus immobilize the metal ions again (Brynhildsen and Rosswall, 1997).

Mixed bacterial cultures or *Wolinella succinogenes* use perchlorate or chlorate as electron acceptors for respiration (Wallace et al., 1996; van Ginkel et al., 1995) and thus detoxify these chemicals.

SULFATE REDUCTION AND METAL ION PRECIPITATION

Sulfate-reducing bacteria are biotechnologically relevant to sulfate removal or heavy metal precipitation in wastewater or waste and to the elimination of SO_2 during off-gas purification.

An overview of applications of sulfate-reducing microorganisms in environmental biotechnology is given by Lens et al. (2002). Sulfate is the terminal electron acceptor and is reduced to sulfide, with reducing equivalents derived from the degradation of lactic acid or many other organic compounds (Widdel, 1988). Alternatively, some sulfate reducers can also use molecular hydrogen. Sulfate reducers gain energy in an anaerobic electron transport chain (Hansen, 1994), leading to sulfide, a weak dibasic acid, which dissociates according to Eq. 35.

$$H_2S \text{ "!}^{K1} H^+ + HS^- \text{ "!}^{K2} 2\,H^+ + S^{2-}$$

$$K_1 = 1.02 \times 10^{-7},\ K_2 = 1.3 \times 10^{-13}\ (25\ ^\circ C) \qquad (35)$$

The total dissociation is described by Eq. 36:

$$K = \frac{[H^+]\,[S^{2-}]}{[H_2S]} = K_1K_2 = 1.3 \times 10^{-20} \qquad (36)$$

For precipitation of heavy metal ions, sulfide ions are necessary (Eq. 37):

$$Me^{2+} + S^{2-} \text{ "! } MeS \text{ (or) } 2\,Me^+ + S^{2-} \text{ "! } Me_2S \qquad (37)$$

The concentration of sulfide is pH-dependent. At acid pH only those metal sul-fides of very low solubility can be precipitated. Thus, at acid pH, HgS, As_2S_3, CdS, CuS, and PbS form precipitates, whereas at a more alkaline pH, ZnS, FeS, NiS, and MnS form precipitates. Al_2S_3 and Cr_2S_3 are water soluble and cannot be removed by precipitation or sedimentation. Zinc removal from zinc-contaminated groundwater by microbial sulfate reduction and zinc sulfide precipitation in a 9-m^3 sludge blanket reactor was demonstrated and has been transferred to a full scale reactor of 1800 m^3 (White and Gadd, 1996).

AEROBIC AND ANAEROBIC DEGRADATION OF XENOBIOTICS

Except for pesticides and insecticides, which are widely used in horticulture and farming and small amounts of which are washed into the groundwater, many xeno-biotics are spilled in the environment, by spot contamination or contamination of large areas. Biological remediation of soil and groundwater contaminated with gasoline (e.g., Yerushalmi and Guiot, 1998) and the volatile fractions of diesel oil (e.g., Greiff et al., 1998), even at low temperatures (Margesin and Schinner, 1998), seems to be no problem.

Results of many laboratory and field studies with a variety of substances are available (e.g., Arendt et al., 1995; Hinchee et al., 1995a, b; Kreysa and Wiesner, 1996). Except for studies in complex field or wastewater environments, many xenobiotics can be degraded by aerobic or anaerobic pure or defined mixed cultures (Table 1.7).

These include monoaromatic and polyaromatic substances with or without chloro substituents. Whereas the two-ring compound naphthalene is relatively easily degradable by *Pseudomonas* sp. and *Rhodococcus* sp., the four-ring compounds fluoranthene and pyrene are much less degradable by *Rhodococcus* sp. (Bouchez et al., 1996).

Aromatic compounds such as phenol and benzoic acid are degradable by mixed consortia at rates up to 1g L^{-1} d^{-1} in either the presence or absence of oxygen (Mörsen and Rehm, 1987; Knoll and Winter, 1987; Kobayashi et al., 1989).

A potent population is required, which can be obtained by preincubation. Even PCP is biodegradable by a methanogenic mixed culture from UASB granules (Juteau et al., 1995; Wu et al., 1993; Kennes et al., 1996). Some pure cultures and mixed cultures are capable of dechlorinating aromatic or aliphatic compounds (Table 1.7, second part).

As for the aerobic and anaerobic degradation of phenol, the rates of dechlorination of 2-chlorophenol under aerobic and anaerobic conditions are the same order of magnitude, 102 and 128 mg L^{-1} d^{-1}, respectively (Kafkewitz et al., 1996; Dietrich and Winter, 1990).

A pure culture of *Pseudomonas pickettii* was used for aerobic dechlorination, but for anaerobic degradation a mixed culture was used. The main problem in degradation of xenobiotic compounds in wastewater is a too short residence time in the reactors, which does not allow selection or adaptation of bacteria for dechlorination or degradation.

Only if a permanent pollution is prevalent, the degradation potential may develop with time. Alternatively, biofilm reactors should be used to enrich dechlorinating and xenobiotic-degrading bacteria.

Table 1.7 : Aerobic and anaerobic degradation or dechlorination of xenobiotics.

Reaction	Rate	Microorganisms	Reference
Substance	$(mg\,L^{-1}d^{-1})$		
Aerobic degradation			
2-Hydroxy-benzothiazole	138	*Rhodococcus rhodochrous*	De Wever et al. (1997)
Naphthalene	57	*Pseudomonas* sp.	Bouchez et al. (1996)
Fluoranthene	6.6	*Rhodococcus* sp.	Bouchez et al. (1996)
Pyrene	6.6	*Rhodococcus* sp.	Bouchez et al. (1996)
Pyrene	0.56	*Mycohacteriumjlavescens*	Dean-Ross and Cerniglia
Toluene	57	*Pseudomonas putida*	Heald and Jenkins (1996)
Phenol	188	*Bacillus* sp. A2	Mutzel et al. (1996)
Phenol	1000	mixed immobilized culture	Mörsen and Rehm (1987)
Cresol (*o, m, p*)	259	mixed immobilized culture	Mörsen and Rehm (1987)
2,4-Diphenoxy-acid	33	*Alcaligenes eutrophus*[a] JMP134 (pJP4)[b]	Valenzuela et al. (1997)
2,4,6-Trichlorophenol	15	JMP134 (pJP4)[b]	Valenzuela et al. (1997)
Anaerobic degradation			
Pentachloropheno (PCP)	107	methanogenic mixed fixed film reactor	Juteau et al. (1995)
PCP	90	methanogenic mixed culture UASB	Wu et al. (1993)
PCP	4.4	methanogenic granules	Kennes et al. (1996)
PCP	22.7	methanogenic mixed	Juteau et al. (1995)

Reaction	*Rate*	*Microorganisms*	*Reference*
Substance	*(mg L 1*		
Benzene	0.029	sulfate-reducing mixed culture	Edwards and Gribic-Galic (1992)
Phenol	1000	methanogenic mixed culture	Knoll and Winter (1987)
Phenol	31	syntrophic mixed culture	Knoll and Winter (1989)
Phenol	200	syntrophic mixed culture	Kobayashi et al. (1989)
Benzoic acid	600	syntrophic culture	Kobayashi et al. (1989)
Toluene	0.1-1.5	sulfate-reducing mixed culture	Edwards et al. (1992)
Toluene	4.6	methanogenic mixed culture	Edwards and Gribic-
Xylene	0.1-1.5	sulfate-reducing	Edwards et al.
Xylene	5.3	methanogenic mixed culture	Edwards and Gribic-Galic (1992)
Aerobic Dechlorination			
2-Chlorophenol	102	*Pseudomonas pickettii*	Kafkewitz et al. (1996)
4-Chlorophenol	41	*Pseudomonas pickettii*	Kafkewitz et al. (1996)
1,3-Dichloropropanol	671	*Pseudomonas pickettii*	Kafkewitz et al. (1996)
Tetrachloroethene	35.8 total'	anaerobic mixed culture	Wu et al. (1995)
Anaerobic Dechlorination			
2,6-Dichlorophen	38.4	methanogenic mixed culture	Dietrich and Winter (1990)
4-Chlorophenol	0.43	sulfate-reducing consortium	Häggblom (1998)
2-Chlorophenol	128	methanogenic mixed culture	Dietrich and Winter (1990)

Reaction	*Rate*	*Microorganisms*	*Reference*
Substance	*(mg L⁻¹d⁻¹)*		
Tetrachloroethene	1.64	strain TT 4B	Krumholz et al.
	dichlor		(1996)
	ethene[c]		
Tetrachloroethene	2.05	strain MS-1	Sharma and
	dichlor		McCarty (1996)
	ethene[c]		
DCB, TCB, TeCB[e]	1.24	methanogenic mixed culture	Middeldorp et al. (1997)

[a] *Alcaligenes eutrophus* = *Ralstonia eutropha*. [b] pJP4 = 2,4-dichlorophenoxy acetic acid-degrading plasmid.

[c] Dehalogenation product: total dehalogenation or partial dehalogenation to the corresponding deha-logenation product. [d] 2,3,4,5,6-CB = 2,3,4,5,6-chlorinated biphenyls. [e] DCB = dichlorobenzene, TCB = trichlorobenzene, TeCB = tetrachlorobenzene.

BIOAUGMENTATION IN WASTEWATER TREATMENT PLANTS FOR DEGRADATION OF XENOBIOTICS

In biotechnology and pharmacology, mutants of bacteria or fungi or genetically engineered organisms are widely used in the production of citric acid, gluconic acid, as-corbate, and pharmaceuticals such as penicillin, insulin, and blood coagulation factors. Bacteria and fungi have also been adapted or genetically transformed for soil remediation (Atlas, 1981; Margesin and Schinner, 1997, Korda et al., 1997; Megharai et al., 1997). For wastewater and sludge stabilization however, successful use of genetically modified bacteria or of bacteria that can serve as donors for plasmids encoding degradative enzymes has been rather rare (van Limbergen et al., 1998). Usually, natural selection of the most suitable microorganisms from a complex flora, simply by adapting process parameters, is used. The limited reports on successful bioengineer-ing for wastewater treatment may result from any of several factors:

- The plasmids were unstable or the genes are not expressed in the new environment.

- Inoculated strains did not survive or, if they survived, metabolic activity was too low for successful competition with autochthonous strains.
- Inoculated strains, serving as a gene source, survived, but other strains were not competent for gene transfer.
- Wastewaters normally contain a complex spectrum of carbon sources that are better than xenobiotics, and so organisms do not express genes for degrading xenobiotics.

To increase the survival potential in wastewater, a selected flora should have the desired degradative ability, tolerance to cocontaminants, and a natural spatial and temporary abundance (van der Gast et al., 2003). Another possibility would be to add organisms containing plasmids having a broad host range, permitting conjugation and DNA exchange between different species or genera of bacteria. To enhance degradation of organic compounds in activated sludge or by a biofilm, selected specialized bacteria, genetically modified bacteria, or bacteria as plasmid donors for degradative pathways can be added (McClure et al., 1991; Frank et al., 1996). Plasmid exchange from donor to recipient cells would be advantageous to the recipient bacteria, because the plasmids harbor genes whose products function in pathways for xenobiotic degradation, which would thus extend the substrate spectrum of the recipients. The transfer of naturally occurring mercury-resistance plas-mids between *Pseudomonas* strains in biofilms was shown to occur rapidly (Bale et al., 1988).

Selvaratnam et al. (1997) added a phenol-degrading strain of *Pseudomonas putida* to an activated sludge SBR reactor, which had removed 170 mg L^{-1} of phenol before being augmented with the *Pseudomonas putida* strain. Whereas the original phenol-degrading activity was partially lost in the nonaugmented reactor upon further operation, the augmented reactor almost completely degraded the phenol. A more convincing approach would have been to use non-phenol–degrading activated sludge for this experiment, although the survival of the catabolic plasmid *dmpN* of *Pseudo-monas putida* and its expression in the reactor biomass was demonstrated for 44 d by molecular biology techniques under steady-state conditions in the laboratory. Successful bioaugmentation experiments in an upflow anaerobic sludge blanket reactor were reported by Ahring et al. (1992), who introduced a suspension of a pure culture of

Desulfomonile tiedjei or a three-member consortium into an UASB reactor. They observed a rapid increase in the dehalogenation of 3-chlorobenzoate, whereas nonamended parallel incubations had no dehalogenating activity. Even after several months at 0.5-d hydraulic residence time, which was shorter than the generation time of *Desulfomonile tiedjei*, dehalogenating activity was still observed, and *Desul-fomonile tiedjei* could be found within the biofilm by the use of antibody probes. More recently, an UASB reactor was supplemented with *Dehalospirillum multivorans* to improve its dehalogenating activity (Hörber et al., 1998). In contrast, Margesin and Schinner (1998) found, for biological decontamination of fuel-contaminated wastewater, that stimulation of the autochthonous flora by adding a mineral mix enhanced biodegradation to a larger extent than bioaugmentation with a cold-adapted mixed inoculum containing *Pseudomonas* sp. and *Arthrobacter* sp.

Bioaugmentation with a complex inoculum, which naturally occurs in metalwork fluids and contains strains of *Clavibacter* sp., *Rhodococcus* sp., *Methylobacterium* sp. and *Pseudomonas* sp. is very effective in degrading COD in wastewater. The augmented consortium degraded 67% of the COD (48 g L^{-1}) and was therefore 50%–60% more effective than the indigenous flora. In-situ analysis showed that 100 h after the introduction, the augmented consortium constituted more than 90% of the population (van der Gast et al., 2003).

Degradation of many xenobiotics in anaerobic or aerobic pure cultures or complex ecosystems has been demonstrated. Whereas for 'intrinsic sanitation' of polluted soil, the time is not limited, so long as the pollutants are adsorbed tightly to the

soil matrix, degradation of xenobiotics in wastewater must be completed during the residence time in the treatment system. Thus, merely the presence of a degradation potential within a wastewater ecosystem is not sufficient, but degradation rates must be high enough, and degradation must be faster than the residence time of bacteria in suspended systems. Supplementation with microorganisms as a potential tool to increase the degradation speed or to increase the degradation potential in wastewater cannot in general be considered a state-of-the-art procedure yet.

2

Industrial Wastewater Sources and Treatment Strategies

INTRODUCTION AND TARGETS

This chapter deals with the wastewater flows discharged from industrial plants and offers a synopsis of the applicable treatment methods.

The central topic of this book being biotechnology, the main emphasis of this chapter is on industries emitting wastewater with organic pollutants, since these can be treated biologically. Next, the possible wastewater flow fractions occurring in industrial plants are listed. According to each type of industry and individual local conditions, certain wastewater flow fractions do not occur, are disposed of, or are treated in a different manner. Then, various wastewater pollutants are investigated with regard to their direct importance for certain industries. This is followed by a typical treatment sequence for wastewater. In the main section, wastewater composition and possible treatment strategies for the individual industries are examined, with particular emphasis on the most important branches of the food processing industry.

We should note that there are not only substantial differences between the various industrial branches, but that even within one branch wastewater composition and appropriate treatment methods are determined by the following factors:

- production methods
- water supply and water processing
- technical condition and age of the production site
- training and motivation of employees

- use certain additives and cleaning agents, etc.
- number of shifts, seasonal differences (campaign operation)
- effluent requirements (direct or indirect discharge)
- extent of production-integrated environmental protection means
- number of wastewater treatment facilities

WASTEWATER FLOW FRACTIONS FROM INDUSTRIAL PLANTS

Synopsis

Due to the multitude of products and production methods in industrial plants, there is also a wide range of different wastewater flow fractions for which the respective industrial branches have coined their own particular terms (e.g., 'singlings' is a term used only in the distillery business). The wastewater flow fractions listed below represent the most important wastewater sources, without each fraction being necessarily produced by each single branch:

- rainwater
- wastewater from sanitary and employee facilities
- cooling water
- wastewater from in-plant water preparation
- production wastewater (the following flow fractions are in some branches considered part of the production water): - wash and flume water - fruit water - condensates - cleaning water

RAINWATER

Rainwater can periodically constitute a substantial proportion of wastewater, depending on the amount of sealed surface. It is important to differentiate between nonpolluted to slightly polluted rainwater, such as that coming from roofs, which should be percolated or can be discharged directly into the storm sewer or waterways, and rainwater that is collected from sealed areas where product handling or vehicles contribute to contamination of rainwater, making treatment of rainwater necessary. The amount of rainwater Q_R (in L s^{-1}) can be calculated by the following formula:

$$Q_R = r_{D,n} \cdot Ø_S \cdot A_E \quad (1)$$

where A_E (in ha) is the catchment area, i.e., all areas that channel runoff into the rainwater canal in the event of rainfall. $Ø_S$ (dimensionless) is the runoff coefficient, which indicates the percentage of fallen rainwater that actually increases the runoff flow (i.e., the portion that does not percolate or evaporate or is not held back by low-lying areas). This amount varies greatly, depending on the surface conditions of the catchment area. For sealed industrial areas it is safe to use a runoff coefficient $Ø_S$ = 1. $r_{D,n}$ represents the rainfall intensity in L s^{-1} ha^{-1}. For a 10-min rainstorm (with a sewer flow time of >10 min, the standard design rainfall intensity), which in this intensity occurs only once a year, this value amounts in Germany to 100–200 L s^{-1} ha^{-1}. If sewer overflow is not permissible once a year, but only once every five years, the given amounts need to be increased by a factor of 1.8. A detailed design capacity for the rainfall amount can be found in ATV (1992).

The nature of the pollutants and the resulting pollutant load in the rainwater depend mainly on the prevailing degree of air and surface pollution. According to ATV (1992), the average COD value in rainwater runoff is 107 mg L^{-1}. Peak values, which occur especially after long dry periods at the onset of a rainfall, are substantially higher.

WASTEWATER FROM SANITARY AND EMPLOYEE FACILITIES

Wastewater from sanitary and employee facilities consists of the water used by the employees for washing and for flushing toilets and the wastewater from other employee facilities. If there is a large cafeteria, the wastewater from this source should be evaluated separately.

Wastewater from sanitary and employee facilities has the same basic composition as domestic wastewater and should therefore be kept separate from the effluent emerging from the production line. This flow fraction should be discharged into the municipal sewage system, but treatment in the factory's own treatment plant is also possible.

The amount of wastewater per employee and shift is approx. 40–80 L, but the condition of the plumbing fixtures and the degree of dirt involved in the operation (e.g., use of showers at the end of a shift) can have a major impact on the amount of wastewater produced. The load per employee and shift can be assumed to be 20–40 g BOD_5, 3–8 g N, and 0.8–1.6 g P.

COOLING WATER

If cooling is necessary and done with water, one must differentiate between continuous flow (high water consumption) and recirculation (increase in salt concentrations).

No general amounts can be given for the quantity of cooling water considered necessary, because the need for cooling water varies greatly from one industry to the next. As a first approach, one can say that, for industries using recirculation cooling towers, approx. 3%–5% of the water capacity (depending on the salt concentration in the cooling water, this ratio may even be higher) needs to be extracted to prevent excessive increase in pollutant concentrations.

If there are no leaks in the a continuous-flow cooling tower and no chemical additives are used in the cooling water, the composition of the water does not change, but its temperature increases. In recirculation cooling towers the concentration of pollutants increases with evaporation of the cooling water.

WASTEWATER FROM IN-PLANT WATER PREPARATION

Wastewater from in-plant water preparation can result from the preparation of drinking water from well water or from water softening, decarbonation, or desalination systems. The contents of this water depend on the characteristics of the raw water, of the treatment method(s) used, and of the chemicals used.

Production Wastewater

Production wastewater is a generic term, which includes a variety of flow fractions. Exact specifications can be made only in relation to a particular industry. Certain flow fractions arising in specific industries have been designated with a particular name (e.g., 'singlings') and are not listed here. The following wastewater flow fractions are either investigated as a separate flow fraction or as part of the production wastewater:

- *Produce washing water* is also used in many food processing industries as *flume water* for transport of the produce.
- *Fruit water* is the term used in the food processing industry for that water that is extracted from the processed fruits and vegetables, such as the water extracted from potatoes during starch production.
- *Condensates* are the exhaust vapors that have been condensed after having been removed during an evaporation or drying process.
- *Cleaning water* results from washing the production lines (pipes, containers, etc.), cleaning the production facilities, and cleaning the transportation containers (bottle washing).

KINDS AND IMPACTS OF WASTEWATER COMPONENTS

Below, the most important wastewater components are listed, with their influence on the value retention of the production facilities and their impact on the necessary wastewater treatment measures.

Temperature

The temperature has a major influence on the construction material. High temperatures are not suitable for synthetic materials; e.g., they may cause damage to gaskets. Thus, the temperature of wastewater that is discharged into municipal sewage systems is restricted (in Germany the standard discharge temperature is <35 °C). With regard to the corrosion of metallic materials, the temperature is a major factor, next to the chloride and oxygen contents. Another aspect is that volatile components are easily removed from the wastewater and volatilized at higher temperatures.

An increased wastewater temperature has a positive influence on biological wastewater treatment methods, since an increase in temperature also increases the activity of microorganisms. On the other hand, any temperature increase results in a lower oxygen input capacity of the aeration system.

pH

Similar to the temperature, the pH value has an impact on

determining the suitable construction materials and the activity of microorganisms. To avoid damage to the sewage systems and the connected treatment plants, in Germany the pH value of the discharged effluent should be between 6.5 and 10. In treating wastewater, it is of importance which factors have influenced the pH. A low pH, for example, might result from organic or inorganic acids. Inorganic acids should be neutralized; organic acids should be biologically removed.

For many microorganisms the ideal living conditions are at a relatively neutral pH value. Anaerobic wastewater treatment processes are especially sensitive to fluctuations in pH. It is important to keep in mind that organic acids can, at suitable organic loads, be degraded by biological plants without having to be neutralized. This, however, does not apply to mineral acids.

Obstructing Components

With regard to wastewater treatment, obstructing components are large inorganic particles, such as glass shards, plastic parts, cigarette butts, sand, etc., which are biologically inert and need to be removed mechanically to avoid damage, clogging, or caking in the subsequent treatment process.

TOTAL SOLIDS, SUSPENDED SOLIDS, FILTERABLE SOLIDS, SETTLEABLE SOLIDS

The content of solid particles has a substantial effect on the amount of organic matter. One differentiates between total solids (TS), which consist of suspended solids (SS, all particles that do not pass through a membrane filter with a pore size of 0.45 ìm), and filterable solids (FS). Settleable solids (unit: mL L^{-1}) are the solids that will settle to the bottom of a cone-shaped container; therefore, they do not include all of the suspended and floating solids.

Organic Substances

Organic substances constitute the main pollutant fraction in most industrial plants. To prevent direct oxygen consumption in the waterways into which the effluent is discharged, organic substances need to be eliminated as far as possible. A variety of parameters can be used to determine the content of organic matter in a given waste-water sample: BOD, COD, TOC, DOC, etc. These sum parameters, however, do not include any indication of the kind of organic substances measured.

The COD has developed into a major parameter, because the results of COD analysis are available much more quickly than those of BOD analysis. The use of cuvette tests gives an excellent cost–benefit ratio and requires less effort, space, and time to obtain results.

The COD/BOD ratio is an important value in determining the biodegradability of the pollutants in a particular wastewater. If the ratio is <2, the load is considered easily biodegradable.

Nutrient Salts (Nitrogen, Phosphorus, Sulfur)

Nutrient salts are inorganic salts such as NH_4, PO_4, SO_4, which are considered vital for the growth of plants and microorganisms. Since nitrogen and phosphorous can cause massive growth of biomass and may, therefore, lead to eutrophication of waterways into which the effluent is discharged, in the European Union nitrogen and phosphorous must be eliminated before wastewater is discharged into sensitive waterways.

To eliminate nitrogen and phosphorous biologically, sufficient organic pollutants must be present. Therefore, not only is the concentration of these substances in the industrial wastewater important, but also the ratio of their concentrations to the COD or BOD.

Some kinds of industrial wastewater have such low nitrogen and/or phosphorous concentrations that nitrogen (in the form of urea) and/or phosphorous (as phosphoric acid) must be added to obtain the necessary minimum nutrient ratio for growth of the microorganisms needed for biodegradation.

HAZARDOUS SUBSTANCES

Hazardous substances are a generic term used for those substances or substance groups contained in wastewater which must be regarded as dangerous because they are toxic, long-lived, bioaccumulative, or have a carcinogenic, teratogenic, or mutagenic impact. In industrial wastewater, the following substances are of major importance:

- absorbable organic halogen compounds (AOX)
- chlorinated hydrocarbons and halogenated hydrocarbons

- hydrocarbons (benzene, phenol, and other derivatives)
- heavy metals, in particular mercury, cadmium, chromium, copper, nickel, and zinc
- cyanides

Whether a substance is regarded as toxic or hazardous (according to the definition given above) is primarily a matter of concentration. Many heavy metals are vital as trace elements for the growth of microorganisms, but toxic in higher concentrations.

In Germany, the regulations for hazardous substances are so extensive that certain industrial branches not only have to comply with the required discharge quality of the effluent of the entire plant, but also must meet further requirements for the locations where certain flow fractions emerge before they are mixed with the eventual effluent (fractional flow treatment). Some substances have been banned entirely, which requires a specific design and schedule of particular production steps.

Corrosion-inducing Substances

The evaluation of which substances are corrosion-inducing in what concentrations depends, not only on the substances themselves, but also on the choice of material.

Foı cement-bound materials three kinds of corrosion are distinguished: swelling impact through sulfates, dissolving impact through acids, and dissolving impact through exchange reactions, e.g., with chloride, ammonium, or magnesium. A sufficient concrete resistance is given when the following limits are not exceeded with quality concrete and long-term exposure: SO_4 <600 mg L^{-1} (for HS concrete <3000 mg L^{-1}; inorganic and organic acids pH >6,5; lime-dissolving carbonic acid <15 mg L^{-1}; magnesium <1000 mg L^{-1}; ammonium nitrogen <300 mg L^{-1}). Biocorrosion may occur when organically highly polluted wastewater with a neutral pH becomes anaerobic. Then H_2S and, in consequence, H_2SO_4 (which is aggressive to concrete) are produced in the gas phase.

Corrosion of metals is an electrochemical process for which a conductive liquid must be present, e.g., water. For metallic materials problęms arise particularly with high concentrations of chloride, which can lead to corrosion even when high-grade steel is used. It is not possible to determine any general chloride concentrations, because the potential for corrosion depends on a number of parameters, such as the material quality, redox potential, gap width, flow velocity, temperature, and manufacturing quality.

Synthetic materials are commonly regarded as largely corrosion-proof. Some synthetics, however, are not stable toward organic or inorganic acids, alkalis, solvents, or oils, so that when dealing with aggressive media one has to consult resistance tables and check the producers' advice.

Cleaning Agents, Disinfectants, and Lubricants

In industrial factories a great number of cleaning agents, disinfectants, lubricants, dyes, etc., are used. If they occur in high concentrations, many of these materials have an inhibiting or even toxic impact on biological treatment methods. It is also possible that they may contain components that cannot be eliminated in the waste-water treatment plants, e.g., AOX.

Although unrestricted production flow is the guiding principle for industrial companies (e.g., in food industry factories becoming unsterile must be entirely ruled out), samples tested in practice have shown that consumption control systems or replacement of particularly polluting substances have allowed for useful and cost-effective improvements.

GENERAL PROCESSES IN INDUSTRIAL WASTEWATER TREATMENT CONCEPTS

General Information

To an increasing extent, wastewater treatment plants have changed from being pure 'end-of-pipe' units to being modules that are fully integrated into the production process, which is referred to as production-integrated environmental protection. The technological basis of this tendency is that production residues can often be used in other ways than disposal, that the wastewater flow often presents some 'product at the wrong place', and that it is simpler and more cost-effective to clean the single flow fractions individually and at higher concentrations. Thus, the general process of wastewater treatment by industrial companies can be roughly divided into production-integrated environmental protection and post-positioned wastewa-ter purification. The borderline between these areas is not clear-cut. The first step in any procedure of developing wastewater treatment concepts is a detailed stocktaking of the situation of the company with regard to production methods, water supply, and wastewater production. For instance, the production-specific amounts of water, wastewater, and pollutant loads should be ascertained, as well as the characteristics of the different flow fractions of the company and the places where alkalis, acids, detergents, etc. are used.

The next step includes the gathering of various propositions for production-integrated measures and the examination of the different options for the post-positioned wastewater purification unit. The following sections provide further in-depth information on this point. The last step is the comparison and evaluation of the various propositions and options, the most important criteria for the evaluation being operational safety, economic viability, possibilities for sustainable production, and consideration of the overall concept (combination of industrial pretreatment and post-positioned municipal wastewater treatment plant).

Production-integrated Environmental Protection

The following methods should be examined with regard to their suitability as production-integrated measures. The main principle should be that avoidance should take precedence over utilization and utilization over disposal.

- careful treatment of raw materials (short storage periods, careful handling)
- changes in the transport facilities (dry conveyance, establishment of conveyance circuits)
- changes in the production methods (reduction of water demand, substitution of water, improvements in the production organization)
- avoidance of surplus batches and production losses
- product recovery, for example, by cleaning pipes
- production circuits and multiple use of water (flume and washing water circuits, reverse-flow cleaning, lye recirculation in CIP (cleaning in place) plants, cooling water recirculation)
- utilization of raw materials from production residues (protein coagulation, valuable substance recycling, byproduct yield, forage production)

- separate collection of residues
- extensive retention of production losses in collection containers and utilization separate from the wastewater flow
- cleaning in different steps: (1) dry cleaning, e.g., with high-pressure air; (2) washing; (3) rinsing
- useful treatment of the flow fractions
- general operation and organization (training of staff, control of water and waste-water amounts, installation of water-saving devices, use of high-pressure cleaning tools, etc.)

TYPICAL TREATMENT SEQUENCE IN A WASTEWATER TREATMENT PLANT

A typical treatment sequence in a wastewater treatment plant consists of the stages listed below. Most industrial factories, however, have only a few of these operation stages, either because they do not have to cope with the respective pollutants in their wastewater or because they are exempted from particular treatment steps due to specific regulations, which occurs, e.g., with indirect dischargers.

- removal of obstructing substances (screens, grit chamber)
- solids removal (strainers, settling tank, flotation)
- storing equalization cooling
- neutralization or adjustment of the pH
- special treatment (detoxification, precipitation/ flocculation, emulsion cracking, ion exchange)
- biological treatment or concentration increase (evaporation) or separation (membrane methods)
- Wastewater Composition and Treatment Strategies in the Food Processing Industry

General Information

In view of the great variety of industrial branches, this section is by no means comprehensive in examining all areas of industry, but concentrates on the most important branches of the food processing industry.

When examining specific wastewater amounts and pollutant concentrations, it is important to consider the points already mentioned in Section 2.1 (e.g., age and technical state of the equipment used at the plants). One crucial aspect mentioned in the introduction as well is training and motivation of the employees, which can have a substantial impact on the amount of product loss (spillage, etc.) during the production process, since these losses have a considerable impact on the concentration of pollutants in the wastewater.

Apart from the hard statistical facts about production processes, a conscientious plant designer should, when planning the layout of the wastewater treatment units, also try to consider all operational factors of the particular plant.

The general pressure to remain cost-effective is prodding the industry to find ever new solutions, which makes for ongoing optimization. This has a considerable impact on the amount and composition of the wastewater produced and thus directly on the treatment methods.

Two basic tendencies have resulted from this: the first is the attempt to reduce the amount of water used, e.g., by recycling or reusing water in other processes. The result is a decreased amount of wastewater, but with a higher concentration of pollutants. The second tendency is to separate the fractions and to reduce the specific load (kg COD t^{-1} of product), e.g., by disposing of the dried solid matter (e.g., as nutrients for agricultural use). A detailed description of what is generally referred to as *production-integrated environmental protection* is presented in the following section.

To make precise statements about wastewater amount and composition for any particular industry, one needs to obtain the latest data pertaining to the particular plant.

Apart from the relevant periodicals dealing with this topic, the most important data sources in Germany are the *Handbücher zur Industrieabwasserreinigung* (manuals on industrial wastewater treatment) published by the Abwassertechnische Vereinigung ATV (Association for Wastewater Technology, Germany, today ATV-DVWK) (ATV, 1999, 2000, 2001). Furthermore, relevant data can be found in the reports, codes of practice, and leaflets developed and issued by the single ATV-DVWK commissions and ATV-DVWK working groups.

Sugar Factories

Sugar can be produced from sugarcane or sugar beets. In Europe sugar is extracted from sugar beets. The average sugar content of sugar beets is 18%. The processing of sugar beets is seasonal (campaign operation) and generally takes place from September to mid-December.

In recent years, the amount of wastewater has been greatly reduced from 18 m^3 to approx. 0.8 m^3 t^{-1} of sugar beets by water-saving methods and by extensive sealing of the water circuits. In modern plants the water derives almost exclusively from the sugar beets themselves (sugar beets have approx. 0.78 m^3 of fruit water per ton).

According to ATV (2004), a typical sugar factory produces the following wastewa-ter flow fractions (Table 2.1).

The most important wastewater components are the high organic loads derived from the sugar. In contrast, the amounts of nitrogen and phosphorous are comparatively low; because growing ecological awareness has led to a more controlled fertilization of sugar beet fields, the amounts of these pollutants are ever decreasing. In Germany, lime milk is added to the flume water and at the juice purification step to prevent becoming unsterile. Therefore, the wastewater has an increased calcium content. Table 2.2 shows the concentrations of the most important components. Due to the recirculation of water in partially closed cycles, the concentrations increase steadily during the course of the campaign operation.

For the treatment of sugar factory wastewater, the following processes are common:

- soil treatment
- long-term batch processing
- small-scale technical processes, usually consisting of anaerobic pretreatment and aerobic secondary treatment

Agricultural soil treatment is primarily geared toward utilization of the contained nutrients and water. The simultaneous degradation of the organic substances is of less importance; it does not form the basis of dimensioning. If large quantities of ion-exchange waters occur, the salt tolerance of the irrigated plants has to be considered: 90–120 mm of total annual wastewater irrigation can be regarded as a standard value, but the maximum single occurrence should not exceed 30 mm. In Germany, the total amount of wastewater irrigation is partly restricted to <50 mm per year, depending on factors such as the water consumption of the plants and the water storage capacity of the soil, with the result that, because of the high area demand, these methods are no longer economically viable. In Germany only anaerobically pretreated wastewater or condensate are used in irrigation.

Table 2.1 *Wastewater amounts in m^3 t^{-1} of sugar beets (ATV, 1990, ATV-DVWK, 2004).*

Wastewater Fraction		*Specific Wastewater Amount*		*Specific COD Load*
		(m^3 t^{-1})		*(kg t^{-1})*
Surplus condensates		0.4–0.6		0.1-0.15
Soil sludge transport water		0.15-0.25		2–4
Cleaning water		~0.02		<0.1
Water from ion-exchange unit		0.05-0.13		0.15-0.3
Surplus water from wet dust collection		~0.02		~0.1
of the pulp-drying vapors				
Pump sealing water and cooling water		varying (0.4–0.7 (ATV, 1990))		-

Table 2.2 *Concentrations of pollutants in sugar factory wastewater (Jördening, 2000).*

Kind of wastewater	*Amount*	*pH*	*COD*	*Ninorganic*	*Calcium*
	(m^3 t^{-1})		*(mg L^{-1})*	*(mg L^{-1})*	*(mg L^{-1})*
Condensate	0.3	8.5-9.5	200-400		100-300
Soil transport water,	0.3	6-11	6000-14 000	20–40	80-2500
washing and flume water					

With long-term batch processing, the wastewater is discharged into sealed ponds. The degradation period lasts until the summer of the following year and consists of an anaerobic phase succeeded by an aerobic phase (if necessary, aeration equipment is used). If the batch depth does not exceed 1.2 m the COD concentration can be reduced to less than 300 mg L^{-1}. The disadvantages of this process are the great area demand and the emergence of noxious odors in the spring time.

In recent years, mainly anaerobic wastewater treatment processes have become established in the sugar industry. In comparison to the processes described above and to the aerobic biological treatment, anaerobic methods have a number of distinct advantages: less area demand, lower sludge production, low energy consumption, energy generation from biogas, no noxious odors. In Germany, mainly anaerobic contact sludge processes are used due to the high calcium contents, whereas in the Netherlands, e.g., where caustic soda is used instead of lime milk, many UASB reactors are used. Anaerobic fixed-film reactors have not been tried yet. The successful operation of a fluidized bed reactor has been described by Jördening (1996, 2000). In properly working reactors, the desired pH range of 6.8–7.5 automatically remains stable, the operating temperature normally is 37 °C. With a volumetric load of 5–10 kg COD m^{-3} d^{-1} (for UASB up to 15 kg), a COD reduction efficiency of approx. 90% is achieved. Because of the lime, nothing needs to be done to decrease the phosphorous concentrations to the limits required for effluent quality. Nitrogen is decreased only to a small extent by integration into the excess sludge; thus, further treatment is necessary before direct discharge of the effluent is possible. As a rule of thumb, nutrient salts are eliminated in anaerobic reactors in the ratio COD:N:P = 800:5:1. To prevent operational difficulties with wastewater having high calcium concentrations, for contact sludge processes decanter centrifuges have proved to be most suitable for separating the calcium carbonate particles from the bacterial sludge.

If direct discharge into a waterway is planned, aerobic secondary purification is necessary, ideally by an activated-sludge system. The condensates should be directly fed into the aerobic stage.

Starch Factories

Starch is produced from potatoes, corn, and wheat. Depending on the original raw material the wastewater fractions, amounts, and loads emerging during starch production vary considerably.

Corn starch: fractional flow sources: maceration station, germ washing, starch milk dewatering, gluten thickener, glue of gluten dewatering, and chaff dehydration. The various fractions of wastewater are mainly recycled and used as processing water. The wastewater fractions that have to be treated are

- processing water

- the condensates resulting from evaporation of the maceration water

Wheat starch: during wheat starch production, wastewater is derived from the separation step and from thickening of the secondary starch. All other flow fractions are returned into the process water. The wastewater flow fraction that has to be treated is referred to as process water.

Potato starch: during potato starch production, washing water (flume and transport water), fruit water (sometimes also condensates from a fruit water evaporation plant), and production wastewater are produced. By recycling it has been possible to reduce the washing water demand from 5–9 $m^3\ t^{-1}$ to 0.3–0.6 $m^3\ t^{-1}$ (ATV-DVWK, 2002). Fruit water separated from the potatoes is usually fed into the protein recovery unit. Approx. 50% of the proteins contained in the fruit water are coagulated and separated subsequently. Protein production from fruit water is always economically viable, since the price for the protein produced is approx. 0.5 € kg^{-1}, whereas biological treatment, particularly for the elimination of nitrogen (10 g of protein contains 1.7 g N), is quite expensive (approx. 2–5 € kg^{-1} of N).

According to ATV-DVWK (2002), the specific wastewater amounts of starch production are as shown in Table 2.3.

Wastewater from starch factories has a high organic load and usually consists of easily degradable matter. The undissolved organic contents are mainly carbohydrates and proteins. The fat content is normally ~10%. Usually, this kind of waste-water does not contain any toxic substances.

The substrate ratio COD:N:P is satisfactory; actually, there may even occur an excess of N and P, so that it is not necessary to add nutrient salts. Table 2.4 shows standard wastewater values for corn, wheat, and potato starch wastewater, which have distinct differences.

The following processes are used for treatment of starch factory wastewater:

- soil treatment
- pond processing
- small-scale technical processes (anaerobic, aerobic, evaporation)

Until recently, the wastewater from most starch factories in Germany was used to irrigate fields. A summary of the results of this practice can be found in Seyfried and Saake (1985). However, a lack of sufficient agricultural areas and the low amounts permitted to be used put an end to this practice.

Pond processing in batch operation is possible only for production of potato starch, since this is a campaign operation. Continuously operating ponds are rare, since they require additional aeration, due to the high load concentration. They can only be recommended as a secondary treatment method, because the demands for area and aeration are too high.

Anaerobic wastewater treatment has become established alongside conventional activated sludge processes. Fixed-film reactors and UASB reactors are mainly used, which at loads between 7–30 kg COD m^{-3} d^{-1} can achieve degradation rates of 70%–90%. To maintain operational stability, a separator for solids is usually placed upstream of the reactor. Furthermore, a separate pre-acidification stage with a sludge removal system is recommended. The amounts of available phosphorous and nitrogen are sufficient for the anaerobic treatment. Sometimes, trace amounts of cobalt and nickel need to be added. The pH should not exceed 7.0, since at higher pH values MAP (magnesium ammonium phosphate) might precipitate.

In the potato starch industry a further possibility for fruit water treatment is reduction of the wastewater by evaporation to a solids content of 70%. The dried solids can then be utilized, e.g., as fertilizer. To save evaporation energy, a membrane process can be used to increase the concentration prior to evaporation, which would be done as a cascade operation under vacuum conditions.

Aerobic secondary treatment is always required if the company intents to discharge its wastewater directly into waterways.

VEGETABLE OIL AND SHORTENING PRODUCTION

In the vegetable oil industry, one differentiates between the following branches: extraction plants for extraction of raw fat and oil, refining plants for refining of raw fat and oil, plants for further processing of the nutrient fats, e.g., into margarine, which consists of approx. 80% fat, 20% water, plus some other ingredients. The process technology for nutrient fat and oil production largely depends on the raw materials, depending on whether oil is extracted from seeds (soy, sunflower, coconut, rapeseed, etc.), animal fats from tallow and fat liquefiers (tallow or lard), and fruit flesh fats (palm oil, olive oil, which due to its poor storage stability is usually extracted near the site of production), and fats from marine animals.

The processing of seed oils consists of the following stages: cleaning, peeling/shelling if required, masticating, conditioning (heating and moistening), pre-pressing with ensuing extraction or direct extraction without prepressing. Extraction is accomplished by means of a solvent-oil mixture (emulsion), followed by removal of the solvent (usually hexane) by steam. The vapors are condensed and the hexane is separated from the water in static separators. In a further distillation step, the remaining hexane is removed from the wastewater. The wastewater amount produced in seed oil extraction processes is less than 10 m^3 t^{-1} of seeds. Data for the wastewater pollutant concentrations are available only for COD, which is in the range of 700-2000 mg L^{-1}.

Extraction of animal fats is accomplished by masticating fatty tissues and heating the macerate, followed by a separation process. Wet and dry melting processes are distinguished. The dry melting process does not produce any wastewater, whereas the wet process produces approx. 0.35 m^3 t^{-1} raw material, which mainly consists of glue water and pump sealing water from the separators. Depending on the extraction method and the cleaning procedures used in the production plant, the concentration of pollutants in the wastewater from tallow melting plants can vary considerably. For wastewater that has passed the fat separators with topped sludge catcher implements, one can assume the values shown in Table 2.5 (the ratio of emulsified fats, however, may be dramatically higher than given here).

In refining plants, the raw oil is purified (refined) by removing undesired ingredients. The basic process steps consist of desliming, neutralizing, bleaching, and deodorizing (steaming). Depending on the raw material and the desired end product, further processes such as winterizing, fractionating, transesterification, or hydrogenation may be added. In addition to this, other waste products such as saponification water (soapstock) are processed. Wastewater fractions occur during desliming/neutralizing, oil drying and cooling, steaming (condensates), as well as during soap cracking (acidic water). The amount and composition of the wastewa-ter depends mainly on the characteristics of the fresh water, with regard to temperature and degree of hardness, the mode of process operation (continuous or discontinuous methods, process temperature and pressure), the type and quality of raw materials, and the frequency with which the raw materials are changed. The data given in the reference literature vary greatly, due to the multitude of factors involved. A standard value for wastewater of a refining plant which recirculates the falling water is $<10\ m^3\ t^{-1}$ of raw material.

Provided that no falling water recirculation or static fat separators are used in the wet chemical refining process, the total wastewater of a refinery has the following characteristics (Table 2.6).

For margarine production, wastewater results only from the cleaning circuits of the CIP plants and amounts to approx. 1-3 $m^3\ t^{-1}$ margarine. After the rinsing and cleaning water has passed the fat separator, the wastewater has the following characteristic parameters (Table 2.7).

Production-integrated environmental protection must be the central part of the wastewater treatment concept, with the major factors being the efficiency of the production process and prevention of product loss during the process.

Wastewater treatment processes usually consist of a physical-chemical pretreat-ment by fat separators or flotation systems to decrease the amounts of undissolved solids and lipophilic substances. Whereas installation of fat separators is only a minimal pretreatment concept, because the efficiency of these systems may be completely reduced by a hot water surge, a more expensive flotation system using additives also allows the elimination of emulsified, mainly lipophilic, substances. Particularly effective are pressure flotation systems designed for a surface load of 4–5 $m^3\ m^{-2}\ h^{-1}$ with a recirculation flow of 10%-40% and operating at 4–7 bar.

Often a mixing and equalizing (M+E) tank is installed behind the flotation system to equalize pH value and temperature peaks and to allow a more constant loading of the subsequent biological treatment stage. In biological wastewater treatment, aerobic activated sludge treatment with a sludge load of approx. 0.1 kg

BOD kg $MLSS^{-1}$ d^{-1} has proved to be effective. To prevent flotation of sludge and development of scum layers, the fat contents of the wastewater should be <200 mg L^{-1}.

Potato Processing Industry

Potatoes are used as fodder or feed potatoes, as industry potatoes (starch production, distilleries), or as market potatoes.

Potato processing can be divided into three main production methods: fresh products (peeled potatoes, precooked potatoes, potato salads, sterilized potatoes, potato products), dried products (dehydrated potatoes, instant mashed potatoes, raw dehydrated potatoes), and fried products (French fries, chips, sticks).

Prior to the final processing the potatoes must be dry cleaned and sorted, sometimes stored for some time and then transported to the processing plant. The conveyance to the processing plant can be wet or dry. Then the potatoes are washed and peeled (mechanically and/or with steam). In the fried production process, peeling is followed by cutting, sorting/washing, blanching, steaming (drying), dewatering, frying and, if necessary, cooling.

For each of the different production methods, wastewater occurs during washing, peeling, cutting, sorting, blanching and steam drying. The specific wastewater amounts and the contents of the fractions of each process step are shown in Table 2.8. The most significant wastewater fraction results from the potato fruit water, owing to the contained starch: a starch concentration of 1 g L^{-1} is equivalent to approx. 1230 mg BOD_5 L^{-1}. The wastewater load depends mainly on the type of potato (cell size), the growth and storage conditions, as well as on the care in handling (cut and bruised potato cells increase the loads). Usually, the COD/BOD ratio is between 1.6 and 2.0, which is favorable for biodegradation. The C/N ratio is also advantageous for denitrification. Wastewater from the potato processing industry contains comparatively much nitrogen and phosphorous. Nutrient salt limitations occur only in exceptional cases. Wastewater treatment systems often consist of the following sections:

- grit chamber, screening system, settling tanks for purification of the flume, and washing water recirculation
- production-integrated screening systems and separators to recover organic solids that have been separated from

the production wastewater and dewatered, to recycle valuable substances (e.g., cattle forage)

- fat separators for wastewater containing fat, when deep-fat fryers are used in the production process
- biological treatment for pretreatment and full treatment

Although there are large scale applications for the entire range of aerobic and anaerobic treatment methods, good results have been achieved using activated sludge systems, which are designed as either one-stage or cascade units and which can cope with a sludge load of 0.1 kg BOD kg $MLSS^{-1}$ d^{-1}. A problem that can arise is bulking sludge, which can be reduced by using the cascade design. In recent years, more anaerobic plants have been built, with the UASB reactor and the EGSB reactor being the most common type in the potato processing industry. To guarantee stable operation of these reactors, it is imperative to limit the amount of filterable solids in the wastewater by installing separators or settling tanks preceding the anaerobic treatment. A relatively stable and neutral pH value is also essential. Because of the large amount of starch particles, the reactors should be preceded by an acidification unit having a retention period of more than 6 h.

SLAUGHTERHOUSES

Slaughterhouses and meat processing plants can be divided into four categories according to their different production processes.

- slaughterhouses for hogs and cattle
- slaughterhouses for poultry
- meat-cutting plants
- meat-processing industry

Local butcher shops are not considered, due to their small turnover volume.

The following statements refer only to wholesale slaughterhouses that process up to 8000 hogs per day. In the slaughtering process, not only meat from muscle tissue, but also byproducts and residues are produced. The meat and the organ meats (such as liver, etc.) are fit for human consumption and can be traded freely. The residues produced in the slaughtering process are divided into two categories:

- Residues that have commercial value and are tradable, such as fat and bones, which find use as raw materials in feed plants or in the pharmaceutical industry.
- Nontradeable residues, such as meat unfit for human consumption and other byproducts, which need to be treated in animal carcass disposal plants. Additional waste products include primary waste (stomach and intestine contents) and secondary waste (solids from wastewater screening and flotation sludge).

The primary wastewater and waste product sources are divided into three production areas:

- truck washing and animal sheds (green line)
- slaughter and cutting (red line)
- stomach, intestine, and entrails cleaning (yellow line) - the latter, however, are often not done on the slaughterhouse grounds

The waste occurring in trucks and animal sheds consists of bedding material, feces, and urine, which amount to 2.0 kg per hog and 10 kg per cow, if the stabling time is kept short. These materials should be removed without the use of water and spread on agricultural land. Sparing water consumption during truck cleaning can keep the washing water down to 100 L per truck. This wastewater should be screened to remove large particles and should then be fed into the main wastewater stream.

The specific amounts and contents of wastewater (red line) are shown in Table 2.9. However, the presented data can be achieved only so long as blood retention is approx. 90% (the COD of blood is 375000 mg L^{-1}. The total blood volume is approx. 5 L per hog and approx. 30 L per cow).

In slaughterhouses, wastewater pretreatment is mainly done with mechanical procedures. Up to now, the number of plants for which physicochemical or biological operational steps have been added is comparatively small. The main cleaning effect of mechanical and physical procedures consists of retention and separation of solids with the help of stationary strainers, rotating screening drums, separators, fine rakes, screening catchers, or fat separators with a preceding sludge catcher. In wastewater from slaughterhouses, part of the organic matter consists of oils and fats in emulsified form. Thus, it may be wise to add a physical-chemical stage to the mechanical pretreatment, which would consist of a precipitation/flocculation stage and a flotation unit.

Although most of the slaughterhouses operating in Germany do not have their own biological treatment stages, the wastewater from the slaughterhouses is suitable for biological methods, because of its composition. The following biological methods have until now been used successfully on an industrial scale:

- large space biological methods (oxidation ponds, frequent formerly)
- various activated sludge systems (single-stage, cascade, two-stage)
- anaerobic biological methods

For activated sludge systems the sludge load should not exceed 0.15 kg BOD_5 kg $MLSS^{-1}$ d^{-1}. Direct anaerobic treatment in contact sludge reactors or joint treatment in municipal digestion tanks is particularly suitable for fats, floating materials, stomach and gut contents, and the liquid phase from the dewatering of rumen contents.

DAIRY INDUSTRY

Dairy products are classified into drinking milk, cream products, sour milk and milk mix drinks, butter, curd products, hard and soft cheeses, condensed milk, and dried milk. The difference between the listed products and the entire delivery amount is mainly due to the return of skimmed milk and whey and to the extraction of exhaust vapors during coagulation and drying of milk and whey.

For milk processing, the delivered raw milk is first – regardless of the production schedule – cleaned with separators, separated into cream and skimmed milk, and pasteurized. Cream is mainly used for the production of butter. Skimmed milk is processed into drinking milk, fresh milk products, and cheese, partly by adding cream or bacterial cultures. Skimmed milk and whey are the basic materials for the production of dried milk, lactose, and casein.

The wastewater produced in milk processing plants consists of cooling water, condensation water, sanitation water, and process water. The process water consists of the wastewater from the pretreatment, water losses during production, those residues that can no longer be used economically, washing water, detergents, rinsing and cleansing water, and water processing. In dairies the wastewater derives almost exclusively from cleaning of the conveyance and production implements. More than 90% of the organic solids in the wastewater result from milk and production residues. For the milk processing industry, wastewater discharge is almost always identical with loss of products that could otherwise be utilized or sold. This is a great incentive to decrease the production of wastewater by production-integrated measures. For untreated dairy wastewater, the following data are valid; peak values can even exceed these values (Table 2.10).

Dairy wastewater has only a small ratio of settleable solids. Thus, conventional mechanical procedures, such as settling tanks, are ineffective. Inevitable losses of fats can be retained in fat separators, which, however, have only a limited efficiency if the wastewater temperatures are comparatively high.

One major problem with dairies is the considerable variation in wastewater volume and concentration. Thus, as a first step after straining and a sand trap, it is recommended to install a mixing and equalizing tank (M+E tank). In the M+E tank wastewaters of different concentrations and pH are mixed, the wastewater flow is equalized, and partial biological degradation occurs, which can also result in a biological neutralization. As a minimum volume, approx. 25% of the daily water flow has proved to be a favorable value, but it is also possible to adjust the facilities for daily or weekly equalization. With unaerated M+E tanks there is no biological degradation worth mentioning; instead, substance conversion (acidification) happens, which leads to the emergence of noxious odors. Aerated M+E tanks are mostly operated as washing-off reactors. They are able to reach BOD_5 efficiency rates of 20%-60% for homogenized samples.

As a further pretreatment stage, a flotation implement is recommended, which can either replace the M+E tank or be downstream from it; this facility allows for the removal of fats and proteins, i.e., the major part of the organic pollutants.

Although more than 90% of the milk processing companies in Germany discharge their wastewater indirectly, direct discharge can under certain conditions be economically viable. Direct dischargers mostly have an activated sludge system, which should, if strong variations occur, be preceded by an M+E or a calimity tank. Since dairy wastewater has a tendency to develop bulking sludge, it is recommended to design the plant so that the microorganisms in the activated sludge are intermittently subjected to high loads, which can be achieved by installing an activated sludge system in plug flow design, by a preceding contact tank (selector), or by a SBR method (sequencing batch reactor: the process steps of filling, denitrification, aeration, sedimentation happen one after the other, but in the same tank).

FRUIT JUICE AND BEVERAGE INDUSTRY

Natural mineral waters and spring waters are collected and bottled at the location of the source spring. Table water consists of drinking water or natural mineral water to which salts are added. Refreshment beverages are produced from water, flavoring substances, sugar or sweetener, and carbon dioxide. The technology of fruit juice production can, in a simplified manner, be divided into the production stages of washing, grinding, refining, filtering, heating, recooling, and bottling.

The wastewater produced in these three industrial branches consists of the following streams (some do not occur in every branch): wastewater from cleaning bottles and containers and from bottling, rinsing and washing water, exhaust vapor condensate, wastewater from the production facilities, wastewater from surface cleaning (floors of the production sheds and the parts of the yards where production takes place), and wastewater from cleaning the conveyor facilities.

Wastewater produced in the mineral water industries contains the following components: adhesive materials and fibrous substances, cleaning alkalis and acids, and soiling from the deposit bottles. For soft drinks, one has to consider the fact that the wastewater additionally contains organic pollutants (with a high ratio of carbohydrates, a large part of it being sugar), which derive from residues and product losses. For the fruit juice industry, product losses - in particular the loss of fruit concentrates - and the sugar, which is often added, are a considerable part of the waste-water pollution. The COD of fruit juices ranges from about 50 g L^{-1} (tomato juice) to about 200 g L^{-1} (apricot juice); 1 kg of glucose (or of fructose) is equivalent to 1066 g COD. Besides the wastewater, the fruit juice industry also produces cooler sludge, filtration residues, sludge from clarifying agents, pomace, and kieselguhr. Because of their high pollution potential, these substances should be the focus of production integrated measures. If possible, they should be utilized or disposed of separately.

The specific wastewater amounts and pollutant concentrations of the three industry branches are presented in Table 2.11. For companies in the fruit juice industry, one has to differentiate between those that do only bottling, only processing, and both processing and bottling. It is apparent that the wastewater from the beverage industry has low nitrogen and phosphorous values in relation to the BOD. The pH can range from 3.5–11.5. At the time of contact with the product the pH is mostly within the acidic range.

To meet the discharge limits of the municipal sewer system, it is often necessary to equalize the pH peaks and sometimes to reduce the temperature (discharge limit in most cases: <35 °C). Thus, a wastewater pretreatment plant could - in addition to a straining station - consist of only a neutralization stage. Because of the high cost of chemicals, biological neutralization is usually recommended, e.g., in an aerated mixing and equalizing tank, which, used as a washing-off reactor, achieves BOD_5 elimination rates between approx. 35% (daily equalization) and >50% (weekly equalization). Particular heed, however, should be paid to the alkaline water from the bottle washing machines, as it might be necessary to collect this water in a separate container and to discharge it in controlled doses.

Extensive wastewater pretreatment can be successfully done with anaerobic reactors in the fruit juice industry. Two-stage implements (first stage: acidification reactor with mixing and equalization function; second stage: methane reactor) have proved to be advantageous. At volumetric loads in the methane reactor of up to >10 kg COD m^{-3} d^{-1} the COD elimination rate amounts to about 80%.

For direct discharge into waterways, the activated sludge system with cascade design has proved to be viable; it is operated at sludge loads of <0.1 kg BOD_5 kg^{-1}

MLSS d^{-1}. Because of the low nitrogen and phosphorous amounts in the raw waste-water, it is generally necessary to add these substances. For reuse of deposit bottles, denitrification may be necessary because, as part of the label glue, nitrogen is added to the water. Moreover, one has to deal with the danger of bulking sludge.

BREWERIES

Beer of course contains both alcohol and carbonic acid. In Germany, legal regulations prescribe that it may be produced only from malt (germinated and 'oasted' barley), hops, yeast, and water. The different kinds of beer (lager, stout, top-fermented, bottom-fermented) are produced mainly by varying the original wort concentrations and by using different kinds of malt and yeast.

After malting, the main operation steps of beer production are wort production, fermentation, storing, filtration, and bottling. Prior to its fermentation into alcohol, the starch contained in the malt (which in Germany is obtained from barley) has to be converted into fermentable sugar.

Residues and wastewater flow fractions occur in the brewing room, in the fermentation and storage cellars, in the filter and pressure tank cellar, during dealco-holization, and during bottling (bottle, barrel, other containers). Brewery wastewa-ter is prone to heavy variation with regard to volume and concentration in the single flow fractions. Where production-integrated measures have already been applied, one can assume the following characteristics for the entire wastewater flow of an average brewery (Table 2.12).

Brewery wastewater has a comparatively high temperature (25–35 °C). With decreasing wastewater volume the temperature tends to rise to 40 °C. It is likely that the pH values vary strongly. In companies that reuse deposit bottles, the wastewa-ter from the bottle washing generally has alkaline pH values. Acidic wastewater may at times result from cleaning processes and from regeneration by ion exchange techniques (for water processing). The nitrogen consists mainly of organic nitrogen (albumen, yeast) and to some extent of nitrate (nitric acid). Furthermore, the waste-water is likely to be contaminated by cleaning and detergent agents, as well as by kieselguhr and by particles arising from abrasion of bottles and shards.

Through production-integrated measures, considerable contributions to the reduction of amounts and loads, temperature, solids content, and pH can be achieved. Some very important measures are the retention and separate disposal of cooler sludge, kieselguhr, and yeast and the addition of lye.

For wastewater pretreatment, the first step should be the removal of settleable solids, such as shards, labels, spent hops, bottle caps, etc., by suitable screens and strainers. To neutralize the mainly alkaline wastewater it is common to use carbonic acid from the fermentation or flue gas. It is also possible to biologically neutralize the alkalis with the carbon dioxide that is produced during the BOD degradation. Because of the heavy variations, it is always recommended to use an equalization tank, which can be run as an aerated mixing and equalizing tank with a biological partial purification (the elimination rates of these washing-off reactors range from approx. 35% with daily equalization and >50% with weekly equalization) or which may serve as an unaerated pretreatment tank or acidification reactor for the anaerobic plant. For the anaerobic pretreatment of brewery wastewater the most common implements are UASB and EGSB reactors, which usually are run without heating the wastewater (reactor temperatures are in the range of 24–36 °C).

For the full-scale purification of brewery wastewater to direct discharge quality, aerobic activated sludge systems have proved to be best, because of the need to eliminate nitrogen and phosphorous. The activated sludge system can either be the sole treatment stage or be post-positioned to an anaerobic plant or an aerobic trickling filter unit. Another reasonable solution is the use of SBR methods (sequencing batch reactor), in which all treatment steps are run one after the other, but in the same tank.

DISTILLERIES

Distilleries produce alcohol for human consumption by fermentation and distillation of agricultural products that contain sugar or starch. Some of this alcohol is also used for vinegar production and in the pharmaceutical and cosmetics industries. In companies that produce spirits, the alcohol is diluted to make it potable and is enhanced with flavor additives. Quite a large number of rather small fruit schnapps distilleries exist.

For the production process, it is important that raw materials containing starch be turned into sugar by enzymes, fermented into ethanol, and then distilled, whereas raw materials containing sugar are only fermented and then distilled. Wine is only distilled. Normally, the first steps are mechanical disintegration of the fruit and mashing with water. In some instances, the saccharification must be artificially boosted. After fermentation is finished, the raw spirit (approx. 80 vol.% alcohol) is cleaned of its distillation residues (slops) by a first distillation. In a further refining step, either a so-called fine spirit (approx. 86 vol.% alcohol) is produced by a second discontinuous distillation, or a fine spirit or neutral alcohol (approx. 96 vol.% alcohol) is produced by continuous rectification. The residues of this second refinement step are called singlings.

Depending on the raw product and production methods, distilleries produce washing water, steaming water or fruit water, slops, and cleaning water. The specific wastewater amounts, as well as the concentrations of the major components, are listed in Table 2.13.

Washing water is produced only during the cleaning of potatoes or roots, which is mostly done by the suppliers. During steaming of the potatoes a mixture of condensate and fruit water emerges, which as a rule is added to the mash. Modern methods of unpressurized starch breakdown (DSA methods), however, do not produce any steaming water. Since singlings derive from the distillate of the first distillation stage, they contain absolutely no solids and are hardly polluted. For the bottling of spirits, almost exclusively new bottles are used, so that cleaning water derives only from washing the implements, containers, and factory sheds and is not highly polluted.

Slops contain a high amount of organic acids, proteins, minerals, trace elements, unfermentable carbohydrates, or – especially with fruit slops – high solids ratios (cores, stalks, stones, skins), which result in very high COD and BOD_5 values as well as in low pH.

In wastewater treatment the slops are of particular importance, since the other fractions of the wastewater can normally be discharged into the wastewater sewage without further treatment. Thus, slops should, if possible, be collected and utilized separately from the wastewater flow. The most common utilization method for slops from grain, potatoes, or fruit is direct feeding in cattle farming (if necessary, after thickening with decanters). If direct feeding is not possible, one should consider spreading on agricultural fields (if necessary, after anaerobic treatment of the slops in a factory-owned biogas plant or after injection as cosubstrate into a municipal digestion tank). Only if these two utilization methods are not possible, may the slops wastewater be mixed with the other production wastewater flow. Direct discharge, however, is then possible only with sufficiently powerful municipal waste-water treatment plants. In any case, the wastewater should be neutralized as a major pretreatment step. Another point one has to consider is the danger of bulking sludge development and hydrogen sulfide emission (corrosion, odors).

Slops from molasses distilleries often retain very high residual COD ratios after biological treatment. Here, evaporation of slops to a dry solids content of approx. 75% with ensuing separation of potassium sulfate (fertilizer) and utilization of the evaporated slops as an additive for cattle feed has proved to be a suitable utilization method. The condensed exhaust vapors from the evaporation unit are often subjected to anaerobic secondary purification.

3

Activated Sludge Process

PROCESS DESCRIPTION AND HISTORICAL DEVELOPMENT

Single-stage process

About 1910, investigations started on the treatment of wastewater simply by aeration (e.g., Fowler and Mumford in Manchester). Ardern and Lockett in Manchester conducted similar experiments but after a certain aeration period they stopped aeration, let the flocs settle, decanted the supernatant, added more waste-water, and repeated the cycle again and again. After buildup of a certain amount of biomass they obtained a fully nitrified effluent at an aeration period of 6 h. The settled sludge they called 'activated sludge'. The first technical scale plant was a fill-and-draw activated sludge plant, which today is called the SBR process. Since at that time the process had to be operated manually, they had a lot of operational problems, and therefore, the next plant was built in what is called today the conventional mode (Fig. 3.1).

An activated sludge plant is characterized by four elements:

An aeration tank equipped with appropriate aeration equipment, in which the biomass is mixed with wastewater and supplied with oxygen.

- A final clarifier, in which the biomass is removed from the treated wastewater by settling or other means.
- Continuous collection of return sludge and pumping it back into the aeration tank.
- Withdrawal of excess sludge to maintain the appropriate concentration of mixed liquor.

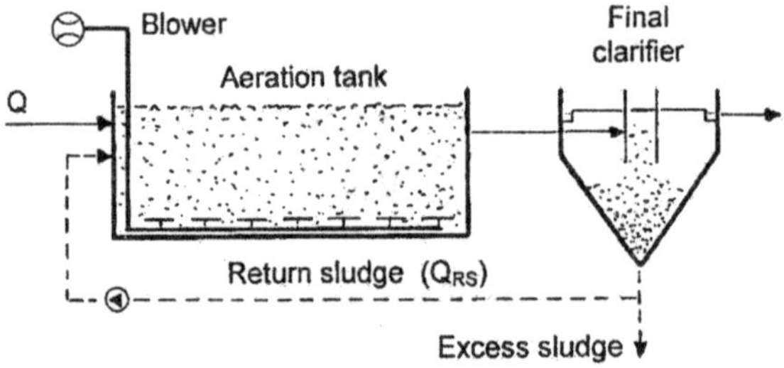

Fig. 3.1 Flow diagram of an activated sludge plant.

If one of the elements fails, the whole process fails.

Primary sedimentation is not required for activated sludge plants. For economic reasons, however, primary tanks are usually operated.

In the early times activated sludge tanks were aerated with fine bubble diffused air. Because of clogging problems in the ceramic diffusers, surface aerators were developed. In 1921 Bolton invented the vertical shaft cone surface aerator at the treatment plant of Bury. Beginning about 1965, cone surface aerators were installed in numerous plants in Germany, the largest one being the Emscher River treatment plant. Another large one is the second stage of the main treatment plant of the city of Hamburg. In the Netherlands in 1925, Kessener constructed the horizontal axis brush aerator, which was installed in spiral flow aeration tanks as they were used for diffused air aeration. In the 1960s brush aerators were frequently used in Germany in high-rate activated sludge plants. Pasveer installed a brush aerator in the oxidation ditch for aeration and circulation of mixed liquor. Starting about 1965, the horizontal axis mammoth rotor, diameter 1.00 m, was installed in closed-loop aeration tanks. The carrousel tank with cone surface aerators represents another closed-loop aeration tank. Both systems are still used in small as well as large plants.

After membrane diffusers were developed around 1970, diffused air aeration became popular again. Usually, aeration should create sufficient turbulence to prevent mixed liquor from settling. To minimize the power requirements for aeration at plants with a low oxygen uptake rate, Imhoff installed a horizontal axis paddle in a tank with diffused air aeration as early as 1924. After Pasveer and Sweeris had postulated that oxygen transfer was considerably increased if the air bubbles rise in a horizontal flow,

Danjes developed a system in which diffusers were fixed on a moving bridge. This system was marketed as the Schreiber Countercurrent Aeration System. As an answer to the Schreiber system, around 1970 the firm Menzel installed slow propellers in circular tanks with fine bubble diffused aeration. Today the combination of membrane diffusers in circular or closed-loop tanks with propellers creating a circulating flow is favored for intermittent aeration to remove nitrogen. Recently in some plants with EPDM (ethylene-propylene dimer) membranes after short operating periods of 1–2 years, a sharp increase in the pressure drop was observed. This is attributed to biodegradation of the plasticizer of the EPDM membrane.

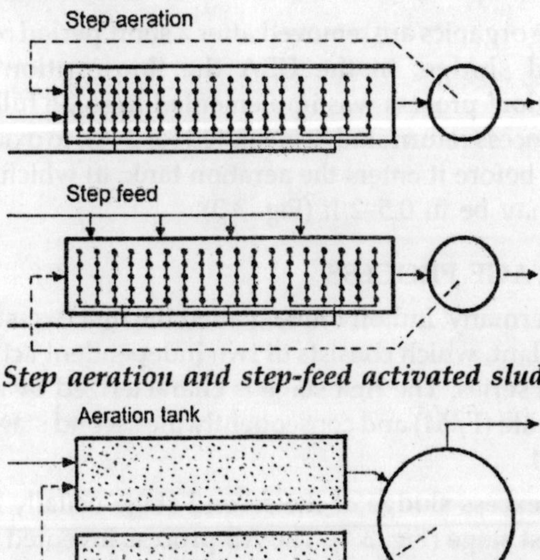

Fig. 3.2 ***Step aeration and step-feed activated sludge plants.***

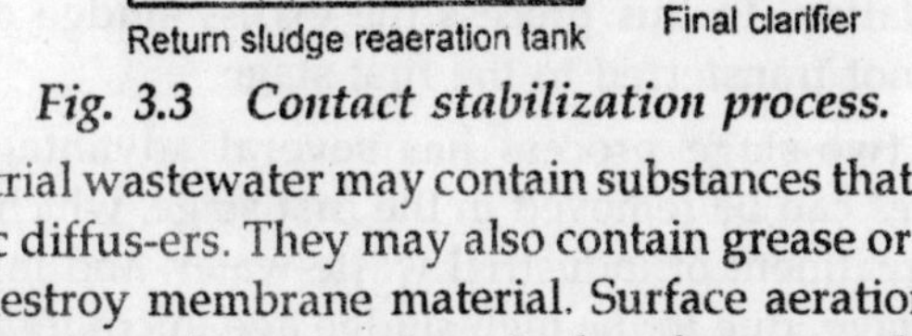

Fig. 3.3 ***Contact stabilization process.***

Industrial wastewater may contain substances that precipitate on ceramic diffus-ers. They may also contain grease or substances that can destroy membrane material. Surface aeration or coarse bubble aeration with static mixers is therefore a good choice. For deeper tanks the rotating turbine aerator, which is a combination of coarse bubble aeration and a mixer to break up the large bubbles into smaller ones, has been used successfully. In a jet or ejector diffuser, mixed liquor is pumped through a venturi nozzle into which air is introduced. Very fine bubbles are released by the shear stress. Early aeration tanks were rectangular with evenly distributed diffusers along the tank. Wastewater and return sludge entered the tank at one end, and mixed liquor left the tank at the other end.

Because of the high oxygen uptake rate, the dissolved oxygen concentration in the inlet zone was almost zero. To overcome this problem the diffusers at the inlet zone were arranged in a higher density than at the outlet zone.

This was called 'step aeration'. 'Step-feed', in which the return sludge is introduced at one end and wastewater is distributed along the tank, has been used in tanks having evenly distributed diffusers (Fig. 3.2).

Since organics are removed after a short period of contact with activated sludge, in the USA the 'biosorption' or 'contact stabilization' process was implemented in some full-scale plants. In this process return sludge is aerated for 2–4 h to oxidize adsorbed organics before it enters the aeration tank, in which the retention period may be in 0.5–2 h (Fig. 3.3).

TWO-STAGE PROCESS

In Germany, Imhoff implemented the first two-stage activated sludge plant, which consists of two independent activated sludge plants in series. The first stage is characterized by a high sludge loading rate (F/M) and consequently the second stage has a rather low F/M.

The excess sludge of the second stage usually is transferred to the first stage (Fig. 3.4). The AB process invented and patented by Böhnke is a two-stage activated sludge plant without primary sedimentation. In this process the excess sludge of the second stage is not transferred to the first stage.

The two-stage process has several advantages. Harmful substances can be removed in the first stage, which is important for the treatment of industrial waste-water; and in the low-load second stage, due to the high sludge age microorganisms can be maintained that are able to remove slowly biodegradable organics or to oxidize ammonia.

Furthermore, bulking sludge is only rarely observed in either stage. The disadvantages are that about twice as many clarifiers are needed as in the one-stage process and that nitrogen removal, as well as enhanced biological phosphate removal, may be inhibited owing to missing organics, which are removed in the first stage.

SINGLE SLUDGE CARBON, NITROGEN, AND PHOSPHOROUS REMOVAL

In the early 1960s three different methods for nitrogen removal were demonstrated (Fig. 3.5):

- post-denitrification
- pre-anoxic zone denitrification
- simultaneous denitrification

Post-denitrification was not successful without the addition of external organic carbon. Bringmann tried a bypass of wastewater to enhance denitrification, but then some ammonia remained in the final effluent.

The first technical scale pre-anoxic zone denitrification process in Germany was implemented at the research wastewater treatment plant of the University of Stuttgart. After Barnard's successful experiments, the first full-scale plant with pre-anoxic zone denitrification and enhanced biological phosphate removal was built in 1974 at Klerksdorp, South Africa. In Germany the first full-scale plant with pre-anoxic zone denitrification was constructed at Biet.

In 1969 the wastewater treatment plant of Vienna Blumental, designed for 300000 p.e., was put into operation. Two 6000-m^3 closed-loop aeration tanks operated in series, each equipped with six twin mammoth rotors, were operated in simultaneous denitrification mode. At that time this was the largest single-stage activated sludge plant in the world for nitrogen removal without the addition of external carbon.

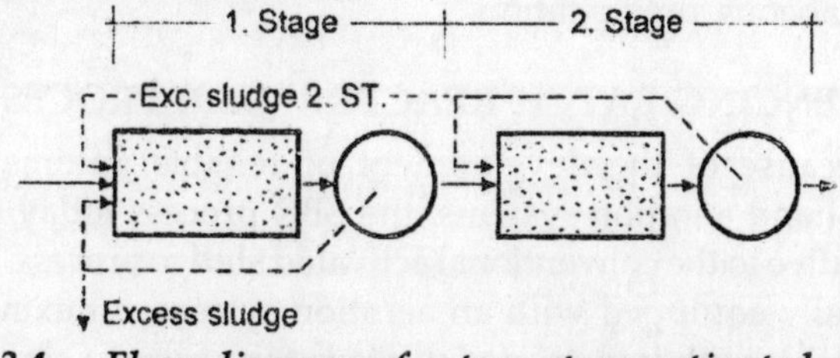

Fig. 3.4 Flow diagram of a two-stage activated sludge plant.

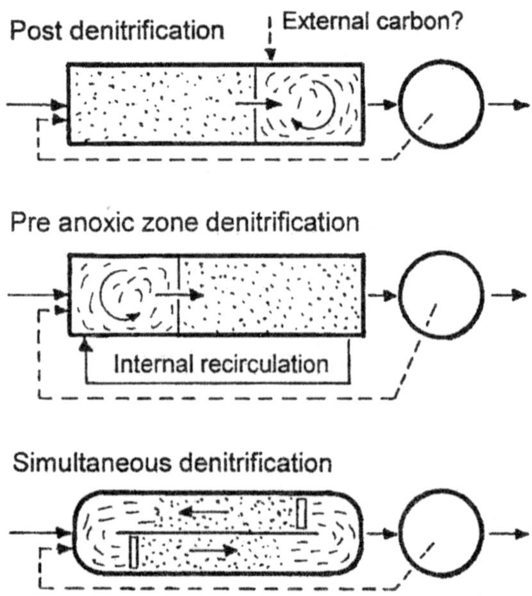

Fig. 3.5 Processes for nitrogen removal.

These and other process developments for nitrogen removal are discussed in detail in Section 3.3.3.

Based on the work of Thomas, phosphorous is easily removed by simultaneous precipitation. Barnard put an anaerobic tank upstream of the biological reactor for enhanced biological phosphate removal. Today most newer plants are built with means for enhanced biological phosphate removal and/or equipment for simultaneous precipitation.

SEQUENCING BATCH REACTOR (SBR) PROCESS

Because of the development of reliable automatic process control and aeration systems, the SBR process today is a perfect alternative to the conventional activated sludge process. The reactor is usually equipped with an aeration system, a mixing device, a decanter to withdraw treated wastewater, an excess sludge removal device, and the process control system. Wastewater treatment is performed by a time series of process phases (fill, react, settle, decant). As in the conventional activated sludge process, the SBR process is capable of carbon, nitrogen, and phosphorous removal. It is used for both industrial and municipal wastewater.

SPECIAL DEVELOPMENTS

Pure oxygen-activated sludge process

Owing to poor aeration systems in many activated sludge plants in the USA, the plants were operated with a low mixed-liquor suspended-solids concentration of about 1-2 kg m^{-3} MLSS and for long aeration periods of 5-8 h just for carbon removal. In the pure oxygen activated sludge process, which was developed around 1970, oxygen transfer is not limited. MLSS can be raised to, e.g., 5 kg m^{-3}, and the retention period can be shortened to, e.g., 2 h to achieve over 90% BOD removal. The covered aeration tanks necessary to recycle the oxygen gas are advantageous, since the plant looks clean and no emissions are released. The disadvantage is the high carbon dioxide concentration in the gas, which may cause corrosion of the concrete and, furthermore, nitrification may be inhibited by a too-low pH. In Germany only a few pure oxygen activated sludge plants were built in the 1970s. Most of them have since been converted to nitrogen removal plants with diffused air aeration.

Today in some conventionally aerated activated sludge plants, pure oxygen is used at periods of peak oxygen demand. The tanks are not covered and oxygen is not recycled. The oxygen gas is either introduced by special hoses with fine apertures, which release very small bubbles, or by jet type aerators. At the new plant of Bremen Farge, pure oxygen in addition to diffused air is used not only during peak loads but also during periods of power failure. This was calculated to be more economical than the installation of one more turbine blower and a much larger emergency power station.

ATTACHED GROWTH MATERIAL IN ACTIVATED SLUDGE AERATION TANKS

To increase the biomass in an aeration tank or to enhance nitrification, elements on which biomass can grow are immersed in the mixed liquor. At first, corrugated plastic sheets like that used in trickling filters, e.g., flocor, was installed (Fig. 3.6). It was believed that nitrifiers would grow on the material. Schlegel, however, demonstrated that almost no nitrifiers were attached, but a high number of protozoa were. He postulated that at such plants nitrification was enhanced because of lower sludge production caused by the high number of protozoa and the possibility to operate with higher MLSS because of the improved settleability (low sludge volume index) of the mixed liquor. Another material installed in aeration tanks is ring-lace, which is vertically fixed cords with loops. However, massive growth of worms attracted by the attached protozoa was observed. In the Linpor® process porous plastic foam cubes occupy 10%-30% of the aeration tank volume. Due to the attached biomass, the total amount of mixed liquor solids can be increased, and since the solids stay in the aeration tanks the clarifiers may not become overloaded. In Japan the ANDP process was developed, by which up to 40% of the volume of the aerobic compartment is filled with pellets (short polypropylene hoses 4 mm in diameter and 5 mm long) which are assumed to contain immobilized nitrifiers.

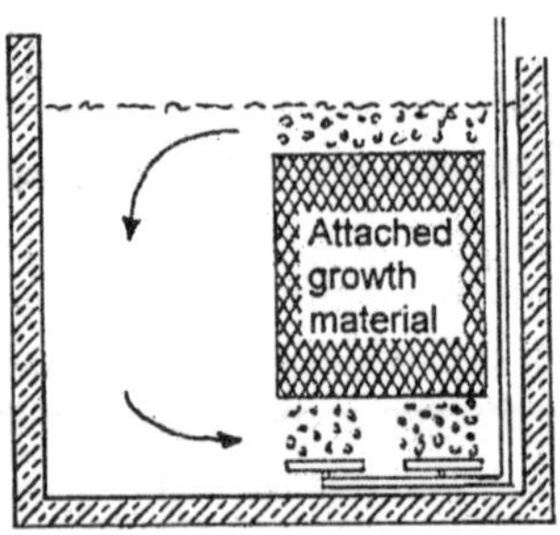

Fig. 3.6 Cross section of an aeration tank with a module for attached growth.

High-rate reactors

High-rate reactors are characterized by a high volumetric removal rate, e.g., 10–60 kg COD m^{-3} d^{-1} and consequently by a high volumetric oxygen transfer rate. Loop reactors are preferred. The ICI Deep Shaft is such a reactor, as is the HCR reactor. In the Hubstrahl reactor several plates with holes oscillate up and down with a high frequency to enhance oxygen transfer and to cause high turbulence. High-rate processes are preferred for high-strength wastewater with a very high fraction of soluble and readily biodegradable organics. Because of the high loading rates used for economic reasons the overall removal is restricted to 60%–80% COD.

Membrane separation of mixed liquor

After Kayser and Ermel successfully applied the membrane technique to separation of sample flow for continuous monitoring of, e.g., nitrate from mixed liquor, Krauth and Staab installed tubular membrane units instead of a final clarifier in a pressurized aeration tank (Fig. 3.7). The process is marketed as the Biomembrat process. As a result of recent improvements in the membrane technique, numerous experiments using microfilter units are underway. The advantages are that it is possible to operate such systems with rather high MLSS (up to 15 kg m^{-3}) and that the permeate is almost free of suspended matter. The disadvantage is that the flux rate is only on the order of 20 L m^{-2} h^{-1}. The process is therefore still costly and can only be used when there are special effluent requirements.

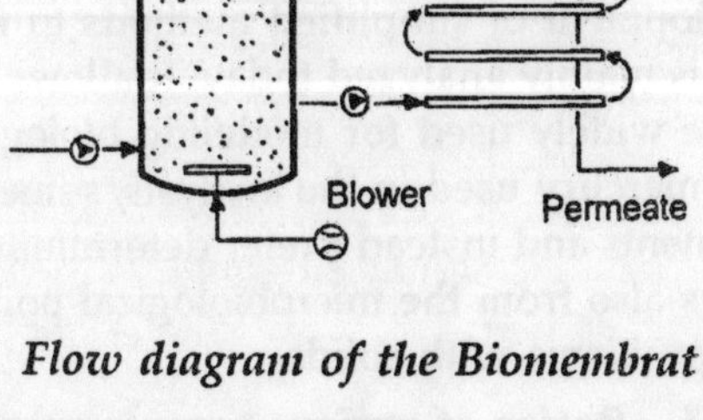

Fig. 3.7 Flow diagram of the Biomembrat process.

TECHNOLOGICAL AND MICROBIOLOGICAL ASPECTS

Wastewater characteristics

Wastewater to be treated can contain organic carbon predominantly as a single soluble substance (e.g., an alcohol), as a mixture of soluble substances, or as a mixture of solids and numerous soluble organic substances. Many industrial wastewaters are mixtures of soluble organic substances, but some may contain mainly one organic substance. Municipal wastewater and wastewater from most food processing industries is always a mixture of soluble and particulate organic matter.

Microbial degradation of organic carbon requires certain amounts of nitrogen, phosphorous, calcium, sodium, magnesium, iron, and other essential trace elements to grow biomass. In industrial wastewater treatment plants, missing elements have to be added. Since domestic wastewater contains all the necessary elements in excess, it is advantageous to treat special industrial wastewater together with municipal wastewater.

The concentration of organic matter in wastewater is measured as the biochemical oxygen demand (BOD_5, or BOD_{20}, incubation period of 5 or 20 d, nitrification inhibited), chemical oxygen demand (COD), or total organic carbon (TOC). Raw municipal wastewater can be characterized by the ratios shown in the first column of Table 3.1. Since BOD reflects only biodegradable matter and COD and TOC also include nonbiodegradable components, the ratios in well treated effluent (BOD_5 = 10–20 mg L^{-1}) differ.

BOD_5 (or in Scandinavia, BOD_7) has been the most common parameter for characterizing wastewater. The advantage of BOD is that it includes only biodegradable organics; the disadvantage is that BOD_5 measures only a fraction of the biodegradable organics because the measurement of BOD_{20} is economically not feasible. After the development of simplified methods to measure COD, this parameter is mainly analyzed today. It allows mass balances and is therefore widely used for modeling biological processes. Because of the mercury used in the analysis, some countries ban COD measurements and instead prefer determining TOC, which is advantageous also from the microbiological point of view but has analytical problems with solids.

Table 3.1 Ratios of various organic parameters.

Ratio	Influent	Effluent
COD/TOC	3.2 to 3.5	3.0 to 3.5
COD/BOD_5	1.7 to 2.0	3.0 to 6.0
BOD5/TOC	1.7 to 2.0	0.5 to 1.0

Removal of organic carbon

Many attempts have been undertaken to describe the removal of organics according to Michaelis–Menten or Monod kinetics. For many single substances the k_m or k_s value is rather small; therefore, in batch experiments zero-order removal of single substances is observed. Mixed substrates like municipal wastewater, however, show first-order removal reactions in batch experiments. Wuhrmann and von Beust [40] explained this phenomena as a series of different zero-order reactions. Tischler later demonstrated the removal of glucose, aniline, and phenol in batch tests. In tests with the separate substances, removal of the substances as well as decrease in COD follow different zero-order reactions (Fig. 3.8, left). It is important to notice that, although the substances are completely removed, a COD of about 30 mg L^{-1} remains. In a test in which the three substances were mixed with adapted mixed liquor, a quasi first-order reaction was observed (Fig. 3.8, right). Again, a nonbiode-gradable COD of about 60 mg L^{-1} remained. The remaining COD can be visualized as nonbiodegradable compounds produced by bacteria; hence, at least a fraction of the nonbiodegradable COD of any wastewater does not originate from the wastewa-ter itself.

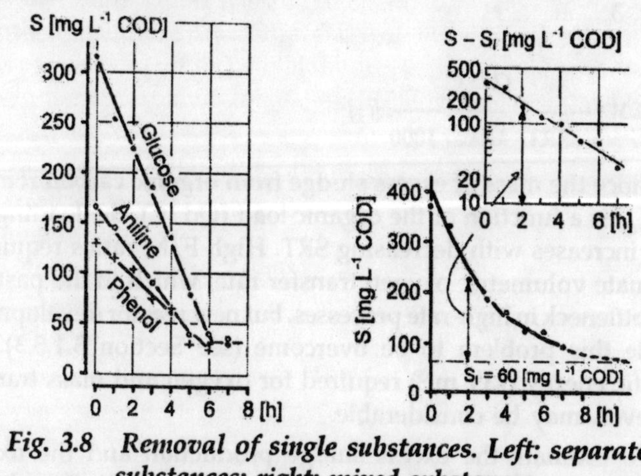

Fig. 3.8 Removal of single substances. Left: separate substances; right: mixed substances.

The rate constant of the first-order removal reaction of organics from municipal and many other types of wastewater depends on the wastewater characteristics as well as on the loading rate (F/M). This is because, even at the same MLVSS, the number and types of microorganisms may be different for various types of waste-water as well as under different load conditions.

Since batch experiments indicate that the removal of organics depends on the retention period and the mixed liquor volatile suspended solids (MLVSS), the food/microorganism ratio (F/M ratio) is widely used for design (Eq. 1).

$$\mathrm{F/M} = \frac{Qd \cdot C}{V \cdot \mathrm{MLVSS} \cdot 1000} = \frac{C}{t^* \cdot \mathrm{MLVSS} \cdot 1000} \quad [d^{-1}] \tag{1}$$

In Germany F/M is expressed as BOD_5 sludge loading rate (B_{TS}) based on MLSS. The extent of removal of organics depends strongly on the F/M ratio. Unfortunately, similar dependencies are observed only when treating the same type of wastewater.

Today, the sludge age or the solids retention time (SRT) is more frequently used in design:

$$\mathrm{SRT} = \frac{V \blacksquare \mathrm{MLSS}}{\;} \quad [d] \tag{2}$$

Combining Eqs. 1 (with MLSS instead of MLVSS) and 2 leads to Eq. 3:

$$\mathrm{F/M} = \frac{\;}{\mathrm{SRT}} \cdot \frac{Qd \cdot C}{M\mathrm{exc} \cdot 1000} \quad [c_{-1}] \tag{3}$$

Since the mass of excess sludge from organic carbon removal ($M_{exc,C}$) is a function of the organic load ($Qd \cdot C$), the loading rate F/M increases with decreasing SRT. High F/M ratios require an adequate volumetric oxygen transfer rate, which in the past was the bottleneck in high-rate processes, but new reactor developments enable this problem to be overcome (see Section 3.1.5.3). The specific energy (kW m^{-3}) required for oxygen and mass transfer, however, may be considerable.

To estimate the excess sludge production and the oxygen consumption for organic carbon removal and to finally calculate the reactor volume, the COD balance can be used. The following calculations are based partly on the activated sludge models ASM1 and ASM3 and on considerations of Gujer and Kayser. Some factors are restricted to almost complete biodegradation of organics, which may be obtained for municipal wastewater by sludge ages of >5 d.

Since the suspended solids of the final effluent are regarded as a fraction of the excess sludge for COD balancing only S_{CO}D,e is of interest.

PLANT CONFIGURATIONS

Typical Tanks for mixing and aeration

Mixing tanks for denitrification can be square, rectangular, or circular and have mixers in the center or propellers (Fig. 3.12). Rectangular tanks can be visualized as a series of square tanks. In closed-loop, tanks either propellers or vertical shaft impellers maintain the circulating flow.

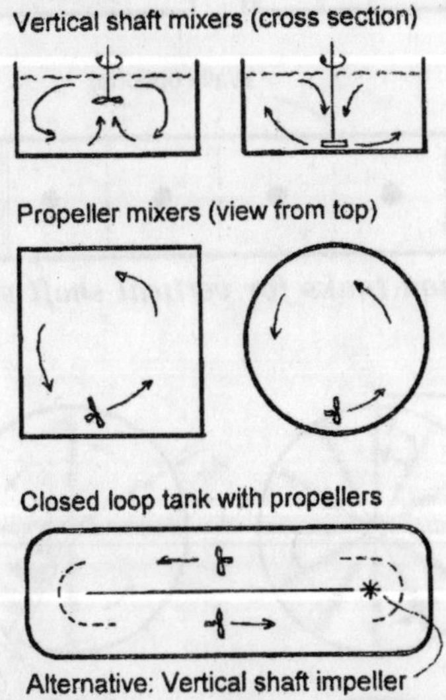

Fine-bubble diffused-air aeration systems can be installed in almost any type of tank. Tanks for vertical shaft surface aerators are either square or rectangular in which the length is a multiple of the width (Fig. 3.13). Tanks for cyclic aeration are preferably circular or of closed loop type. Aeration equipment as well as appropriate mixers must be installed. Mixing can also be performed by rotating bridges on which diffusers are mounted. (Fig. 3.14). Since the aeration is switched off cyclically, only non-clogging aeration systems, e.g., membrane diffusers for fine bubble aeration are appropriate. Simultaneous nitrification and denitrification in practice is performed mainly in closed-loop tanks equipped with horizontal-axis surface aerators, e.g., mammoth rotors or vertical shaft surface aerators, as in the carousel process.

Simultaneous denitrification can also be performed with air diffusers arranged in 'fields' in closed-loop tanks (Fig. 3.15).

Fig. 3.12 Typical mixing tanks for denitrification.

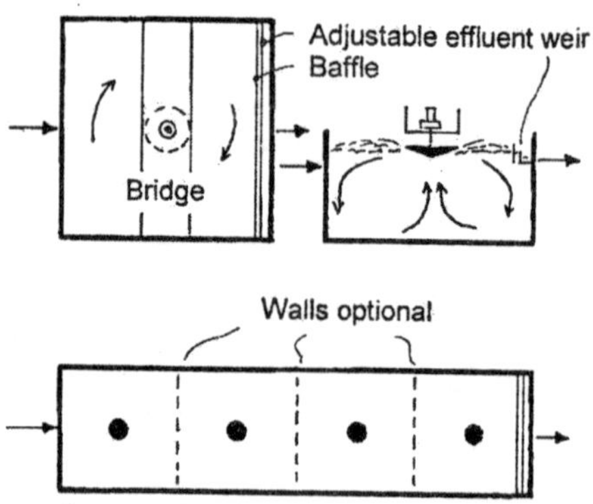

Fig. 3.13 Aeration tanks for vertical shaft surface aerators.

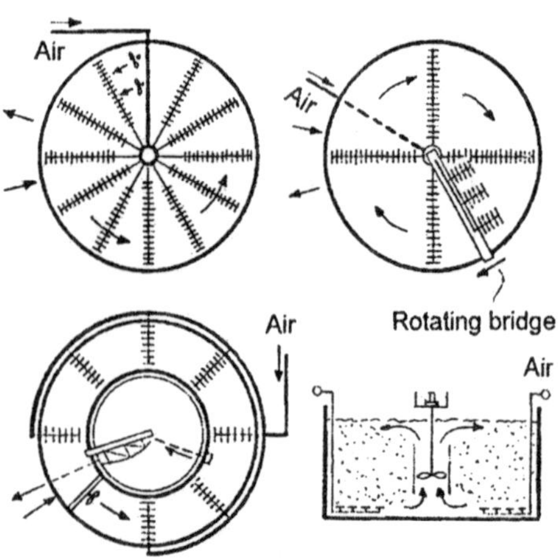

Fig. 3.14 Typical tanks for cyclic aeration.

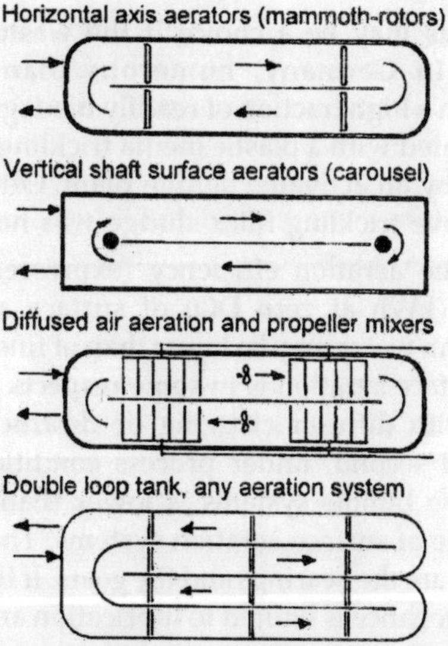

Fig. 3.15 Typical tanks for simultaneous nitrification and denitrification.

Carbon removal processes

In industrialized countries today, removal of both carbon and nitrogen is increasingly required; however, in developing countries and for pretreatment of industrial and trade wastewater, removal of organic carbon only is important.

As a rough design value, a sludge age SRT ~4 d may be chosen to achieve a low effluent BOD_5 of 10–30 mg L^{-1}. Assuming a specific sludge production of 0.4 kg SS per kg COD, the loading rate must be on the order of F/M_{COD} 0.6 kg COD (kg MLSS)$^{-1}$ d^{-1}. For the treatment of specific industrial wastewater a higher sludge age may be appropriate. The mixed liquor's suspended solids concentration may be as high as MLSS 3–4 kg m^{-3}.

In designing, provisions should be made for

- a sludge that settles well
- a sufficiently high volumetric oxygen transfer rate
- a robust aeration system, especially in developing countries and in industrial plants

Sludge settling is improved by plug-flow type aeration tanks, aeration tanks constructed as a cascade, and/or use of a selector.

Two-stage plants may be a choice if the wastewater is highly concentrated. In Germany, numerous plants that receive wastewater with a high fraction of readily biodegradable organics have been operated with a plastic media trickling filter as the first stage followed by an activated sludge plant. Often, intermediate settling to remove trickling filter sludge was not implemented.

Although the aeration efficiency (expressed as kg oxygen transferred per kWh at zero DO) of surface aeration systems measured in clean water may be lower than of fine bubble diffused air systems, surface aeration is in some respects preferable. First, no problems with diffuser clogging or destruction have to be considered; and second, under process conditions the aeration efficiency of fine bubble systems is lower than in clean water, which is not true of surface aeration systems. The weak points of surface aerators are the bearings and the gears. If these are properly designed, maintenance is limited to lubrication and changing gear oil.

NITROGEN REMOVAL PROCESSES

The single-stage activated sludge process for nitrogen removal, when the organic matter of the wastewater is used for denitrification, incorporates the dilution of ammonia nitrogen to a concentration equivalent to the desired effluent concentration of nitrate nitrogen. Consequently, the organics are diluted by the same ratio.

Whether conditions favorable to the development of filamentous bacterial growth are created depends on the wastewater characteristics, the dilution ratio, and the process configuration. Often anaerobic contact tanks for enhanced biological phosphate removal are considered for the purpose of suppressing filamentous growth.

Unfortunately, such tanks are not successful with respect to some detrimental filamentous organisms like *Microthrix parvicella*. The processes for nitrogen removal can be divided into three groups:

- Subdivided tanks with distinct compartments for denitrification and nitrification, e.g., pre-anoxic zone denitrification, step-feed process, or post-denitrification process.

- Completely mixed or closed-loop tanks in which conditions for nitrification or denitrification are established periodically, e.g., intermittent nitrification–denit-rification, alternating nitrification–denitrification (Bio-Denitro process), or intermittent nitrification–denitrification with intermittent wastewater feeding (JARV process).
- Closed-loop tanks in which anoxic zones for denitrification and aerobic zones for nitrification are established at the same time (simultaneous nitrification–denit-rification).

Activated sludge plants for nitrification only can suffer from a too-low residual alkalinity. Especially if the aeration tank is completely mixed due to denitrification in the final clarifier, sludge can float and harm the final effluent quality. To overcome such problems, implementing provisions for some denitrification even when nitrification only is required is strongly recommended.

Pre-anoxic zone denitrification

The activated sludge tank is divided into two main parts, the anoxic zone and the aerobic zone. Since biodegradation of organic carbon follows first-order kinetics, the anoxic zone may be subdivided (Fig. 3.16). Furthermore. the last one or two anoxic compartments may also be equipped with aeration installations, for flexibility.

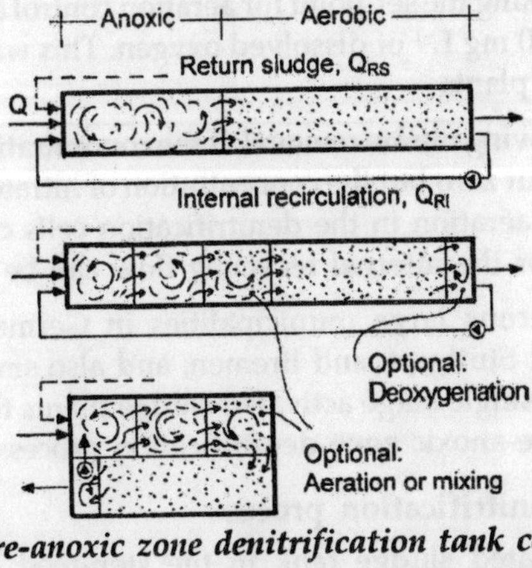

Fig. 3.16 Pre-anoxic zone denitrification tank configurations.

The aeration tank may have any configuration, as shown in Section 3.3.1. Since it is often difficult to keep the dissolved oxygen concentration in the outlet zone as low as desired, a final nonaerated zone, from which the internal recirculation flow is withdrawn, may be appropriate. If the tank is arranged in a U-shape, the recycling pump merely has to push the flow through the dividing wall.

The hydraulic head loss along such activated sludge tanks is in the range of centimeters if the top of the dividing walls end 0.10–0.30 m below the water level.

Process control may be limited to automatic control of the aeration intensity, to maintain a preset dissolved oxygen concentration. If monitors for ammonia and nitrate are installed at the aeration tank outlet or – even better – at the outlet of a group of aeration tanks, the signals can be used for additional control measures, the purposes of which may be:

- Saving energy: If the concentration of ammonia is zero and that of nitrate is in the desired range, aeration of the denitrification cells can be switched off or, if they are already off, the set-point for aeration control can be lowered. If ammonia increases the opposite measures have to be taken.
- Keeping ammonia low in the winter: If at very low temperatures of the mixed liquor the concentration of ammonia increases, one might try to improve nitrification by raising the set-point for aeration control above the usual 1.5–2.0 mg L^{-1} of dissolved oxygen. This was successful at some plants.
- Improving nitrate removal: If the concentration of ammonia is about zero but the concentration of nitrate is at its upper limit, aeration in the denitrification cells can be stopped and/or the internal recycling flow can be increased.
- Numerous large municipalities in Germany, including Berlin, Stuttgart, and Bremen, and also smaller cities are using single-stage activated sludge plants that implement the pre-anoxic zone denitrification process.

Step-feed denitrification process

The activated sludge tank in the step-feed denitrification process consists of two to three pre-anoxic zone units in series: the return sludge is diverted to the first denit-rification zone and the wastewater is distributed to each denitrification zone (Fig. 3.17).

Although the first experiments on this process were performed in the UK and later in Japan, the first results for a full-scale plant were reported by Schlegel in Germany.

To increase nitrate removal in the step-feed process, it is necessary to decrease the fraction of wastewater diverted to the last denitrification zone (decrease x) or to increase the return sludge flow and/or the internal recirculation of the last unit ($Q_{IR,n}$) (Eqs. 40 and 41). In existing plants, however, internal recirculation is generally not used with the step-feed process. Since increasing the return sludge flow (Q_{RS}) can hinder the final clarification, it seems more appropriate to decrease x. This is possible only if the organic carbon contained in the wastewater flow (x Å" Q) is sufficient to denitrify the incoming nitrate load.

Due to the stepwise 'dilution' of the return sludge with wastewater, the MLSS drops from unit to unit. The result is a higher average concentration of MLSS than in the effluent of the last aeration tank. This is considered an advantage, since the MLSS of the effluent determines the size of the final clarifiers. To maintain the same loading rates in the three compartments it is possible to chose appropriate tank volumes or, which is easier, to distribute the wastewater flow appropriately. This would occur when $Q_1 = 0.4\ Q$, $Q_2 = 0.33\ Q$, and $Q_3 = 0.27\ Q$. The MLSS would then be, respectively, 4.3 kg m^{-3}, 3.5 kg m^{-3}, and 3.0 kg m^{-3}. Without internal recir-culation, the ratio C_{COD}/S_{NO3}, which determines the degree of nitrate removal, in the three denitrification zones differs considerably. With $Q_{IR,1} = 1.0–1.5\ Q$, $Q_{IR,2} = 0.4–0.5\ Q$, and $Q_{IR,3} = 0$, C_{COD}/S_{NO3} takes the same value. In the three-step process with $Q_{RS} = Q$, $Q_{IR,3} = 0$, and $x = 0.27$, the denitrification efficiency is 86% (Eq. 41). If with more-concentrated wastewater a low nitrate concentration must be maintained, $Q_{IR,3}$ (Eq. 41) has to be selected. $Q_{IR,1}$ and $Q_{IR,2}$ then have to be increased appropriately.

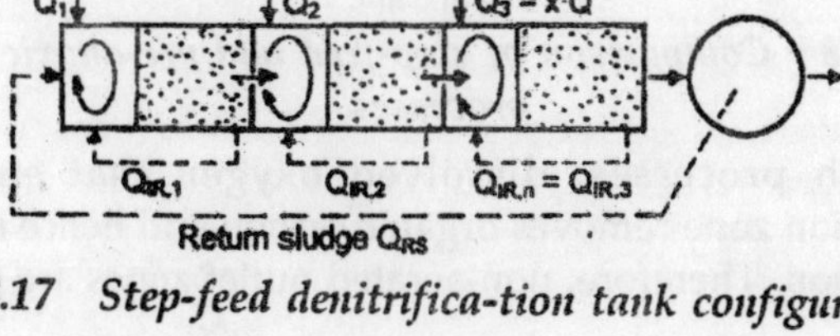

Fig. 3.17 Step-feed denitrifica-tion tank configuration.

The similarity of the pre-anoxic zone denitrification process and the step-feed process is obvious when Eqs. 38 and 41 are compared. To achieve 86% denitrification efficiency in the pre-anoxic zone process, the recycling ratio must be $Q_R/Q = 6.4$. The differences between the pre-anoxic zone process and the step-feed process are illustrated in Figure 3.18.

The advantages of the pre-anoxic zone process are that each of the three tanks is operated independently and that the tanks all have the same water level and depth. In the step-feed process some head loss occurs as the water flows from one tank to the next; therefore, either the water depth differs from tank to tank (same bottom level) or the water depth is kept constant (different bottom levels). For maintenance, it is necessary to have a bypass for each tank in the step-feed process.

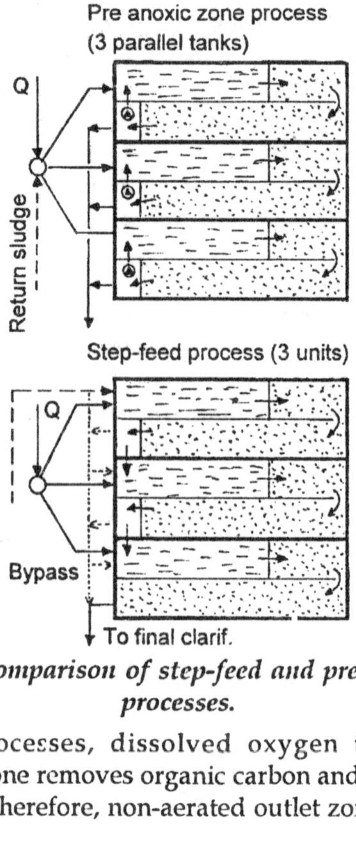

Fig. 3.18 Comparison of step-feed and pre-anoxic zone processes.

In both processes, dissolved oxygen that enters the denitrification zone removes organic carbon and hence decreases denitrification. Therefore, non-aerated outlet zones are shown in the pre-anoxic zone tanks. In the step-feed process only the first and second aeration tanks may be equipped with a non-aerated zone. Several plants with the step-feed process are operated by the Emschergenossen-schaft and, e.g., the cities of Wolfsburg and Bremerhaven.

Simultaneous nitrification and denitrification

The key to nitrogen removal by the simultaneous nitrification-denitrification process is to appropriately set the aerators so as to establish sufficiently large aerobic and anoxic zones simultaneously (Fig. 3.19). Since the load of any wastewater treatment plant fluctuates diurnally, the concentrations of nitrate and ammonia vary inversely when the aerator setting is constant. To achieve the desired nitrogen removal, a process control is therefore required.

Pasveer in 1964 was the first to report on simultaneous denitrification in an oxidation ditch. He achieved this by setting the optimal immersion depth of the surface aerator so as to create a sufficiently large anoxic zone. At the Vienna Blumenta plant (Section 3.1.3), the oxygen uptake rate was continuously measured with a special (homemade) respirometer. The respirometer output was used to switch the appropriate number of aerators to achieve the desired nitrogen removal.

The first real process control for simultaneous denitrification was developed by Ermel. A continuous sample flow was separated from the mixed liquor by ultra-filtration and diverted to a nitrate monitor. At the Salzgitter Bad plant the two closed-loop aeration tanks are operated in parallel. Each tank is equipped with three mammoth rotor surface aerators. One rotor in each tank is operated continuously to create sufficient circulating flow.

The two other rotors of each tank are automatically switched on if the nitrate concentration in the sample flow drops to, e.g., S_{NO3} = 3 mg L^{-1}. The aerators were stopped if, e.g., S_{NO3} reached 6 mg L^{-1} and were switched on again after the set point of S_{NO3} = 3 mg L^{-1} was reached. Figure 3.20 shows a daily time course of ammonia and nitrate levels measured in one of the aeration tanks. Due to the still-low denitrification rate during the period of high ammonia load (8 to 12 AM) the concentration of ammonia rises to about 4 mg L^{-1} N. As the denitrification rate increases after noon, the off-periods of the two aerators become shorter and the ammonia concentration decreases.

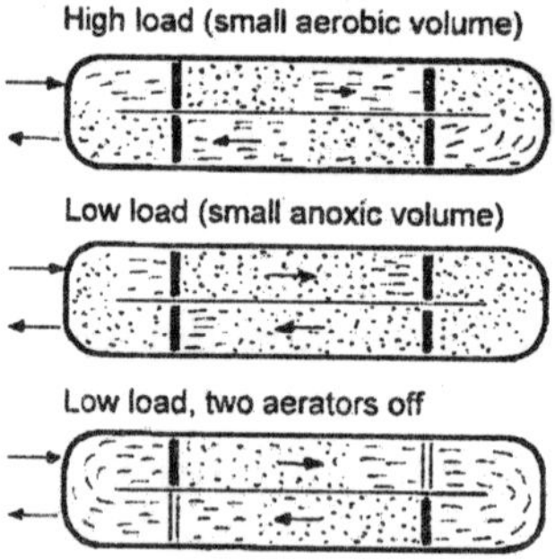

Fig. 3.19 ***Simultaneous nitrification and denitrification under different loading conditions.***

A more sophisticated control system based on monitoring both nitrate and ammonia was used in the wastewater treatment plant in Hildesheim.

In Salzgitter Bad an ORP controller was tested as a very simple, low-cost control method. Since the oxidation–reduction potential (ORP) drops sharply, if at zero DO nitrate reaches zero, the controller switches the additional aerators on at a certain slope of ORP. The additional aerators are then operated for a preset period of time. Figure 3.21 shows the time course of ORP. The effluent during the time when the ORP controller was used was as good as when the nitrate controller was used. At about the same time, similar experiments with ORP were conducted in Canada.

Some newer plants for simultaneous nitrification and denitrification are equipped with propellers (in addition to surface aerators) to maintain a sufficient flow velocity independent of the number of aerators in operation. Such plants can also be operated in intermittent nitrification–denitrification mode.

In addition to the cities already mentioned, plants with simultaneous nitrifica-tion–denitrification are also operated in, e.g., Osnabrück, Münster, Gera, Pader-born, Tel-Aviv, and in numerous smaller communities in which oxidation ditches were converted to the simultaneous mode by means of automatic control.

Whether and how much of the readily biodegradable organics are oxidized by dissolved oxygen (and therefore lost for denitrification) depend on the placement of the wastewater inlet and its distance to the next aerator. It is advisable to introduce the flow near the tank bottom, since anoxic conditions are predominant there.

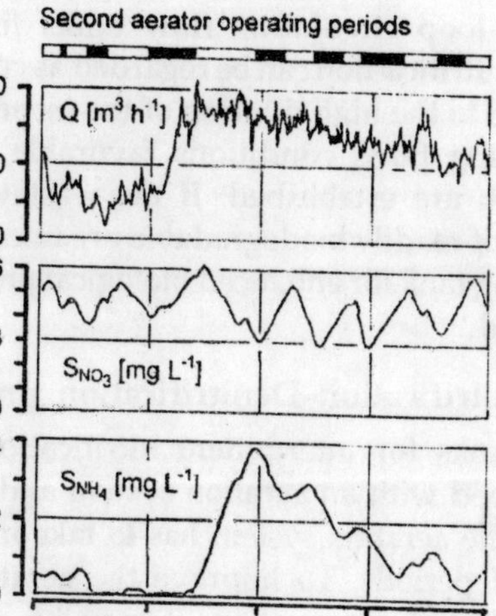

PM 12 Salzgitter Bad plant.

***Fig. 3.20** Time courses of ammonia and nitrate levels in one aeration tank at the*

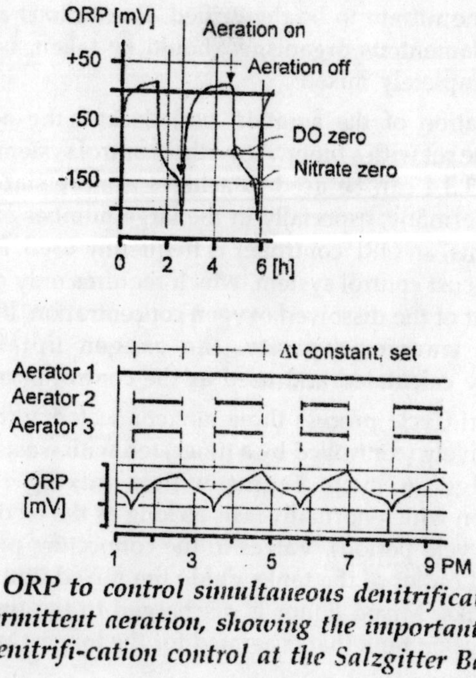

***Fig. 3.21** ORP to control simultaneous denitrification. Top: with intermittent aeration, showing the important points; bottom, denitrifi-cation control at the Salzgitter Bad plant.*

The closed-loop circulating flow tanks for simultaneous nitrification–denitrifica-tion can be regarded as completely mixed. In addition, due to the high dilution of the incoming wastewater by the circulating flow, conditions favorable for filamentous bacterial growth are established. If the wastewater contains a higher fraction of readily biodegradable organics, a selector or an anaerobic mixing tank for enhanced biological phosphate removal is recommended.

Intermittent nitrification–Denitrification process

Aeration tanks for intermittent nitrification–denitrification must be equipped with an aeration system and mixing devices. The design of the aeration system has to take into consideration the aeration-off periods. To improve the aeration efficiency of plants with diffused air aeration, it may be advisable to also operate the propellers during the aeration periods.

In intermittent nitrification–denitrification plants the fraction of readily biodegradable organics, which enters the tank while aeration is operating, may be oxidized by dissolved oxygen and therefore lost for denitrification. This must be considered when calculating the nitrate to be denitrified. Precautions against the growth of filamentous organisms should be taken, because the tanks are completely mixed.

The duration of the aeration periods and the aeration-off periods can be set with a timer. Any other control system described in Section 3.3.3.4 can be used to achieve a more stable effluent quality. In Germany, especially in the large number of extended aeration plants, an ORP controller is frequently used. NitraReg is another low-cost control system, which requires only continuous measurement of the dissolved oxygen concentration. By knowing the oxygen transfer capacity, the oxygen uptake rate is automatically calculated and used as the control parameter.

In the Tri-Cycle process three interconnected aeration tanks are consecutively (controlled by a timer) fed with wastewater and return sludge. A cycle begins with a mixing period for denitrification which normally lasts as long as the feeding period (1/3 of the cycle period). Valves in the connecting pipes and at the inlet and outlet of the tanks guide the mixed liquor through the three tanks. Mixed liquor is discharged to the final clarifier from the aeration tank that is aerated for the longest period. This process is used in at least six plants in Germany. Unfortunately only brochures of the company (GVA, Wülfrath, Germany) that developed this process are available.

The Jülich Wastewater Treatment Process (JARV) was developed to overcome problems with bulking sludge in completely mixed aeration tanks. The key of the process is a rather short feeding period compared to the cycle period. This requires a balancing tank upstream of the aeration tank and an effluent gate to equalize the flow to the final clarifiers. Balancing is avoided if, e.g., four parallel aeration tanks are consecutively fed with wastewater. The effluent from the aeration tanks may contain considerable ammonia peaks. It is, therefore, advisable to build a small post-aeration basin between the aeration tanks and the final clarifiers. Only two plants in Germany are operated by this process.

The differences of the three processes relative to the intermittent nitrifica-tion–denitrification process are that almost all readily biodegradable organics are available for denitrification, that there is a higher concentration gradient by which the sludge volume index can be improved, and that during the discharge period the mixed liquor is aerobic (except in the JARV process if a post aeration tank is omitted). The anoxic tank fraction (V_D/V) can be estimated as for the pre-anoxic zone denitrification process (Eq. 26).

Special processes for low COD/TKN ratio

Wastewater from the food industry may be characterized by high concentrations of organics as well as considerable nitrogen concentrations. Anaerobic pretreatment of such sewages is favorable because of the negligible sludge production and energy requirement. If nitrogen removal is required, the COD/TKN ratio can however decrease too much for sufficient denitrification.

Since denitrification of nitrite requires about 35% less organics than denitrifica-tion of nitrate, a process in which *Nitrosomonas* were inhibited was developed by Abeling. The pre-anoxic zone process was operated with a control system to maintain the pH at about pH = 8 by dosing the aerobic tank with NaOH and to keep ammonia at $S_{NH4} = 10$ mg L^{-1} by appropriate aeration control. According to the findings of Anthonisen et al. and Nyhuis (Fig. 3.10), these are conditions under which *Nitrobacter* are inhibited.

Because there is always some ammonia and some nitrite in the effluent, a second stage using a fixed-film reactor was implemented.

A different method of removing high nitrogen concentrations without any organic substrate was published by Jetten et al. In a continuous-flow stirred reactor as a first stage, about 50% of ammonia was converted to nitrite; and in a second stage a fixed-film reactor converted nitrite to nitrogen gas (N_2) by autotrophic bacteria using ammonia as electron donor. However, this is not regarded as an activated sludge process.

Post-denitrification with external organic carbon

Few plants around the world use external carbon as the sole carbon source for denit-rification in single-stage activated sludge plants. One such plant was constructed to treat the whole wastewater of the Salzgitter Steel Works in Germany.

The wastewater originates from treated blast furnace gas (high ammonia loads), treated coke oven gas (phenols, cyanides, ammonia, etc.), and several other discharges. The total flow of about 50000 m^3 d^{-1} contains about 35 mg L^{-1} ammonia nitrogen. Because soft water is used for cooling, the alkalinity is low. Therefore, experiments were first carried out using the pre-anoxic zone process to gain as much alkalinity as possible. Since the organic carbon content of the wastewater was too low, methanol had to be added to ensure sufficient nitrate removal, but the process was very unstable due to the toxic components of the wastewater.

The process was therefore changed to post-denitrification, with satisfying experimental results. The full-scale plant is shown in Figure 3.25. It is possible to operate the first two aeration tanks (#1 and #2) in parallel, to prevent a strong concentration gradient of the toxic substances, but this has not been necessary. The center zone of tank #4 (1500 m^3), to which methanol is added in response to the measured nitrate concentration in the tank, serves as a denitrification zone. In the final aerated zone (1500 m^3) accidentally overdosed methanol is oxidized. Tank #3, for maintenance purposes, is constructed like tank #4. During normal operation both parts of this tank are aerated.

To remove 1250 kg of nitrate nitrogen per day, 3500 kg of methanol per day are consumed, which is in the practical range of 2.5 to 3.0 kg methanol per kg nitrate nitrogen to be denitrified.

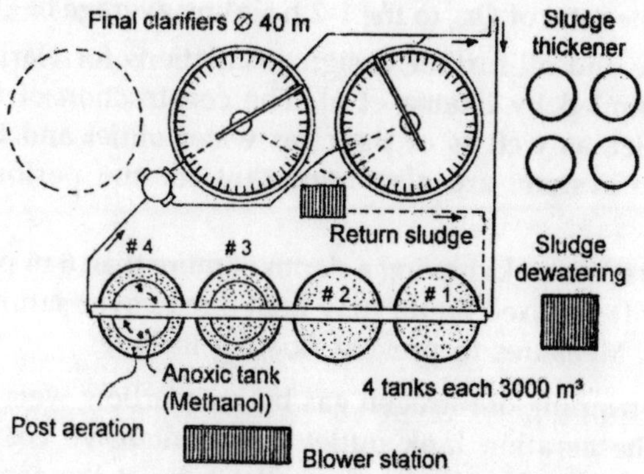

***Fig. 3.25** Flow diagram of the wastewater treatment plant of the Salzgitter Steel Works (post-denitrification).*

Interactions between the biological reactors and the final clarifiers

The biological reactor and the final clarifier, linked by the return sludge flow, form a unit process. The conditions shown in Figure 3.26 for rectangular tanks with scrapers are similar to those in circular tanks with scrapers.

Since MLSS is kept constant by withdrawing excess sludge, the suspended solids concentration (SS_{RS}) of the return sludge increases with decreasing return sludge flow (Q_{RS}). The return sludge flow is the sum of the flow of thickened sludge (Q_{sl} with SS_{sl}) and the short circuit flow (Q_{short} with MLSS).

For return sludge pumping two strategies are common:

- constant flow of Q_{R_S} at least during dry-weather periods
- constant ratio Q_{RS}/Q

Because of the diurnal fluctuation in wastewater flow, at constant Q_{R_S} the bottom sludge layer height h_S and SS_{RS} fluctuate approximately in parallel with Q and MLSS fluctuates inversely to the wastewater flow variation. If the return sludge ratio $O_{RS}/Q$is kept constant SS_{RS} fluctuates only a little. But if, e.g., during sudden storm water flows, the return sludge flow is immediately increased so as to keep Q_{RS}/Q constant, the short circuit flow increases and SS_{RS} decreases accordingly. It therefore makes sense to keep the ratio of Q_{R_S} to the 1-2 h sliding average of Q constant.

These and all further design calculations for clarifiers have been compiled by Ekama et al. The construction of the mixed liquor inlet, as well as of the clear water outlet and the sludge collection system, are also important for the performance of clarifiers.

If aeration tanks having a depth of more than 6 m precede the final clarifier, mixed liquor may float due to over-saturation with nitrogen. Measures to prevent floating include:

- Stripping of nitrogen gas by an overflow weir cascade at the aeration tank outlet or by intensive coarse-bubble aeration in a shallower outlet zone of the aeration tank.
- Applying deep final clarifiers in which mixed liquor is introduced near the bottom.

Design procedure

Detailed design information may be taken from handbooks. The main design steps for single-stage activated sludge plants comprise:

1. Determination of the design loads (e.g., BOD_5, COD, suspended solids, nitrogen, phosphorous), the average alkalinity, the wastewater flow (daily and peak), and the peak storm water flow ($m^3\ h^{-1}$). Existing data should be checked for annual fluctuations in the wastewater temperature, the loads, and the flows. If nitrification is required, the design load should be selected in combination with the wastewater temperature. The time period with the highest two-week average COD load at the lowest wastewater temperature can be selected to determine the critical sludge age and the sludge production. The highest oxygen demand may however have to be calculated for another period (e.g., summer).
2. Required effluent quality as percent removal or as concentrations ($C_{BOD,e}$, $C_{COD,e}$, $S_{NH4,e}$, $S_{NO3,e}$, $S_{P,e}$, SS_e). Mode of inspection, e.g., grab sample or 24-h composite sample. Value to be maintained, e.g., the annual average, 80% of all days, or 80% of grab samples.

3. Selection of the process configuration. Should it be with primary sedimentation? Aerobic selector? Anaerobic mixing tank for enhanced phosphate removal? Phosphate precipitation (and what type of precipitant)? Process for nitrogen removal? Addition of external organic carbon for nitrogen removal - continuously or temporarily? Necessity of adding N, P, and trace elements to specific industrial wastewater? Sludge disposal, separate stabilization, or costabilization of sludge?
4. An aerobic selector can be designed for a volumetric load of 20 kg COD (m^3 d^{-1}). For enhanced biological phosphate removal, an anaerobic contact period of 0.25–0.5 h (based on $Q + Q_{RS}$) can be assumed.
5. Selection of the aerobic sludge age (SRT_{aer}) considering the degree of treatment, e.g., organic carbon removal only; nitrification at any time, at certain time periods, or at periods beyond a certain reactor temperature (e.g., T 10 °C); costabil-ization of sludge. The following values may be used: Organic carbon removal only: SRT = 4 d; nitrification at T e" 10° °C: SRT_{aer} = 8–10 d.
6. For denitrification: estimation of the nitrate to be denitrified (Eq. 24). Assumption of anoxic tank volume fraction V_D/V (Eqs. 26 or 27 or values from Figure 3.11). Calculation of sludge age with Eq. 28.
7. For costabilization of sludge (extended aeration) and nitrogen removal, a sludge age of SRT = 25 d can be assumed.
8. Calculation of the remaining alkalinity with Eq. 33 and, if aeration tanks deeper than 6 m are planned, checking of the resulting pH (Section 3.2.6.2).
9. Determination of the MLSS considering the sludge volume index ISV to be expected. It is recommended to first check the final clarifier design to decide upon the appropriate MLSS. Generally, MLSS = 3.0–5.0 kg m^{-3} is used in design calculations. Higher values should be used only if a sludge volume index of ISV = 100 mL L^{-1} or less can be expected.
10. Calculation of the daily mass of excess sludge with Eqs. 12 ($M_{exc,C}$) and 32 ($M_{exc,P}$). For settled municipal wastewater,

as a rough estimate one can assume 0.4 to 0.5 kg excess sludge solids per kg COD influent. Finally, the reactor volume is calculated with Eq. 14.

11. For nitrogen removal only: estimation of the required internal recycle flow (Eq. 37) or the wastewater distribution in the step-feed process (Eq. 40) or the cycle period for intermittent nitrification–denitrification processes (Eq. 44).
12. Design of the aeration installation, considering the minimum and maximum oxygen uptake rates (Eqs. 13, 16, and 25).
13. Design of the final clarifier. As a rough estimate for the surface area of horizontal flow clarifiers, a volumetric sludge surface loading rate of q_{SV} d" 450 L m^{-2} h^{-1} (Eq. 50) can be assumed. The side wall water depth should not be less than 3.00 m, and the average water depth should be in the range of 3.50–4.50 m (except, e.g., downstream of deep aeration tanks).

For larger plants it is recommended to check the results of static dimensioning with dynamic simulation. This should be considered with the collection of load data.

4

Modeling of Aerobic Wastewater Treatment Processes

INTRODUCTION

The trend of improving the effluent quality from wastewater treatment plants leads to an increasing complexity in the design and operation of the plants. To design the plants and optimize and control the operation, it is necessary to use dynamic models. Most models used for wastewater treatment plants today are deterministic, the exception being some models for control, which can be of the black-box type. The deterministic models aim to give a realistic description of the main processes of the plant. However, models are never true in the process sense and always simplify the complicated processes occurring in a biological treatment plant. The models we have at hand today include the phenomena for which we think we have a reasonable explanation. A major gap in modeling is lack of knowledge about the development of the microbiology in treatment plants. Thus, phenomena like bulking and foaming are still awaiting more basic understanding before we can develop reliable models for them. Below, various elements of modeling are discussed. For further information on modeling in general and on modeling of biofilters, please see Chapter 13, Volume 4, of the Biotechnology series (Rehm et al., 1991).

PURPOSE OF MODELING

Models are used for several purposes with regard to wastewater treatment plants:

- design
- control

- operational optimization
- teaching
- organizing tool

The intended use of a model has implications for its structure. Models used for design and for control need not be identical.

Models are no better than the assumptions upon which they are built. Several factors influence their behavior. The way they handle detailed wastewater composition is important. Wastewater characterization has a strong impact on real plant behavior as well as on its modeling. Errors in characterization of the wastewater or changes in the composition of the wastewater can result in erroneous modeling results.

ELEMENTS OF ACTIVATED SLUDGE MODELS

An activated sludge model consists of various elements:

- transport processes
- components
- biological and chemical processes
- hydraulics

To this can be added a framework of component conversion and data presentation tools. The amount of detail needed depends on the intended use of the model and on the amount of information available on the wastewater and the treatment plant.

TRANSPORT PROCESSES AND TREATMENT PLANT LAYOUT

Transport processes deal only with movement of water and do not include any chemical or biological processes. The flow scheme of the treatment plant, which describes the movement of water and sludge, must be known, and a model of the flow scheme must be part of the overall model. Often it is necessary to simplify the flow scheme, due to a high complexity of the plant or to limitations to the number of tanks that can be applied in the model. Simplification of a flow scheme can be very beneficial for improving the overview of the situation in the plant. Parallel tanks can be modeled as one tank, and tanks in series might also be modeled as one. However, one must be aware that the more simplified the flow scheme model is, the greater the model calculations may deviate from the real world.

The flow pattern of wastewater and sludge must be known. Not all treatment plant operators can give this information directly, at least not correctly.

Aeration

Aeration in each of the tanks must be described, either with a fixed oxygen concentration or as an aeration coefficient, K_La, operating uncontrolled or controlled together with a control strategy. Aeration of tanks without mechanical aeration should also be taken into account. The oxygen penetration through the surface of, e.g., de-nitrification tanks can be significant.

The use of a fixed oxygen concentration is a simplification that does not allow for simultaneous nitrification-denitrification processes to be modeled, nor the impact of oxygen in recycle flows. Thus, the K_La model is recommended for professional modeling.

Components

Components are the soluble and suspended substances that one wants to model, including substances present in the raw wastewater as well as substances found within the treatment plant. The components to model depend on the purpose of the model. If the purpose is to model a nitrifying plant, one phosphorous component will suffice, but if modeling of biological phosphorous removal is the objective, then at least two phosphorous components are needed: polyphosphate in the biomass (X_{PP}) and a soluble component, orthophosphate (S_{PO4}).

Processes

Processes include modeling of chemical and biological processes. The model to be used is always a strong simplification of reality, but these simplified models often give reasonable modeling results, but sometimes not. For example, a simple phosphorous precipitation model, like the one applied in ASM2 (Henze et al., 1995), can model the part of phosphorous removal that is not related to assimilation and biological excess uptake. On the other hand, a model that does not account for the denitrification that occurs in nitrification tanks, the so-called simultaneous denitrifica-tion, gives effluent nitrate concentrations that are too high. Thus, the degree of simplification must be considered. If one wants to model denitrification, there must be at least one process for this (anoxic growth of heterotrophic biomass). But it is also possible to apply many processes for the description of denitrification. This occurs for a model that is aimed at predicting intermediates like nitrite, dinitrogen oxide, nitrous oxide, etc., in the denitrification process.

Hydraulic Patterns

The hydraulics of the various tanks have to be modeled. Any tanks can be modeled as ideal mixing, but some may need to be modeled as a series of ideally mixed tanks. More complex models of the hydraulics are seldom needed.

PRESENTATION OF MODELS

The complex interrelationship between the various components and processes are best presented in a matrix. A very simple model for an activated sludge process for removal of organic matter is shown in the matrix in Table 4.1. With this table it is possible to obtain a quick overview of the conversions in the described process.

Table 4.1. Simple model matrix for activated sludge organic removal[a].

Process	Component			Process Rate
	S_{O2}	S_S	X_H	
Aerobic	±1 +1		+1	$b_H X_H$
growth Decay			-1	

S_{O2}: soluble oxygen, g O_2 m^{-3}; S_S: soluble organic substrate, g COD m^{-3}; X_H: biomass, g COD m^{-3}; Y_H: yield coefficient, g COD g^{-1} COD; $m_{m,H}$: maximum growth rate, d^{-1}; K_S: half saturation constant, g COD m^{-3}; b_H: decay constant, d^{-1}.

MASS BALANCES

The rows in the matrix give the mass balance of the process. The second row in Table 4.1 shows, e.g., that decay removes biomass, X_H (the stoichiometric coefficient is negative, –1), and produces soluble substrate, S_S (the stoichiometric coefficient is +1).

Rates

The rate equations of the processes are found in the right column (Table 4.1). To find the rate for the change in biomass in relation to decay, r_{XH}, the rate equation must be multiplied by the stoichiometric coefficient in the matrix; that is:

$$r_{XH} = -1 \cdot b_H X_H \tag{1}$$

Component Participation

The columns in the matrix (Table 4.1) give an overview of which processes the various components participate in (according to the model). The second column shows that the substrate, S_S, is removed by aerobic growth and is produced by decay.

The Activated Sludge Models Nos. 1, 2 and 3 (ASM1, ASM2, ASM3)

Most models for activated sludge processes are based on the IAWQ Activated Sludge Model No. 1, called ASM1 (Henze et al., 1987). This model is used as a platform for further model development and is today the international standard for advanced activated sludge modeling. Because the ASM contains only a very simplified model, most modelers expand the ASM1, depending on the degree of complexity needed to model the actual problem. In some situations more complex kinetic equations are needed, in others more processes or more components have to be included. Nutrient limitation of the growth processes is usually included.

Activated Sludge Model No. 1 (ASM1)

The ASM1 model describes activated sludge processes with nitrification and denit-rification. It is the experience of more than 10 years of use that the model gives a good description of the processes, as long as the wastewater has been characterized in detail and is of domestic or municipal origin. The model was not developed to fit industrial wastewater treatment. When used for industrial wastewater, great care should be taken in calibration and in interpretation of the results. The ASM1 can calculate several details in the plant:

- oxygen consumption in the tanks

- concentration of ammonia and nitrate in the tanks and in the effluent
- concentration of COD in the tanks and in the effluent
- MLSS in the tanks
- solids retention time
- sludge production

As with all models, ASM1 also gives erroneous results if it is fed erroneous or overly simplified information. Table 4.2 shows the process matrix for ASM1. All processes, reaction kinetics, mass balances, and stoichiometry in the model are included in the matrix. If understood, the matrix notation is a useful tool to obtain an easy overview of the model.

In the ASM1 the processes for organic matter removal and nitrification are slightly coupled, as seen in Figure 4.1.

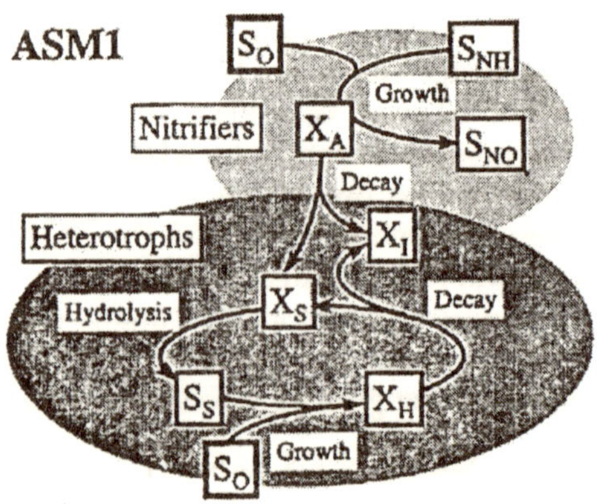

Fig. 4.1 Processes for heterotrophic and nitrifying bacteria in the Activated Sludge Model No. 1 (ASM1) (Gujer et al., 1999).

Activated Sludge Model No. 2 (ASM2)

The ASM2 model incorporates biological phosphorous uptake (Henze et al., 1995). Its combination with denitrification results in a model that is much more complex than ASM1. To describe the life of PAOs (phosphate-accumulating organisms), internal storage compounds of phosphorous and organic matter are needed.

Modeling the growth of the heterotrophic organisms requires at least three different organic substrates:

- acetic acid-like compounds, S_A
- fermentable substrate, S_F
- slowly degradable substrate, X_S

The ASM2 assumes that growth occurs only on substrate S_A and that the other organic substrates are hydrolyzed and fermented so as to be converted to S_A.

Activated Sludge Model No. 3 (ASM3)

The ASM3 model represents an alternative process description for heterotrophic bacteria. Under transient loading conditions, heterotrophic bacteria can store organic matter as polymeric compounds like polyhydroxyalkanoate (PHA) or glycogen (GLY). This storage can influence the overall process of activated sludge by supplying organic material under starvation conditions.

The Activated Sludge Model No. 3 (ASM3) includes this storage in its processes and applies a simplified maintenance/decay process. Figure 4.2 shows the processes used to describe heterotrophic bacteria; as can be seen, the substrate flows through the organisms during oxygen consumption for storage, growth, and maintenance.

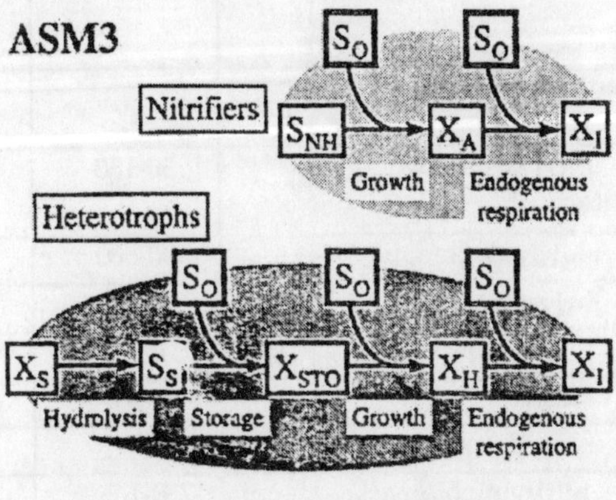

Fig. 4.2 Processes for hetero-trophic organisms in the Activated Sludge Model No. 3 (ASM3) (Gujer et al., 1999).

Wastewater Characterization

Wastewater characterization is an important element in dealing with models. The detailed wastewater composition has a significant influence on the performance of the treatment processes (Henze, 1992).

Table 4.3. Wastewater components in ASM2. Note that modeled levels of soluble organic material are higher than analytically determined levels.

Symbol *Component*		*Typical Level*	*Unit*
'Soluble' compounds:			
S_F fermentable organic matter		20-250	g COD m^{-3}
S_A acetafe and other fermentation products		10-60	g COD m^{-3}
S_{NH4} ammonium		10-100	g N m^{-3}
S_{NO3} nitrate + nitrite		0-1	g N m^{-3}
S_{PO4} orthophosphate		2-20	g P m^{-3}
S_I inert soluble organic matter		20-100	g COD m^{-3}
'Suspended' compounds:			
X_I inert suspended organic matter		30-150	g COD m^{-3}
X_S slowly degradable		80-600	g COD
X_H heterotrophic		20-120	g COD
X_{PAO} phosphorous-	(PA	0-1	g COD
X_{PP} stored		0-0.5	g P m^{-3}
X_{PHA} stored organic		0-1	g COD
X_{AUT} nitrifying biomass		0-1	g COD m^{-3}

The degree of detail needed in the wastewa-ter characterization depends on the objective of modeling. Figure 4.3 shows a detailed fractionation of municipal wastewater in relation to biological phosphorous removal. As can be seen, what is considered 'soluble' in the model (substances with the symbol S) is not equivalent to analytically determined soluble material, because part of the particulate organic material is easily degradable. Thus, from a reaction point of view, it cannot be distinguished from the analytically soluble material.

Table 4.3 shows a detailed fractionation of wastewater, which allows for modeling denitrification as well as biological phosphorous removal processes.

The characterization of wastewater can be simplified by combining existing data on BOD, COD, soluble fractions, etc. An example of this is from the Dutch river boards, which use the procedure shown below (Roeleveld and Kruit, 1998).

Influent:

$COD_{total} = S_S + S_I + X_S + X_I$ $COD_{soluble} = S_S + S_I$ (0.1 ìm filter) CODsuspended = XS + XI

(2) (3) (4)

where S_I = soluble COD (0.1 ìm filter) in the effluent from a low loaded biological treatment plant.

The figure shows a typical composition of primary settled municipal wastewater. Various analytical methods that can be used for the determination of single components are shown. Organic inert suspended material, X_I, and organic, slowly degradable suspended material, X_S, can be determined only by modeling and calculation (Henze et al., 1995). At present, no methods exist to directly determine these two fractions independently.

For inert suspended organic matter, X_I, the reason is that its concentration in the sludge originates in two sources: it is a component of the raw wastewater and is also produced during the decay of microorganisms. These two contributions cannot be separated analytically at present. Slowly degradable suspended organic matter, X_S, cannot be determined analytically except from calculation based on determinations of the other fractions of organic matter.

Fig. 4.3 COD fractionation in the Activated Sludge Model No. 2 (ASM2).

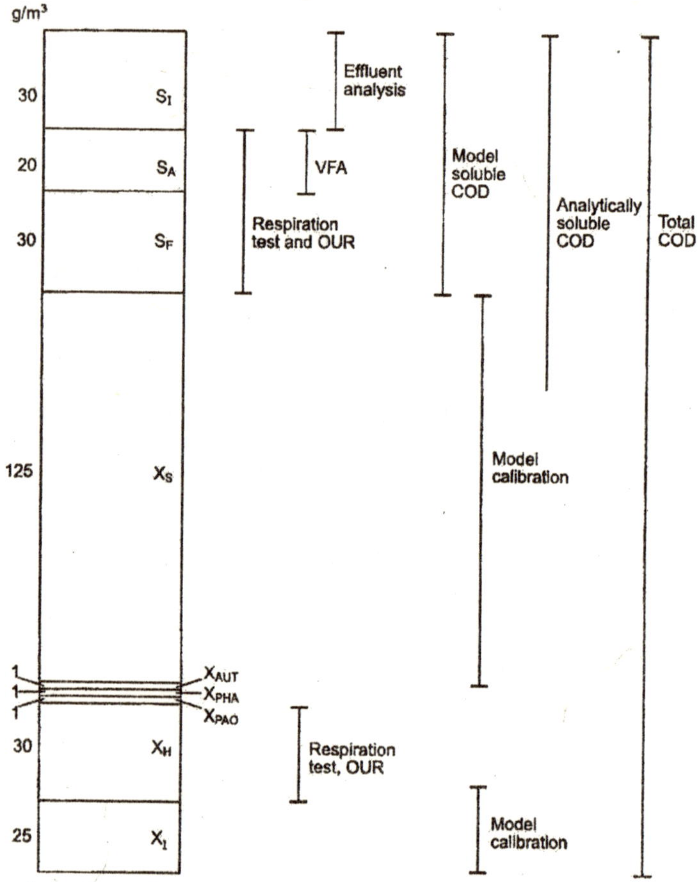

$S_S + X_S$ is determined from a BOD_5 measurement or from a BOD_{20} measurement (or calculation):

$$S_S + X_S = 1.5\ BOD_5 \tag{5}$$

$$S_S + X_S = BOD_{20}/0.85 \tag{6}$$

A simplified evaluation of the nitrogen components is done based on the content of nitrogen in the organic components:

$$TN = f_{NX} \cdot X_S + f_{NS} \cdot S_S + S_{NH4} \tag{7}$$

where f_{NX} and f_{NS} are the fractions of nitrogen (g N g^{-1} COD) and are typically around 0.03 g N g^{-1} COD (Henze et al., 1997).

MODEL CALIBRATION

Calibration of models is difficult. It is mandatory for a successful calibration that the content and the functioning of the model be understood. When calibrating by hand, it is important to follow a strategy and be aware of which parameters are to be used for which part of the calibration.

It is equally important to know the realistic intervals within which the various parameters should vary, in order to still have a realistic model.

Table 4.4 shows the steps to follow for calibration of the Activated Sludge Model No. 1. Constants not shown should, under normal circumstances, not be changed.

For processes without changes in performance or loading, calibration is easy but not very reliable. Often, many sets of calibration constants give a nice model fit. The

Table 4.4. Calibration steps for the activated sludge model no. 1 (ASM1).

Parameter	*Calibration*	*Comments*
Based on:		
Heterotrophic growth rate, $m_{H,max}$	OUR	often kept unchanged
Half saturation constant, K_S	COD in effluent	used to model the hydraulics of the tanks
Growth rate for nitrifying biomass, $m_{A,max}$	NH_4 in effluent	if NH_4 for all conditions is low, m should not be changed
Half saturation constant, K_{NH4}	NH_4 in effluent	only if NH_4 is low
Half saturation constant, $K_{O,A}$	NH_4 in effluent	only if S_{O2} varies
Denitrification factor, h_{NO3}	NO_3 in effluent	
Half saturation constant, K_{NO3}	NO_3 in effluent	only if NO_3 is low

more dynamic the data for calibration, the better the calibration will be, and the greater the chance will be for the model to respond correctly to situations outside the range of those used in the calibration. Many treatment plants have only small dynamic changes. For such plants, single dynamic events (overloading, mechanic breakdown, snow melt, etc.) are excellent for calibration purposes.

Computer Programs

Several computer programs that implement various models exist, and many include one or more of the models in the ASM family. Table 4.5 gives a short overview.

Use of Models

Models can be used for many purposes. An important field is control of treatment plants, for which it is often possible to use simplified models.

Complex processes, like nitrification- denitrification combined with biological phosphorous removal and external carbon source addition, can make it necessary to use even more complex models than those in the ASM family (Meinholt et al., 1998).

Optimizing the operation of a treatment plant is another use for models. Figure 4.4 shows a model calculation for a treatment plant that receives varying loads of ammonia from the sludge treatment.

This often creates a problem with overload of the nitrification process, resulting in breakthrough of ammonia peaks into the effluent from the plant. A model calculation can help find the optimal operational strategy for handling ammonia-rich sidestreams.

Table 4.5. Selected simulation programs for activated sludge plants.

Program	*Models Included*	*Characteristics*
ASIM	ASM1, ASM2, ASM3	simple program, allows for quick modeling
EFOR	ASM1, ASM2	program with a detailed wastewater calibration model, in which available data (including BOD) is used for calculation of both raw and treated wastewater composition; choice between various settler models
GPX	ASM1, ASM2, etc.	program in which different models can be selected for the simulation of both biology and settling
SIMBA	ASM1, ASM2	program widely used in the Netherlands and Germany based on Matlab-Simulink

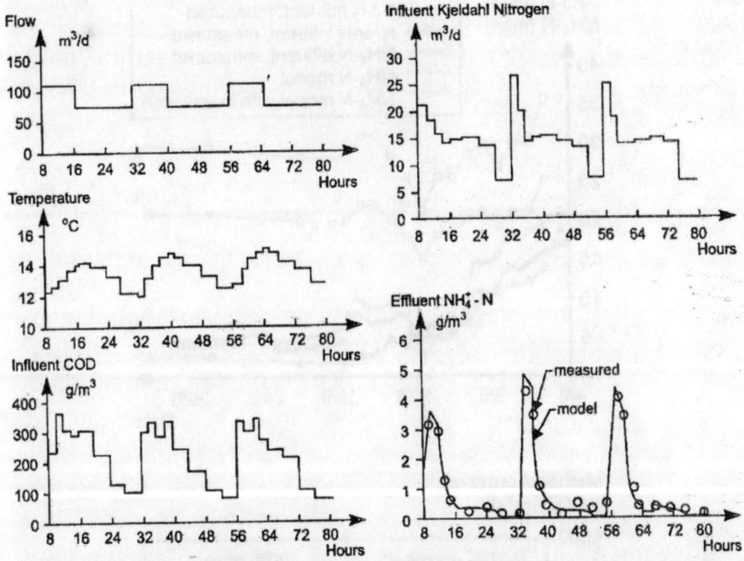

Fig. 4.4 Use of ASM1 for modeling effluent variations for ammonia dynamically loaded with ammonia-rich supernatant (Gujer, 1985).

Figure 4.5 shows a model calculation with ASM1 in relation to startup of a nitrifying activated sludge treatment process. The calculations are made to evaluate the possible effect of inoculation with nitrifying biomass. The results show that the inoculation should have no significant impact on the startup.

Figure 4.6 shows a model calculation of a process for denitrification with metha-nol. The process has an aerobic and an anoxic tank. By using two heterotrophic populations with different growth characteristics during modeling, a result is obtained that explains the differences in methanol removal rate. If the process is run solely aerobically for a period, the group of organisms that, under aerobic conditions, metabolizes methanol quickly will increase. This group has a slow methanol conversion rate under anoxic conditions.

In the second part of the experiment, from day 40 onward, the process is operated with 30% anoxic reaction time and 70% aerobic reaction time. Under these operational conditions, the other group of organisms will dominate, resulting in higher methanol conversion rates under anoxic conditions.

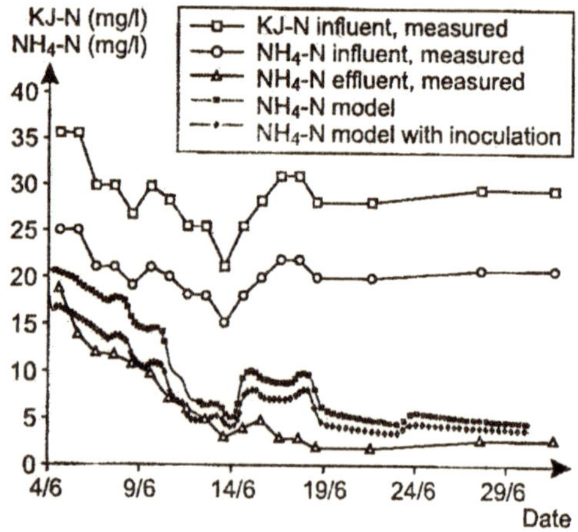

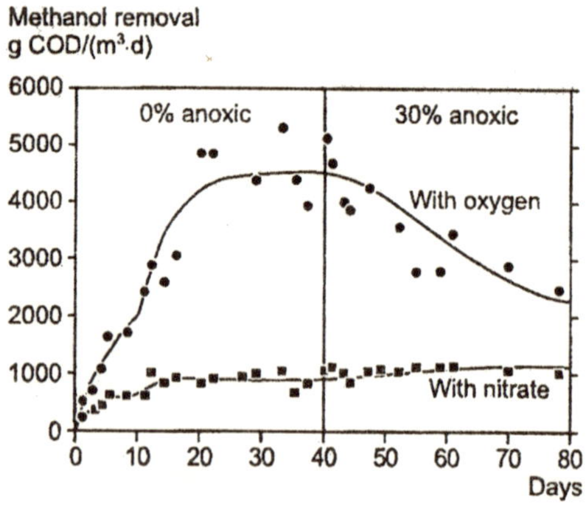

***Fig. 4.5** Model calculation of startup of an activated sludge process with and without inoculation with nitrifying organisms (Finnson, 1994).*

***Fig. 4.6** Modeling denitrification rate in the presence of methanol under varying operational conditions in an activated sludge process (Purtschert and Gujer, 1999).*

5

High-rate Anaerobic Wastewater Treatment

INTRODUCTION

Anaerobic wastewater treatment is a very old method of water purification. The Su-merians were already familiar with this method of wastewater purification. The first full-scale application of the anaerobic treatment of domestic wastewater is described for the 1860s (McCarty, 2001).

Anaerobic wastewater treatment has some advantages in comparison to aerobic treatment. The specific productivity of an anaerobic system is much higher and the engineering is simple. Whereas much energy is needed for aeration in aerobic wastewater treatment plants, anaerobic treatment produces energy in the form of usable biogas. Anaerobic treatment produces only low amounts of excess biomass (5% on COD reduction in comparison to nearly 30%–50% in aerobic wastewater treatment) and the nutrient requirements are therefore small compared with aerobic treatment. On the other hand, this also means that the growth of anaerobic bacteria is slow, and for this reason in particular the start-up of an anaerobic plant is slow. Anaerobically treated water usually cannot be released directly into the environment. The COD concentration in the effluent is usually not as low as is achievable with aerobic plants and is often odorous. For this reason high-loaded wastewa-ters are often treated by a combination of anaerobic and aerobic treatment. The second (aerobic) step is then, if necessary, designed also for N-elimination.

Anaerobic treatment of wastewaters includes acid formation and methane formation, which differ significantly in terms of nutrient needs, growth kinetics, and sensitivity to environmental conditions (Demirel and Yenigün, 2002).

Figure 5.1 shows some basic types of reactor for methane formation.

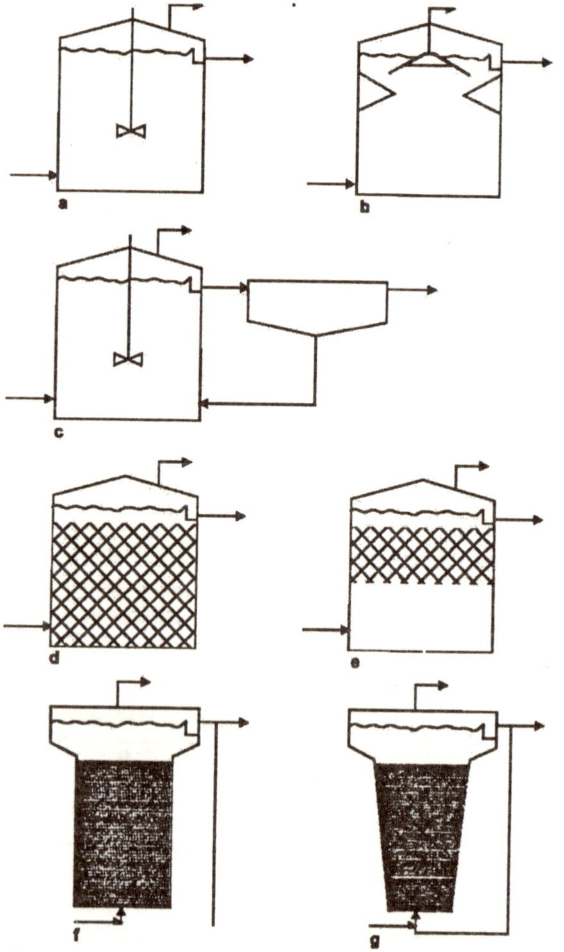

Fig. 5.1 Reactor systems for anaerobic wastewater treatment. a, Completely stirred tank reactor; b, upflow anaerobic sludge blanket; c, contact process; d, fixed film stationary bed; e, combination of a and d; f, fluidized bed; g, tapercd bed.

Therefore, these two steps are preferentially separated physically. For many industrial wastewaters and hydraulic retention times (HRT) that are not too short, acid formation can easily be done without specific installations for bacteria retention or recycling, whereas these procedures are absolutely necessary for methane formation. The classical digester or completely stirred tank reactor (CSTR) (Fig. 5.1a) without biomass retention is hardly used except in the treatment of sewage sludge. Industrial wastewater treatment always aims to be highly productive, and for that purpose, high concentrations of the biocatalyst, as is possible with the reactor systems shown in Figure 5.1b–g, are required.

The most widely used system worldwide is the upflow anaerobic sludge blanket (UASB) (Fig. 5.1b) (McCarty, 2002). The incoming wastewater is equally distributed over the cross section by a system of tubes. At low superficial upflow velocities (1–2 m h^{-1}) the wastewater flows vertically through a sludge bed. A three-phase separation unit, which prevents disintegration of the sludge pellets, is integrated in the upper part of the reactor. A disadvantage of this system is the limited knowledge concerning the formation of sludge pellets. These pellets are essential for the success of the system, but are not always formed with every wastewater. To avoid long times for start up, it is desirable to 'seed' new plants with sludge pellets from existing plants treating similar wastewaters. The productivity lies in the range of 10–15kg m^{-3} d^{-1} COD-degradation.

The so-called contact process (Fig. 5.1c) includes a CSTR and an external device for separation and recycling of anaerobic bacteria. For the separation, settling tanks or a lamella clarifier are used. Bacterial aggregates with adhering biogas bubbles cannot be held back by these methods. Therefore, a degasser is installed between the anaerobic reactor and the settling unit. Furthermore, a reaction in the settling unit has to be avoided, which can be achieved by low COD concentrations or a decrease in temperature. COD degradation in the whole plant (including the settling unit) ranges from 3 to 6 kg m^{-3} d^{-1}. An interesting report concerning this process and its application is given by Kroiss and Svardal (1999).

Fixed- and fluidized-bed reactors offer the advantage of high-load systems, requiring much less volume and space, and hence less investment than conventional systems. Furthermore, these systems tend to operate more stably under transient conditions such as fluctuations in substrates and pH. For these reasons, this chapter deals especially with these modern systems for high-rate anaerobic wastewater treatment.

The advantages mentioned are of interest to those industries that produce large amounts and/or highly concentrated wastewaters, notably the food, paper and pulp industries. Several fixed-film system reactor configurations are shown schematically in Figure 5.1d–g. Although most fixed-film systems can be associated with this scheme, the number of variations is high as regards the flow mode (up- or down-flow), the fluid distribution system at the reactor inlet, the support material and expansion (for fluidized beds), and the configuration of the reactor outlet (gas-liquid- support separation). Recycling is in general provided for dilution of substrate and fluidization.

Several problems, however, have hindered the application of these systems. These are longer startup times if no specific inoculum is available, requirement for a more sophisticated process control, and the cost of the support material (Weiland and Rozzi, 1991). Appropriate solutions are, in principle, available to overcome these problems.

Nevertheless, there has been considerable progress in application as a result of research and pilot plant investigations, as well as data published on industrial systems. A large amount of literature has accumulated, mainly over the last two decades, so that only part of it can be mentioned here. This chapter concentrates on basic principles of anaerobic fixed- and fluidized-bed systems and on recent experience accumulated on the laboratory, pilot, and industrial scales. One should, however, keep in mind that industrial applications must be based on pilot plant experience at the factory site for every new substrate or new source of wastewater or any specific problem.

A very broad and most successful application of high-performance anaerobic treatment in fixed- and fluidized-bed reactors relates to wastewater from industries based on agricultural and forestry products, which typically have high concentrations of organic substrates readily degraded by anaerobic bacteria (Austermann-Haun et al., 1993). They may result from raw material washing procedures, blanching, extraction, fermentation, or enzyme processing. Original substrates are usually carbohydrates, such as sugar, starch, cellulose and hemicellulose proteins, and fats, which readily undergo bacterial degradation to fatty acids, mainly acetic, propionic, butyric, and lactic acids. The majority of installations are in the potato, starch and sugar industries, in fruit, vegetable, and meat processing, in cheese, yeast, alcohol, citric acid, and pectin manufacturing and in the paper and pulp industries. The concentrations of substrates are typically in the range 5–50 kg (COD) m^{-3}, which are diluted by recirculation (loop reactor) to less than 2 kg (COD) m^{-3}.

In some countries, such as China, systems for the treatment of domestic sewage also play a major role (Yi-Zhang and Li-Bin, 1988). In the chemical and petrochemical industries, the implementation of anaerobic treatment plants for complex wastewaters started in the 1990s (Macarie, 2001). Furthermore, considerable efforts were made also to treat inhibitory or toxic substances.

Thus, cyanide-, formaldehyde-, ammonium-, nickel- and sulfide-containing wastewaters were investigated, and it was shown that methanogens can accommodate to rather high concentrations of such toxins, depending on the retention time (Parkin and Speece, 1983). Furthermore, organochlorine compounds in kraft bleaching effluents and in pesticide-containing water, including chloroform, chlorophenols, chlorocatechols and similar compounds, as well as chlorinated resin acids, could be treated to the stage of mineralization by adapted biofilms (Salkinoja-Salonen et al., 1983). These positive results were obtained on the laboratory scale. The degradation of furfural in sulfite evaporator condensate can proceed to a conversion of about 90% (Ney et al., 1989).

BASIC PRINCIPLES

Reactors are tubes with fixed bed internals or fluidized suspended particles, which serve as a support for biomass immobilization. The dimensions range from 10 to 500 m^3 with a ratio of height to diameter of 1–5. In general, an external loop recycles part of the effluent to the inlet, where mixing with the wastewater provides for its dilution to noninhibitory substrate concentrations and pH. Rarely, tapered beds have been used; most of the fluidized beds are provided with a settling zone with a larger diameter at the top of the reactor.

BIOFILM FORMATION

The basis for the use of packed-bed and fluidized-bed systems is the immobilization of bacteria on solid surfaces. Many species of bacteria (and other microorganisms) have the ability to adhere to supporting matrices.

Although immobilized bacteria have been used in aerobic wastewater treatment since the beginning of the 20. century, the application of these systems to anaerobic wastewater treatment is relatively new.

The fundamentals of bacterial adhesion to and growth on solid surfaces are discussed by Wingender and Flemming (1999). Here, only some aspects concerning anaerobic fixed films are considered. The preconditioning of solid surfaces is influenced by both environmental conditions (e.g. pH, temperature) and the surface itself (e.g. hydrophobicity, surface charge). The initial anaerobic biofilm attachment can be improved by the addition of cationic polymers (Stronach et al., 1987; Diaz-Baez, 1988) or slime-producing bacteria (Diaz-Baez, 1988), but the biofilm development is worse than in systems lacking these components. Jördening (1987) reported a positive effect resulting from supplementation of calcium. The primary adhesion of cells to the surface is due to hydrogen bonds, van der Waals forces, and/or electrostatic interactions. This reversible form of adhesion can become irreversible due to the production of exopolymeric substances (EPS), which act as a glue (Wingender and Flemming, 1999). Experiments on the first steps of the formation of anaerobic biofilms have given different results: although Sanchez et al. (1996) found facultative anaerobic bacteria to be primary colonizers, Sreekrishnan et al. (1991) observed that biofilm formation was initiated by methanogenic bacteria.

After a lag phase, which seems to be necessary for adaptation of the microorganisms to the new environment, exponential growth of bacteria begins. The growth rate is mainly determined by substrate transport and temperature (Heijnen et al., 1986).

BIOFILM CHARACTERISTICS

In view of the wide range of possible biofilm compositions, it is obvious that biofilm thickness does not correspond to the activity of the biocatalyst. Hoehn (1970) reported that the highest biofilm density occurs when the total biofilm thickness corresponds to the active biofilm thickness, i.e., the substrate-penetrated part of the biofilm.

KINETICS AND MASS TRANSFER

The reaction kinetics for any process changes with immobilization of the catalyst. In general, the following mass transfer processes have to be considered:

1. transport of substrate from the fluid to the surface of the support through the boundary layer (external mass transfer)
2. transport of substrate from the surface into the pores of the biocatalyst
3. reaction
4. 5. transport of products in the opposite direction of steps 1 and 2

The transport of substrates and products through the reactor is related to the hydro-dynamic characteristics of the system and is generally much faster than steps 2–4. Mass transfer is mostly reduced by diffusion limitation.

Depending on the mode of limitation, one can distinguish between film diffusion and pore diffusion and combined limited systems. Figure 5.2 schematically illustrates the resulting substrate profiles. For the description of the activity changes resulting from immobilization, an effectiveness factor is used, defined as observed reaction rate

$$\varsigma = \quad (1)$$

reaction rate in bulk liquid conditions

5.2.3.1 External Mass Transfer

In passing a solid surface, the fluid characteristics change from turbulent to laminar flow and produce a boundary layer around the surface. The flux j_1 through the boundary layer is equal to the mass transfer coefficient k_e and the concentration gradient from the outer shell c_{is} to the particle surface c_{bi}:

$$j_1 = k_e\,(c_{is} - c_{bi}) \quad (2)$$

An analytical solution for k_e can be given only for the ideal case of a single particle at infinite dilution. The mass transfer coefficient is given by

$$D$$

$$k_e = 2 \qquad (3)$$

$$d_ñ$$

with D-diffusion coefficient and d_p-particle diameter.

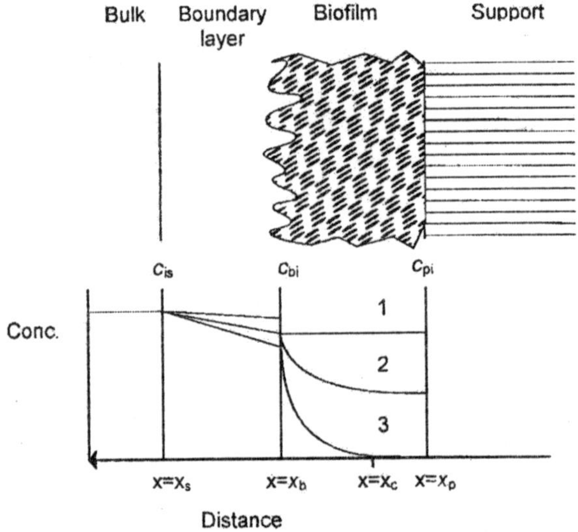

Fig. 5.2 Substrate concentration profiles at an immobilized bio-catalyst surface. 1, Reaction rate-controlled system; 2, combination of reaction rate- and diffusion-controlled system; 3, diffusion-controlled system.

For more complex systems, such as packed- or fluidized-bed reactors, the external mass transfer is usually described by dimensionless analysis, which leads to the correlation characterized by the Sherwood number Sh:

$$ke\ d_ñ$$

$$Sh = f\,(\mathrm{Re, Sc}) = \qquad (4)$$

$$d_ñ\ uñ$$

$$ç$$

$$Sc = ç$$

$$Dñ$$

$$D \qquad (5)\ (6)$$

with the Reynolds number (Re) and the Schmidt-number (Sc).

Mulcahy and La Motta (1978) calculated the external mass transfer for a fluidized biofilm with a correlation given by Snowden and Turner (1967):

$$Sh = \frac{0.81}{\text{å}} Re^{0.5} Sc^{0.33} \qquad (7)$$

Gonzalez-Gil et al. (2001) showed that the external mass transfer does not play an important role for superficial liquid velocities higher than 1 m h^{-1}.

Support

Many support materials have been investigated in laboratory-scale reactors for use in packed- or fluidized-bed systems (Henze and Harremoes, 1983). Despite this, the number of supports that are used even in technical-scale systems is rather low. Certainly, one big problem for the implementation of new processes is due to the difficulty of cooperation with manufacturers. But the problems often result from shortcomings in the studies with respect to requirements of large-scale application. For successful use of any material as a support in fixed-film stationary or fluidized-bed reactors on the technical scale, the following general requirements should be met:

- availability of the material in large quantities (>1000 m^3)
- low cost of the material (related to the achievable performance; it should in general be less than 150 $US m^{-3})
- inert behavior (mechanically and microbially stable) without toxic effects and easy disposal
- low pressure drop (low energy demand for mixing or fluidization)

Stationary-bed Reactors

A selection of supports, which seem to have been applied successfully on the pilot and industrial scale, is summarized in Table 5.1; examples are shown in Figure 5.4.

The biofilm thickness is of limited significance in fixed-bed reactors since it makes up a minor part of the biomass. Published data are mostly in the range 1–4 mm, the upper limit relating to the inflow zone (top of a reactor operated in downflow) (Switzenbaum, 1983; Andrews, 1988).

More important is the biomass concentration in the reactor, which is distributed into two fractions, one immobilized in the biofilm, the other suspended in the void volume of the reactor (Hall, 1982; Weiland and Wulfert, 1986). The organic dry bio-mass in pilot reactors is mostly in the range 5–15 kg m^{-3} (Henze and Harremoes, 1983). Gradients in the concentration of biomass are observed, with the maximum near the reactor inlet [e.g., about 15 kg m^{-3} in the lower and 4 kg m^{-3} in the upper part for upstream operation (Weiland and Wulfert, 1986)]. Gradients were also found by Hall (1982), which depended on the flow direction: 6 kg m^{-3} of fixed bio-mass and 9 suspended for upstream, and 9 fixed and 4 suspended for downstream operation (all in kg m^{-3} organic dry matter). For an industrial starch-processing plant a biomass concentration of 20 kg m^{-3} was reported (Schraewer, 1988). A high biomass concentration was reported for a special support, sintered glass fillings (expensive): up to 65 kg m^{-3} in laboratory-scale experiments, of which 31 kg m^{-3} was found to be immobilized within the inner pores of the support (Ney et al., 1989).

FLUIDIZED-BED REACTORS

The energy demand for fluidization of the support is often said to be very high, in contrast to the energy requirements of other anaerobic techniques. In general, much higher volumetric flow rates have to be achieved in comparison to those in a CSTR. Nevertheless, the energy demand is relatively low, because only the additional pressure drop of the support has to be overcome. Hence, with respect to higher loading rates, the overall energy demand is in the same range or lower than in CSTRs, depending on the support density. Table 5.2 shows some materials that have been tested for use as supports in anaerobic fluidized-bed systems. All materials have particle diameters significantly less than 1 mm, which results in a greater surface area for colonization, decreased superficial upflow velocity and no diffusion limitation, even for porous materials.

Porous materials have the advantage of lower superficial upflow velocities than nonporous materials have. In addition, biomass gradients mainly occur in reactors filled with nonporous materials (Anderson et al., 1990; Jördening, 1987). Franklin et al.

(1992) reported that a sand fluidized-bed reactor contained only uncovered bare sand in the bottom part. They attributed this to the extreme shear forces, which have a large influence on bacteria on the surface. Bacteria in pores are protected against shear forces, and therefore, such pronounced gradients are not known when porous materials are used. Figure 5.5 shows some porous and nonporous supports. Nakhla and Suidan (2002) showed close agreement for the detachment of bacteria in different reactors by normalizing the coefficients of the shear force and the daily methane production per unit biofilm area.

A special type of fluidized system uses granular pellets without a solid support. These pellets, used in so-called expanded granular sludge beds (EGSB) have a diameter of 1–3 mm and can therefore also be expanded by higher superficial upflow velocities of up to 20 m h^{-1} (Lettinga et al. (1999)).

WASTEWATER

Wastewater should be acidified to a high degree (>80%, related to COD). Otherwise, acidifying bacteria could lower the pH, overgrow the methanogenic biofilm and thus reduce the methanogenic activity. Thus two-stage systems are considered superior, since their performance in terms of stability and space-time yield is superior to that of one-stage systems. The load of reactors fed with volatile fatty acids (in a system with a separate acidification reactor) can be higher by a factor of 4–5 than that of reactors fed with complex substrates (Henze and Harremoes, 1983).

Inhibitory substances such as sulfur compounds may play a major role, as in yeast processing (Friedmann and Märkl, 1994). It is also essential that results concerning load refer to an average of a stable continuous process rather than to a singular maximum. Even results obtained in laboratory reactors differ in general from pilot-plant and full-scale reactors operating at the factory site with variations in substrate quality and concentrations and additional fluctuations.

Solids in Stationary Fixed-film Reactors

Suspended solids and even suspended biomass can cause reactor clogging, which can be reinforced by extracellular polysaccharides secreted by acidogenic bacteria (Ehlinger et al., 1987). Therefore, backwash and excess sludge removal must be provided for in the reactor design. Gas-phase desorption and transport through the reactor must be possible. Fixed-bed systems are not feasible for wastewater having high solids content or components that tend to precipitate, such as calcium ions.

Solids in Fluidized-bed Reactors

Solids from the wastewater can cause clogging, especially at the entrance region of the reactor. Holst et al. (1997) recommend solids concentrations <0.5 kg m^{-3} to prevent problems of clogging in the distribution system, but Mösche (1998) reported that even solid concentrations up to 1.7 kg m^{-3} did not cause problems. This difference can be explained by differences in the composition of the solids as well as in the construction of the reactor inlet.

Some inorganic compounds, such as calcium carbonate and ammonium magnesium phosphate, precipitate mainly onto the support in the reactor, when the actual concentrations are beyond the equilibrium. At higher concentrations of precipitated solids on the support, diffusion limitation occurs. In such situations it is necessary to enable removing this material and replacing it with uncovered new support. Sand and other materials with a high settling velocity in relation to the support must either be removed before entering the reactor or be removed by a device at the bottom of the reactor (as described under the first subheading in section 5.3.4.2).

REACTOR GEOMETRY AND TECHNOLOGICAL ASPECTS

Fixed-bed Reactors

Upflow reactors tend to be favored, because they allow clumps of biomass to be retained in the filter by gravity, and the start-up period may be shorter (e.g., 3–4 months compared to 4–6 months for downflow reactors) (Andrews, 1988; Weiland et al., 1988). The height is limited by the gradients of the biomass and reaction rate.

Fixed-bed reactors do not require major specific design considerations. The ratio of height to diameter is usually in the range 1–2. The inlet must provide equal distribution of the wastewater by means of distribution devices, generally a system of tubes with nozzles, about one for each 5–10 m^2 (Lettinga et al., 1983). The fluid flow should in general be about 1 m h^{-1}, up to a maximum of 2 m h^{-1} (Austermann-Haun et al., 1993).

Fluidized-bed Reactors

Fluidized-bed reactors are taller than agitated tanks or stationary-bed reactors. The height–diameter ratio for technical plants varies from 2 to 5. Figure 5.6 shows a technical plant with 500 m^3 volume. The ratio of height to diameter should not be too high with respect to axial concentration gradients, which increase with the height of the reactor. But difficulties concerning uniform fluidization of the support increase with increasing reactor diameter (Couderc, 1985). Therefore, a compromise has to be found.

Whereas fluidized bed reactors are mostly cylindrical, the use of tapered fluidized be reactors has also been investigated and showed advantages concerning the performance (Huang et al., 2000)

Technical-scale anaerobic fluid-ized-bed reactor (sugar factory in Clauen, Germany).

Fluidization of the Support

One of the key factors for the development of a fluidized-bed system is the fluidiza-tion zone. This zone has to provide a homogenous distribution of support and substrate by the incoming feed to prevent any dead-zone formation and to avoid high shear forces. Most laboratory-scale reactors work with inlet tubes in the downward direction or sieves, sometimes also with glass beads for providing a uniform upflow distribution. These are not applicable to full-scale reactors. The use of a multitube system could be a solution for technical reactors, but such a system is expensive and may be subject to problems with solids (blocking) or precipitation (lime or other inorganic compounds) (Iza, 1991).

Problems in distribution systems are sometimes discussed in the literature (Franklin et al., 1992; Oliva et al., 1990), but new developments and improvements of existing distribution systems are rarely described in detail.

A fluidized-bed bottom used in a 500 m^3 BMA (Braunschweiger Maschinenbau-anstalt) reactor with sugar factory wastewater is shown in Figure 5.7 (Jördening et al., 1996). It has a conical shape with 12 concentric pipes for the incoming water. Due to an inner double cone, the superficial liquid velocity is twice that of the reaction zone. So only material with a high settling velocity can settle in this part. A valve at the lower end of the cone allows these particles to be removed.

Bed Height and Loss of Support

The fluidized bed's height is determined by the flow rate and depends on the support. It varies over time with growth of the biofilm, the gas production rate and possible precipitates on the support. Changes occur only slightly with time.

Strategies for preventing support loss are different in several systems on the technical scale:

- For the Anitron process (sand as support) the bed height can be controlled by a stationary support/biomass-separating device at the maximum bed height, which contains the removal of support from the reactor by a centrifugal pump which dislodges the biomass from the support. While the support is fed back to the reactor, excess biomass is discarded. The maximum bed height is at least 1.5 m below the overflow section.
- For the Gist-Brocades (sand as support) and the Anaflux

processes (Biolite® as support) the bed height is controlled only by the fluidization velocity. Biocatalyst loss is prevented by means of three-phase separation constructions. Although the Gist-Brocades system does not contain a unit for removing support, the Anaflux and the Anitron systems are provided with a centrifugal pump for removal of excess biomass from the separator. Therefore, automatic control is not necessary, but daily control via a sample port is useful to prevent support loss.

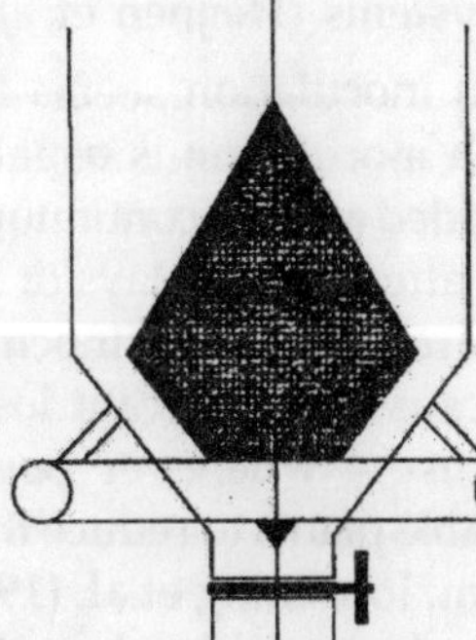

Flow distribution system for fluidized-bed reactors (Jördening et al., 1996).

REACTOR OPERATION

Start-up Procedure

The start-up of fixed-bed reactors is governed by several parameters (Weiland et al., 1988; Burkhardt and Jördening, 1994):

- size and quality of the inoculum, notably the activity of slow-growing methano-gens
- degree of adaptation, mainly the content of bacteria adapted to adhesion
- degree of biomass retention

The limited activity, and thus slow growth of propionic or lactic acid converting bacteria are of crucial importance, and the load must be controlled so as to maintain the substrates below growth-limiting concentrations. The initial load should be low, in the range of 0.1 kg(COD) kg^{-1}(VSS) d^{-1} (Henze and Harremoes,

1983). Start-up is facilitated by Ca^{2+} ions in the concentration range 100–200 g m^{-3}. The load may be increased at a rate of 5%–10% d^{-1}. The overall time required from start-up to full load may be 1–3 months. It can be much less when an adapted inoculum and a sufficient amount of biomass are used. In industries working in campaign periods, restart after storage of the biomass (in the reactor at ambient temperature) is rather straightforward reaches full load within several days.

The time required for the development of a well-attached film on the support in fluidized beds is sometimes very long in contrast to that in suspended systems (Heijnen et al., 1986).

Because continuous inoculation seems to be impractical for technical systems, batch inoculation is usually used. This means that digester sludge is added and the continuous flow of wastewater to the reactor is started after several days or weeks of adaptation. If suspended bacteria are used as an inoculum, the start of the continuous work will cause a significant loss of activity. Hence, it is advantageous to use - whenever possible - immobilized inoculum from comparable plants to reduce the time for adaptation and the loss of inoculum. Jördening et al. (1991) reported that the use of immobilized inoculum could reduce the start-up period by about 30%. Heijnen et al. (1986) showed, by comparing data in the literature, that the loading rate profile is an additional key factor affecting rapid biofilm development: the use of a so-called 'maximum load profile' reduces the start-up time up to a half that achieved with the so-called 'maximum efficiency profile'. The 'maximum load profile' means that the load is increased if the concentration of volatile fatty acids in the reactor is high (>2000 ppm); the 'maximum efficiency profile' means that the load is increased only if the concentration of volatile fatty acids in the reactor is decreased to a minimum (<100 ppm) and therefore conversion to the extent possible has been achieved.

OPERATION RESULTS: STATIONARY BED

Several reviews have been published: e.g., by Henze and Harremoes (1983), Swit-zenbaum (1983) and Austermann-Haun et al. (1993). Table 5.3 shows selected data for typical substrates and carriers on the laboratory and pilot scale, which also seem appropriate for scale-up to the industrial level. One example is included representing very high load, however, with an expensive carrier (Siran®). Most typical loading rates (kg m^{-3} d^{-1} COD) are in the range 3–10 for common wastewater from agricultural and food processes with high conversion (over 80% of degradable COD), but there are also examples of loading rates of about 20 and even 40 kg m^{-3} d^{-1} COD. However, these rather exceptional results may not be suitable for scale-up.

A considerable number of technical-scale systems with volumes of several 10 m^3 to several 1000 m^3 are in operation. The sites are small- and medium-sized agricultural installations, typically treating wastewater from poultry, pig, and cattle farms and distilleries; medium- and large-scale reactors in food industries such as sugar, potato, starch, and dairy processing, paper and pulp manufacturers, and the chemical industry.

Some typical data are summarized in Table 5.4. Acidification often occurs in the wastewater stream prior to feeding it to the methane reactor even when this is not mentioned in detail; notably, for substrates that easily undergo microbial fermentation. For example, this occurs in sugar industry wastewater, containing sucrose as the main substrate, which is stored in lagoons before being fed to a methane reactor. More examples and data have been published by Austermann-Haun et al. (1993).

Overloading may be possible without inactivation of the biomass (if an appropriate pH - least 6 - is maintained), but conversion decreases according to the maximal activity of biomass (in general 1-2 kg COD m^{-3} kg^{-1} dry biomass; Figure 5.8) (Weiland and Wulfert, 1986).

OPERATIONAL RESULTS: FLUIDIZED-BED REACTORS

The performance of fluidized-bed reactors on the laboratory and pilot scale is sometimes excellent: Keim et al. (1989) used Siran® spheres in a fluidized-bed reactor for the treatment of evaporation condensate and reported a loading rate up to 315 kg m^{-3} d^{-1} with 79% removal. Jördening et al. (1991) used another sintered glass (Poraver®) to treat a sugar wastewater with loading rates up to 183 kg m^{-3} d^{-1} and achieved 89% removal. Data from some laboratory- and pilot-scale plants are given in Table 5.5.

Despite these results on the laboratory scale, the data reported for performance on the technical scale (Table 5.6) are in a significantly lower range: 15–50 kg m^{-3} d^{-1} (Fig. 5.9) (see e.g.

Ehlinger, 1994; Franklin et al., 1992; Jördening, 1996; Jördening and Küster, 1997; Oliva et al., 1990).

CONCLUSIONS

As a general conclusion, we can state that both fixed- and fluidized-bed reactors are well established on the industrial scale, notably in the food and related industries (e.g., breweries and distilleries) and in the paper and pulp industry, where the substrates are of natural origin, but also in other areas, e.g., the chemical industry.

Specific limitations, however, must be taken into consideration:

- Acidification inside the methane reactor requires a higher residence time than in two-stage systems with acidification as a first stage; this also provides safer and more stable processing, e.g., when a shock load occurs - a quite common situation in practice.

Wastewater free of suspended solids is required for fixed-bed reactors. No precipitation of solids should occur inside the reactor.

Advantages of both types of systems include higher density of biomass and, therefore, higher reaction rates and a considerably smaller reactor volume required than in conventional systems such as stirred tanks. This is especially true for fluid-ized-bed reactors, since they can provide a much larger support surface and, hence, a high biomass concentration per volume. Much less space is required due to the relatively small reactor volume and the high ratio of height to diameter of the reactors.

For these reasons, investment costs are lower than for systems without biomass immobilization.

6

Modeling of Biogas Reactors

INTRODUCTION

As early as 1973 Graef and Andrews (1973) published a mathematical model of the anaerobic digestion of organic substrates. The authors assumed that the conversion of volatile organic acids by methanogenic bacteria to methane was the rate-limiting step in the sequence of biological reactions and that all volatile acids can be represented as acetic acid. Acetic acid is dissociated to a large extent at the relevant pH range between 6.6 and 7.4. The authors assumed that only the undissociated form of acetic acid is the limiting substrate for the microbial production of methane.

The pH value in this mathematical model is calculated from the ion balance, assuming electroneutrality in the fermentation broth. In this context the concentration of dissolved CO_2, which itself is partly dissociated to HCO_3^- and CO_3^{2-}, must also be known. In the mathematical model of Graef and Andrews, the concentration of dissolved CO_2 is calculated on the basis of the mass transport from the liquid phase to the gas phase of the system. This transport phenomenon proved to be very important for the mathematical modeling of technical biogas reactors, as is shown later in this chapter.

The mathematical model of Graef and Andrews describes a homogenous, completely mixed system as far as the liquid phase of the reactor is concerned.

ELEMENTS OF THE MATHEMATICAL MODEL

This chapter shows that the mentioned elements of the model of Graef and Andrews are an excellent basis for the quantitative analysis of modern biogas reactor systems. In the research work of different groups following this first publication, it was proved that more knowledge is necessary, especially about the microbial kinetics of biogas production (Section 6.3).

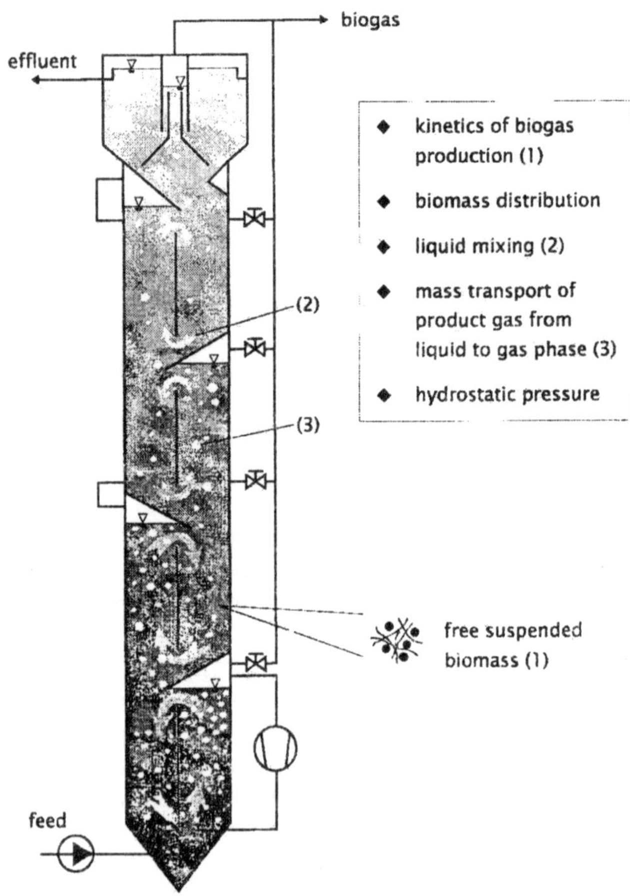

Fig. 6.1 Elements of a mathematical model for a biogas tower reactor (BTR).

Most of the real biogas reactors are far from being completely mixed systems, as demonstrated by the example of a biogas tower reactor (BTR) (Fig. 6.1). This type of reactor is described in more detail by Märkl and Reinhold (1994). The typical features of the

BTR are its tower shape, the modular structure, and the internal installations. Gas collecting devices are used to withdraw the fermentation gas from different levels of the reactor. These gas collectors separate the reactor into modules along the height. By means of these devices, which are equipped with valves, the gas loading and the mixing intensity can be controlled separately in each module. To avoid flotation of active biomass due to excessive gas load, an effective biomass accumulation is generated within the reactor.

The biomass is represented in this reactor by free suspended microorganisms which are associated in the form of sedimentable more-or-less loose pellets (flocs). One very important point, when modeling such a reactor, is to describe the local distribution of active biomass within the reactor (Section 6.4.2).

In a mathematical model the mixing behavior of the liquid phase is of similar importance (Section 6.4.1). The mixing of the BTR is caused by internal airlift loop units. Since the reactor is designed in the shape of a tower and is only fed at the bottom (Fig. 6.1), the question of mixing and supplying the microorganisms in each part of the reactor with nutrients is very important during the scale-up of such a system. Besides, hydraulic mixing is important to prevent toxic concentrations of substrate near the inlet of the reactor.

As pointed out by Graef and Andrews (1973), the mass transport of product gas from the liquid phase to the gas phase is an essential element of the mathematical model. Local transport data as a function of the hydrodynamics for the example of the biogas tower reactor is given for CO_2 and H_2S in Section 6.5 of this chapter. The last element of a mathematical model which is of high importance, especially when discussing tall reactors, is represented by the influence of the local hydrostatic pressure on the kinetics of biogas generation (Section 6.6).

SCALE-UP STRATEGY

Parameters of the mathematical model elements must be identified by experiments, and the models have to be evaluated with respect to their suitability for the design of technical scale biogas reactors. The scale-up strategy is demonstrated in Figure 6.2 with explanations in Table 6.1. Basic experiments are done in the laboratory. The hy-drodynamic behavior and the sedimentation of non-active biomass were studied first in a small reactor unit with a height of 6.5 m. This laboratory reactor has a diameter of 0.4 m and consists of only two modules. To understand the influence of the height of a reactor, a pilot scale biogas reactor was built at the site of a company producing bakers' yeast (Fig. 6.3). The reactor was designed on the basis of the laboratory scale experiments and investigations on the kinetics of wastewater digestion from bakers' yeast production. The characteristic data of the wastewater are given in Table 6.2. The active volume of the reactor is 15 m^3. It is divided into four modules and at the top of the reactor a settling zone is integrated to maintain a high sludge concentration. The pilot reactor is well equipped with instruments for measuring concentrations and velocities along the height of the reactor. Because the pilot scale reactor reaches almost the height of a technical reactor (in Fig. 6.2 two reactor units with a height of 25 m and a diameter of 3.5 m are shown as examples) it is assumed that the mathematical model, which is evaluated on the pilot scale with respect to hydraulics and takes into account the influence of hydrostatic pressure, will permit prediction of the behavior of a technical scale reactor.

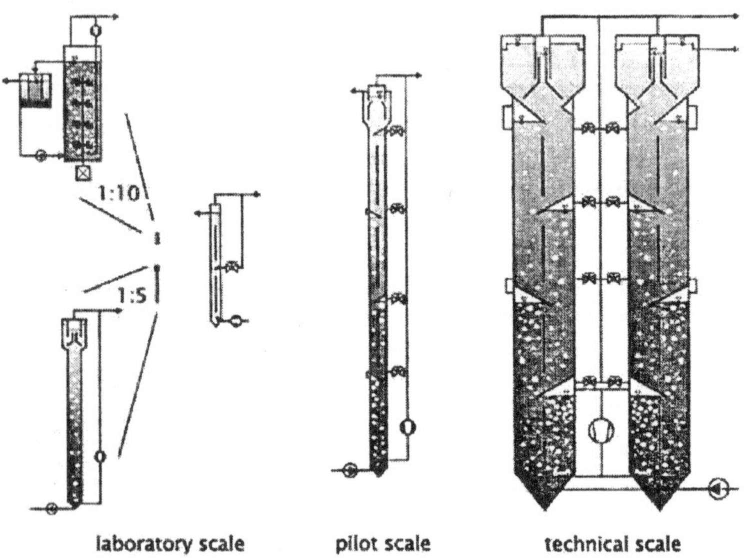

Fig. 6.2 Strategy for scale-up of the biogas tower reactor, specification of reactors according to Table 6.1.

Fig. 6.3 Biogas tower reactor, pilot scale, at the site of Deutsche Hefe-werke in Hamburg, built by Preus-sag Wassertechnik GmbH, Bremen.

Table 6.2 Characteristic data of the wastewater used for the experiments.

	Average	*Range*	*Unit*
Total organic carbon (TOC)	13.8	11-19	g L^{-1}
Chemical oxygen demand (COD)	31	25-36	g L^{-1}
COD (incl. betaine)	44		g L^{-1}
Betaine	5.7	4-10	g L^{-1}
Sulfate	3.9	2.5-6.5	g L^{-1}
Acetic acid	58	0.5-120	mmol L^{-1}
Total suspended solids (TSS)	2.5	0.8-3	g L^{-1}
pH	4.5	4.3-5	-

MEASURING TECHNIQUES

To understand the microbial degradation process and the system behavior of a bio-gas reactor and to establish reliable mathematical models, measuring techniques must be available – if possible – to analyze online special substances in the fermentation broth. Therefore, some new measuring techniques have been developed during the last years.

ONLINE MEASUREMENT USING A MASS SPECTROMETER

The anaerobic treatment of wastewater loaded with high concentrations of sulfate is often accompanied by problems due to inhibition by hydrogen sulfide (H_2S). It is well established that the inhibition is caused by undissociated hydrogen sulfide present in the liquid phase and not by the total sulfide content. This concentration of undissociated hydrogen sulfide depends on sulfate concentration in the wastewater, pH, and ionic strength. The concentration of undissociated hydrogen sulfide in the liquid phase undergoes great changes in the pH range used for anaerobic digestion, which is between 6.6 and 7.4. Since the actual concentration of dissolved H_2S cannot be calculated on the basis of the H_2S partial pressure in the biogas, because gas phase and liquid phase are not in equilibrium as is demonstrated in Section 6.5, this concentration has to be measured.

Measurement on the basis of ion-sensitive electrodes proved to be very problematic, especially with respect to their stability for a long period of time. Meyer-Jens et al. (1995) developed a new type of probe connected to a mass spectrometer. The probe consists of a small tube (outer diameter 0.9 mm, inner diameter 0.7 mm) of poly-dimethylsilicon. The tube can be inserted directly into the fermentation liquid of the biogas reactor. The H_2S dissolved in the liquid phase penetrates the membrane and is transported by a carrier gas (technical nitrogen) to the mass spectrometer.

A very simple silicon membrane probe is shown in Figure 6.4. The silicon membrane tube is arranged in a short bypass loop outside of the reactor. The fermentation liquid flows outside of the tube while the carrier gas passes inside. In Figure 6.5 calibration of the measurement system is demonstrated. The calibration curve is perfectly linear within the relevant H_2S concentrations. The different gradient for desalinated water and wastewater indicates the difference in the solubility (Henry coefficient) of H_2S in desalinated water (78.2 mmol L^{-1} bar^{-1}) and wastewater (68.5 mmol L^{-1} bar^{-1}) at 37°C (data given by Polomski, 1998).

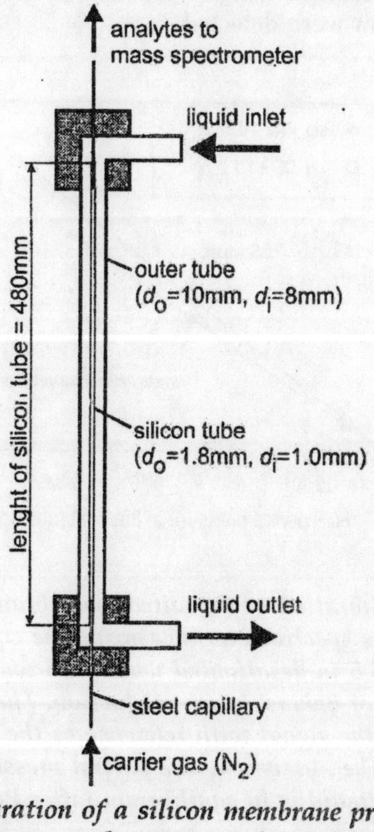

Fig. 6.4 Configuration of a silicon membrane probe operated in a short bypass at the reactor (after Polomski, 1998).

The measurement system can also serve well for the detection of dissolved CO_2 in the biogas reactor. Figure 6.6 shows the calibration curve for CO_2 in a sample of desalinated water. Also with CO_2 the solubility (Henry coefficient) for wastewater ($2.21 \cdot 10^{-4}$ mmol L^{-1} Pa^{-1}) is 12% smaller than the literature data given for desalinated water ($2.52 \cdot 10^{-4}$ mmol L^{-1} Pa^{-1}). Matz and Lennemann (1996) used a similar silicon membrane probe for online monitoring of biotechnological processes by gas chromatographic mass spectrometric analysis. The sensitivity of the probe system could be improved considerably by an instantaneous heating of the membrane to a temperature of 200 °C. This quasi online measuring procedure had a sampling period of 15 min between two successive measuring cycles. Substances like dimethyl-sulfide, butanethiol, cresol, phenol, ethylphenol, and indole at concentrations between 10 and 200 ppm were detected.

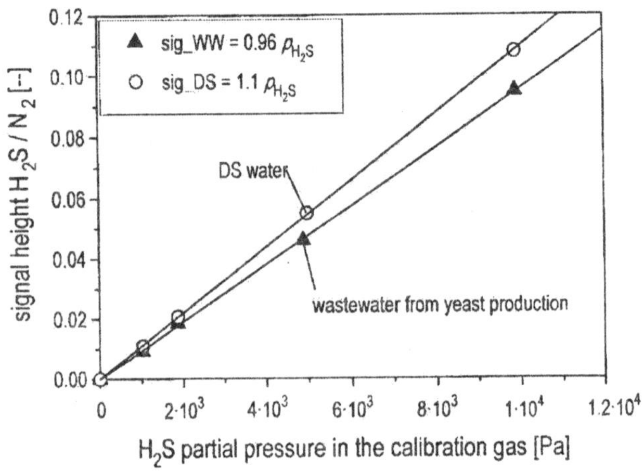

Fig. 6.5 Calibration of the silicon membrane probe coupled with a mass spectrometer measuring the concentration of dissolved H_2S in desalinated water (DS water) and in the wastewater of bakers' yeast production. The ordinate gives the value of the signal with reference to the N_2 signal of the carrier gas. The abscissa is the partial pressure of H_2S, with which the liquid is in equilibrium (after Polomski 1998).

ONLINE MONITORING OF ORGANIC SUBSTANCES WITH HIGH-PRESSURE LIQUID CHROMATOGRAPHY (HPLC)

Zumbusch et al. (1994) reported the simultaneous online determination of betaine (trimethylglycine), *N,N*-dimethylglycine (*N,N*-DMG), acetic and propionic acid during the anaerobic fermentation of wastewater from bakers' yeast production. Ammonia and chloride could also be measured. The determinations were carried out by means of isocratic cation exchange chromatography. For the detection of betaine and *N,N*-DMG an ultraviolet detector was used. All other substances were detected by conductivity.

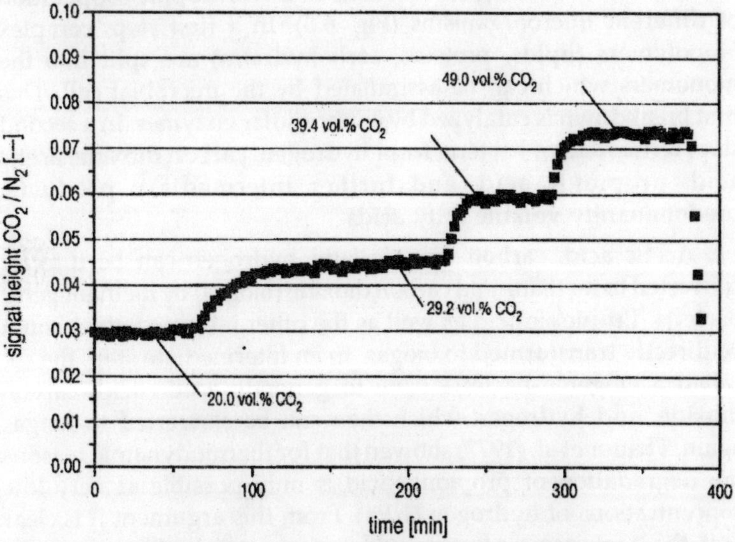

Fig. 6.6 Calibration of the silicon membrane probe coupled to mass spectrometer measuring the dissolved CO_2 in desalinated water (after Polomski, 1998).

Besides other organic components, such as acetic and propionic acid, betaine is the dominant organic substance in the wastewater. Up to 33% of the TOC is represented by betaine. The use of HPLC analysis combined with an automated ultrafil-tration setup for online process monitoring gives interesting information about the dynamic behavior of the anaerobic process, as demonstrated in Figure 6.7.

The graphs show the effect of hydrogen sulfide elimination from the fermentation broth. The concentration of undissociated H_2S was decreased by a factor of 2 (from 300 to 150 mg L^{-1}). During the same time biogas production increased. The concentration of acetic acid decreased while the other acids measured remained more or less stable. Betaine was completely degraded only at lower H_2S concentrations. Interestingly, the concentration of N,N-DMG, which is a metabolic product of the anaerobic degradation of betaine, is also decreased.

Kinetics

The anaerobic degradation of organic substances is performed in a sequence of biological reactions in a synthrophic cooperation of different microorganisms (Fig. 6.8). In a first step, complex biopolymers (lipids, proteins, carbohydrates) are split into the monomers which can be assimilated by the microbial cell. This first breakdown is catalyzed by extracellular enzymes. In a second step, fermentative bacteria form hydrogen, carbon dioxide, acetic acid, propionic acid, and further intermediary products, predominantly volatile fatty acids.

Acetic acid, carbon dioxide, and hydrogen can be directly converted to methane and carbon dioxide (biogas) by methanogenic bacteria. Propionic acid as well as the other intermediates cannot be directly transformed to biogas. In an intermediate step, the so-called acetogenic bacteria have to generate acetic acid, carbon dioxide, and hydrogen which then can be converted to biogas again. Thauer et al. (1977) showed that for thermodynamic reasons the degradation of propionic acid is only possible at very low concentrations of hydrogen (1 Pa). From this argument it is clear that the acetogenic reaction which generates hydrogen can be performed only by a direct and close synthrophic cooperation with methanogenic bacteria which consume hydrogen. Sulfate, a frequent component in almost all food industries' wastewater, is almost totally converted to hydrogen sulfide.

The dynamic behavior of the system is mainly controlled by the conversion of acetic acid to methane and carbon dioxide. This reaction is rather slow and, therefore, it is the bottleneck of the anaerobic digestion, as demonstrated by experiments like those shown in Figure 6.9. Whey which contains about 5% lactose, is continuously digested to biogas. At the beginning of the experiment the concentration of the different volatile acids denoted in Figure 6.9 represent a steady state. In this situation the reactor was heavily overloaded during the next 2.5 h. As a result, the concentration of acetic acid increased by a factor of 5. The concentrations of the other acids remained more or less constant. This finding supports the idea of Graef and Andrews (1973) that the conversion of acetic acid to methane and CO_2 is the rate-limiting step and that a mathematical model of the anaerobic degradation process can be reduced to this dominating reaction.

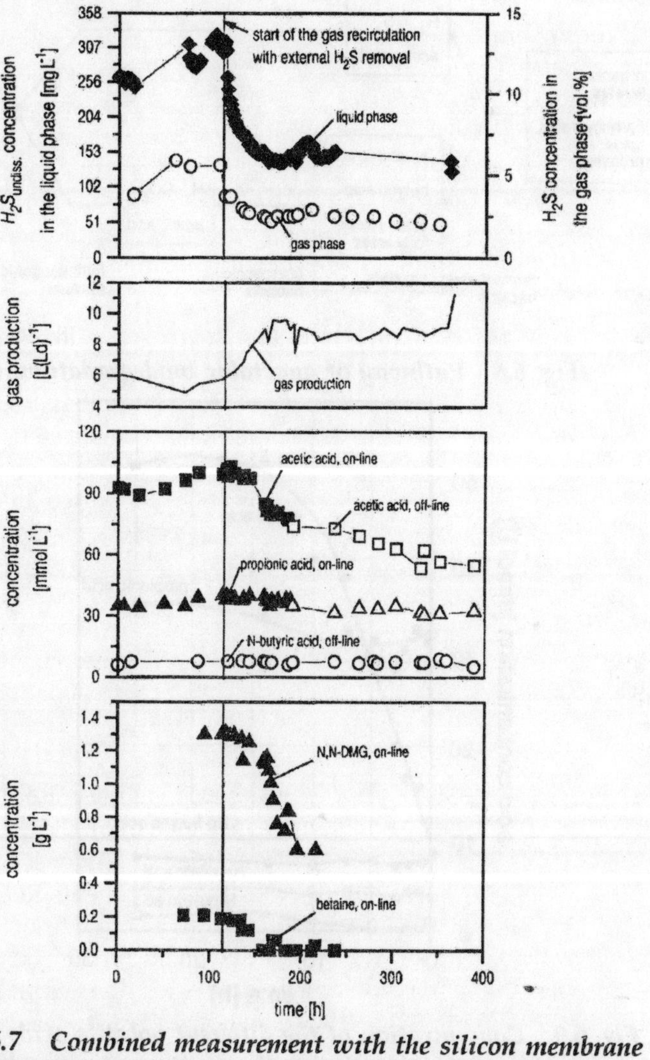

Fig. 6.7 Combined measurement with the silicon membrane probe mass spectrometer and online high-pressure liquid chromatography in a laboratory upflow anaerobic sludge blanket (UASB) reactor with and without elimination of H_2S in an external biogas recirculation loop over a period of some hundred hours (after Polomski, 1998). Online measurements were carried out in cooperation with Zumbusch et al. (1994). H_2S concentrations were detected by the silicon membrane probe and mass spectrometer.

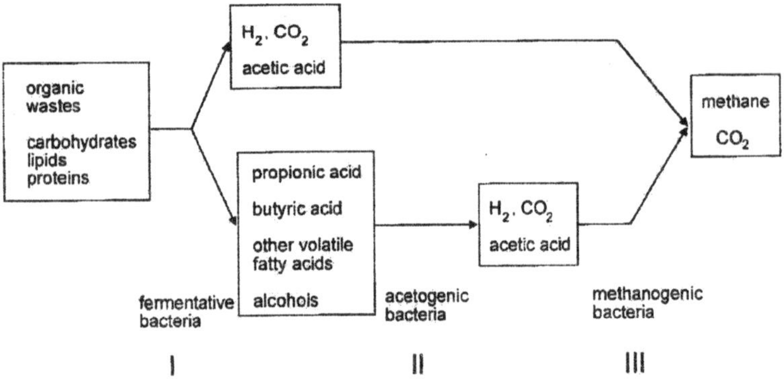

Fig. 6.8 Pathway of anaerobic biodegradation.

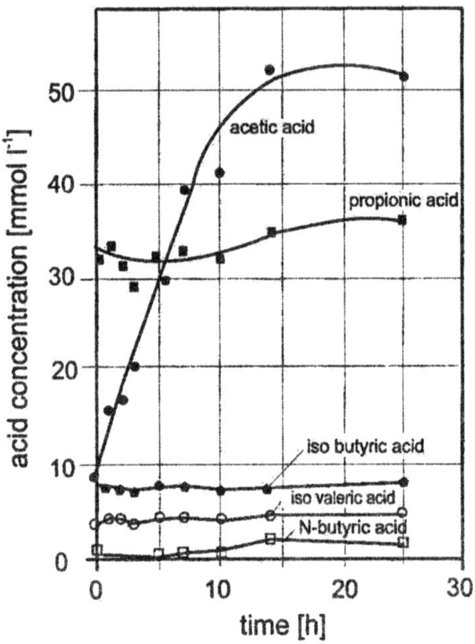

Fig. 6.9 Concentration of the different volatile acids as a function of the time during the continuous anaerobic degradation of whey, a byproduct of cheese production (after Märkl et al., 1983). The experiments were performed in a 20 L stirred tank reactor. The graph shows the dynamic behavior of the system after being heavily overloaded with whey during the first 2.5 h of the experiment.

This simple idea is expressed in Figure 6.10 and Eqs. 1 and 2, which describe the concentration of microorganisms x and the concentration of acetic acid Ac as a function of time.

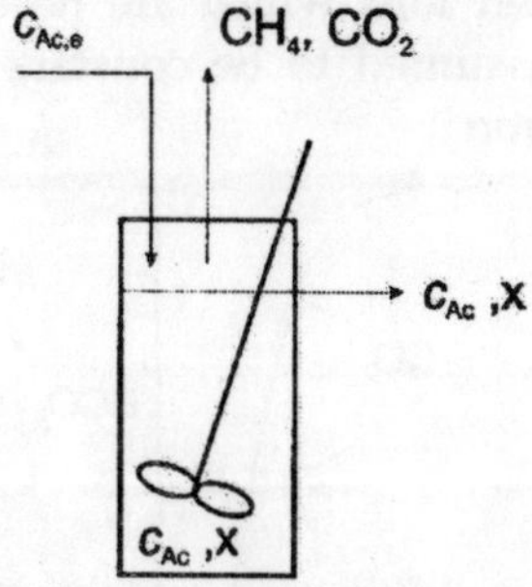

Fig. 6.10 Mathematical model of anaerobic digestion in a stirred tank reactor. The reactor is directly fed by acetic acid (concentration in the inlet: $c_{Ac,e}$). The concentration of acetic acid in the reactor is c_{Ac}, x denotes the concentration of biomass.

The reactor is directly fed by acetic acid $c_{Ac,e}$. The growth rate of the microorganisms is denoted as $\mu(c_{Ac}, c_i)$, and the biogas production can be assumed to be directly proportional to μ. At a first glance, this model looks very simple. The real problem when solving the equation is that we need information on the kinetics of the reaction. The growth rate μ is a function of the acetic acid concentration c_{Ac} but may also depend on the concentrations of other substances c_i. Before going into detail of formulating this kinetic equation one should understand more about the physico-chemical state of the fermentation broth.

Acetic acid is dissociated to a large extent in the relevant pH range between 6.6 and 7.4. The pH value is calculated on the basis of the activity of H^+, which equals $\tilde{a}_1 \, c_{H^+}$.

The concentration of H^+ ions c_H can be calculated according to Eq. 3 which rep-+

resents the electroneutrality of the fermentation broth:

(3) $c_{OH^-} + c_{Ac^-} + c_{Pro^-} + c_{HCO3^-} + c_{HS^-} = c_{NH_4^+} + c_{H^+} + Z$

The amounts of negative and positive ions must be balanced.

The most important ion concentrations in this calculation are the concentrations of dissociated acetic acid c_{Ac-} and propionic acid c_{Pro-}, OH^- ion c_{OH-}, hydrocarbon ion c_{HCO3-}, and dissociated hydrogen sulfide c_{HS-}. Besides the H^c ion, the ammonium ion (concentration c_{NHc4}) has a positive charge. Z represents the pool of not extra specified ions which are necessary to balance the equation and are assumed to be constant during the different stages of fermentation.

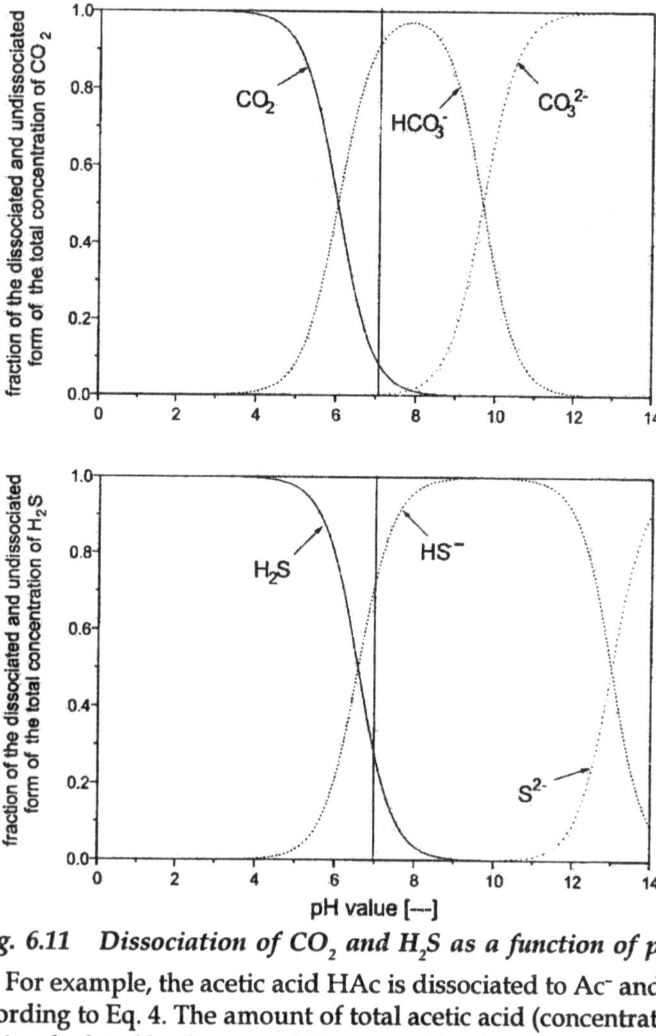

Fig. 6.11 Dissociation of CO_2 and H_2S as a function of pH.

For example, the acetic acid HAc is dissociated to Ac^- and H^+ according to Eq. 4. The amount of total acetic acid (concentration: c_{Ac}) is calculated by the sum of dissociated (c_{Ac-}) and undissociated species (c_{HAc}). From these two equations and the knowledge of the dissociation constant $K_{D,Ac}$ and the activity coefficient $\tilde{a}_1$ the concentration of the dissociated species can be calculated according to Eq. 10. The activity coefficient is calculated by an approximation after Davis which can be found in Loewenthal and Marais (1976). The activity coefficients depend on the ionic strength, which was determined to be 0.235 mol L^{-1} in wastewater from bakers' yeast production. The calculation of the dissociation constants was performed after Beutier and Renon (1978). Data for the discussed wastewater are given in Table 6.3.

The calculation for the dissociation of CO_2 and H_2S is in principal more complex because it is performed in two steps according to Eqs. 6 and 7, which are qualitatively shown in Figure 6.11. But from these graphs it is clear that both the concentrations of CO_3^{2-} and S^{2-} can be neglected in the relevant range of pH between 6.6 and 7.4. Therefore, calculation can be handled like a 1-step dissociation. Eqs. 3, 9–14 give the pH value in implicit form. The pH can be evaluated by a stepwise iterative procedure.

Acetic Acid, Propionic Acid

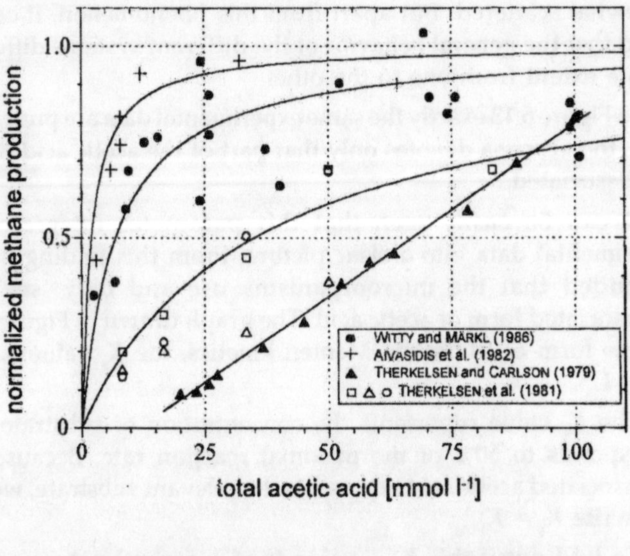

Fig. 6.12 Methane production as a function of the concentration of total acetic acid.

Many experiments have been reported on the growth rate of acetic acid converting organisms with respect to the concentration of acetic acid in the fermentation broth. A reliable collection of those data is presented in Figure 6.12. Because it is very difficult to measure the growth rate of methane producing organisms directly (in a mixed culture it may be impossible) and because it is assumed that this growth rate is directly proportional to the methane production rate, usually the latter value is taken as a measure of bacterial activity. In Figure 6.12 the methane production rate, related to the maximum methane production rate of a biogas reactor, is denoted on the ordinate of the graph.

On the abscissa the concentration of the total acetic acid measured in the fermentation broth is denoted. Data of different systems are collected. Witty and Märkl (1986) reported the digestion of waste mycelium from antibiotics production, Ther-kelsen and Carlson (1979) and Therkelsen et al. (1981) digested a complex artificial substrate, and Aivasidis et al. (1982) studied a pure culture of *Methanosarcina barke-ri* which was directly fed with acetic acid. Due to the complexity of the synthrophic reaction system and also due to the unstable nature of the biogas reaction, the data points reflecting the experimental results of the different authors are somewhat scattered. But apart from this phenomenon, it can be stated that the general behavior of the different systems differs to a large extent from one to the other.

In Figure 6.13 exactly the same experimental data are presented. Here, the abscissa denotes only that part of the acetic acid that is not dissociated.

It can be easily seen that this parameter integrates all experimental data into a clear picture. From this finding it was concluded that the microorganisms use and only 'see' the undissociated form of acetic acid. The graph drawn in Figure 6.13 has the form of Michaelis–Menten kinetics, the K_s value is 0.07 mmol L^{-1}.

The K_s value represents the concentration of substrate that corresponds to 50% of the maximal reaction rate. Because the undissociated acetic acid represents the ıelevant substrate, we can also write $K_s = K_{HAc}$.

To find out if this K_{HAc} value is of a general nature or if it depends on the type of microorganism that is active in the conversion of acetic acid to methane, some more kinetic data of authors who worked with more defined microbial systems are studied. These data are presented in Figure 6.14. It can be seen that experiments performed with *Methanothrix* sp. result in a smaller K_{HAc} value (K_{HAc} = 0.02 mmol L^{-1}) than those performed with *Methanosarcina barkeri*, which correspond to a somewhat higher value (K_{HAc} = 0.12 mmol L^{-1}). This result may be due to the fact that the relative surface of the filamentous *Methanothrix* sp. is larger than that of the rod-shaped *Methanosarcina* sp.

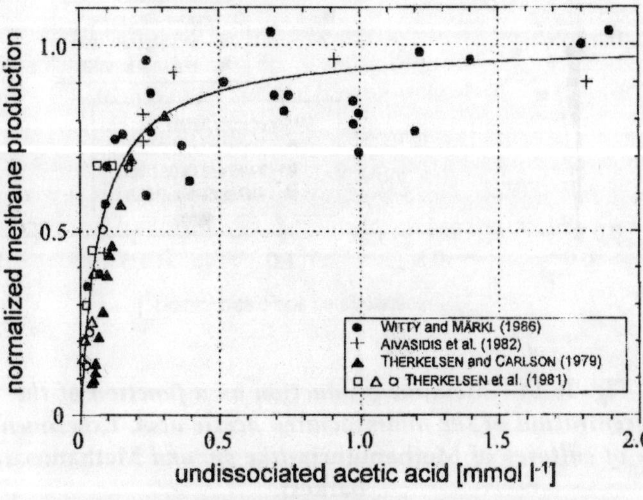

Fig. 6.13 Methane production as a function of the concentration of undissociated acetic acid.

Altogether, the K_{HAc} value based on undissociated acetic acid is roughly in the range between 0.02 mmol L^{-1} and 0.12 mmol L^{-1}. In a mixed culture an average value of 0.07 mmol L^{-1} may be adequate. If this mixed culture contains mainly *Metha-nothrix* sp. to convert acetic acid, the value will be smaller. If *Methanosarcina* sp. dominate, the value of K_{HAc} should be higher. The author of this paper used K_{HAc} = 0.07 mmol L^{-1}.

Witty and Märkl (1986) reported that propionic acid inhibits the conversion of acetic acid to methane and CO_2. Experiments with different amounts of propionic acid resulted in an inhibition coefficient of K_{HPro} = 0.97 mmol L^{-1}. Therefore, a concentration of 0.97 mmol L^{-1} of undissociated propionic acid causes an inhibition of 50% of the rate without propionic acid (Eq. 18).

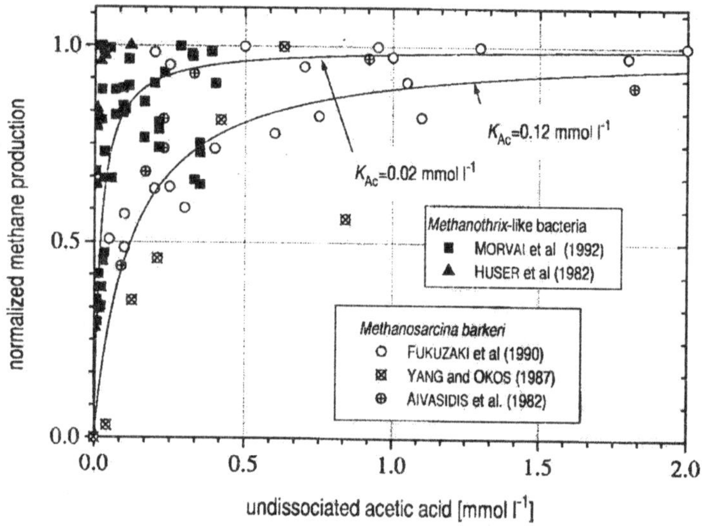

Fig. 16.14 Methane production as a function of the concentration of the undissociated acetic acid. Experimental data of cultures of Methanothrix-*like sp. and* Methanosarcina barkeri.

Hydrogen Sulfide

The inhibition of methane generation from acetic acid by H_2S is well known. Because the medium sulfate concentration in the wastewater from bakers' yeast production is as high as 3.9 g L^{-1}, which is almost totally converted to hydrogen sulfide, the problem of H_2S inhibition is very substantial.

Friedmann and Märkl (1994) reported an inhibition constant of 2.8 mmol L^{-1} (95.2 mg L^{-1}). Recent experiments of Polomski (1998) on both the laboratory and pilot scale (for experimental apparatus see Figure 6.2) resulted in an inhibition constant of 2.5 mmol L^{-1} (85 mg L^{-1}). The results of these experiments are shown in Figure 6.15.

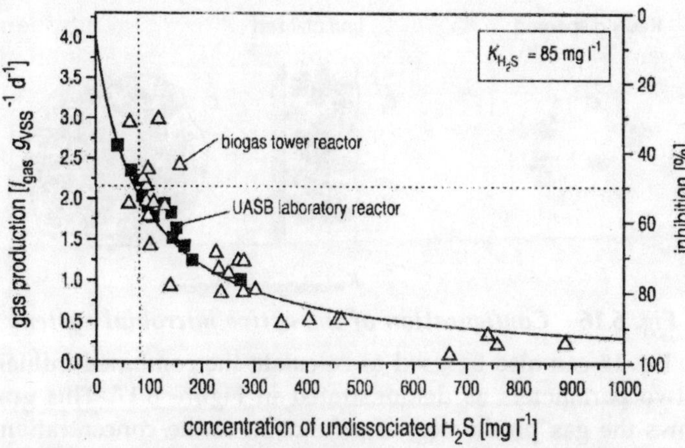

Fig. 6.15 Specific gas production of a UASB laboratory reactor and a biogas tower reactor on pilot scale (for both reactors, see Figure 6.2 and Table 6.1) as a function of the concentration of un-dissociated H_2S. The data of gas production are corrected for the influence of acetic acid and pro-pionic acid concentrations according to Eq. 18. VSS: volatile suspended solids (biomass).

CONCLUSIONS

As far as the kinetics of the conversion of acetic acid to methane and CO_2 are concerned, the results are summarized in Eq. 18. The data given are valid only near the steady state of the system; this means in a pH range between 6.6 and 7.4 and in the usual range of substrate concentrations. If the system was heavily overloaded for some time and was out of the described range, the microbial population might need some recovering time, which cannot be described by Eq. 18. Figure 6.16 shows a sketch of different configurations in which active microorganisms exist in biogas reactors. They can exist in a freely dispersed form, i.e., as single organisms, or as in the biogas tower reactor in the form of loose pellets. The microbial system can also be immobilized in the form of a film on the wall or as a dense pellet. In the second case the conversion efficiency is also influenced by transport phenomena. The data given in Eq. 18 hold only for freely dispersed organisms. When immobilized microorganisms dominate in a biogas reactor the constants (both saturation and inhibition constants) are larger.

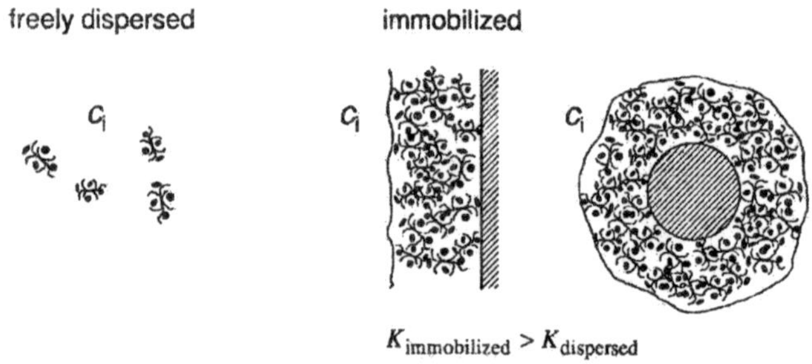

Fig. 6.16 Configuration of the active microbial system.

Eq. 18 can also be used to calculate the combined influence of two parameters as demonstrated in Figure 6.17. This graph shows the gas production as a function of the concentration of total acetic acid. It can be seen that the behavior changes completely if it is compared to the graph in Figure 6.12. Adding H_2S to the fermentation broth changes the kinetics from a Michaelis-Menten type to a substrate inhibition type. The effect can be explained by the continuous decrease of the pH value if the concentration of acetic acid is increased. At smaller values of pH more of the total hydrogen sulfide exists in the form of undissociated H_2S and the inhibitory effect increases along the abscissa.

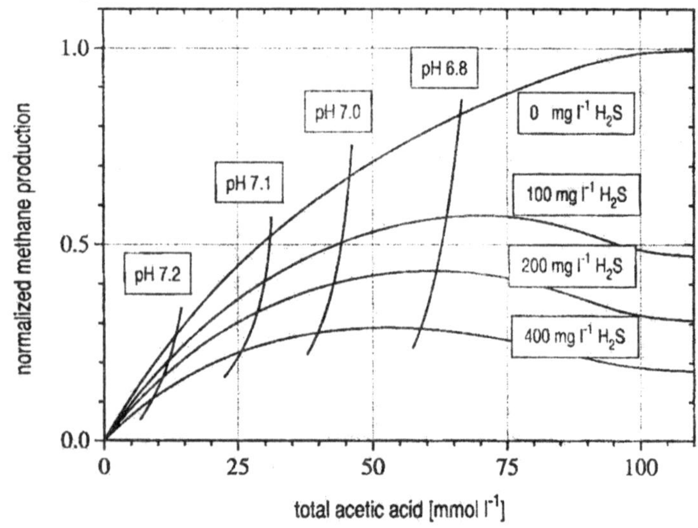

Fig. 6.17 Methane production as a function of the concentration of total acetic acid at different concentrations of total hydrogen sulfide (c_{HPro} = 0).

HYDRODYNAMIC AND LIQUID MIXING BEHAVIOR OF THE BIOGAS TOWER REACTOR

Mixing of the liquid phase with respect to the scale-up of a reactor has to be known to understand the nutrient supply of all of the active reactor regions and to avoid local overloading of the reactor. The biogas tower reactor of Figure 6.1 consists of four modules. The active volume of one reactor unit, as shown in Figure 6.2, is 280 m^3 (height 25 m, diameter 3.5 m). A settler at the top of the reactor helps to maintain high biomass concentrations within the reactor.

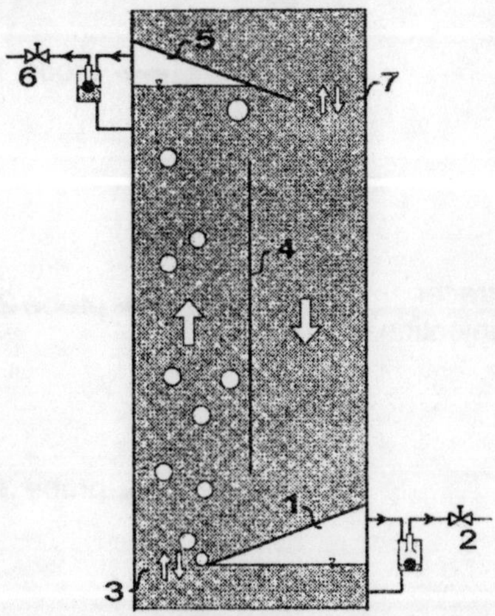

***Fig. 6.18** One module of the BTR (1,5: gas collecting devices; 2,6: gas control units; 3,7: connecting cross-sectional areas; 4: baffle).*

The principal function of one module is described in Figure 6.18. Biogas produced below this module rises and is collected under the collecting device (1), where it can be withdrawn. The quantity of gas withdrawn is controlled by a valve (2). If less gas is taken off than collected, the remaining gas rises through the open cross-sectional area (3) into the next module and into the next gas collecting device (5). The baffle (4) separates the space between two gas collecting devices into two channels joining at the top and the bottom of each module. Because of the rising gas on one side of the baffle, there is a difference in the gas holdup in two channels, which corresponds to a fluid circulation along the baffle (Blenke, 1985). The upflow channel is called a "riser" and the downflowing part is called a "downcomer". The circulation velocity is strongly linked to the amount of gas passing through the open cross-sectional area (3). Hence, by controlling the gas outlets (2) and (6) it is possible to control the liquid circulation velocity and the mixing time in a module. If no gas is withdrawn, both the circulation velocity and the mixing intensity are high.

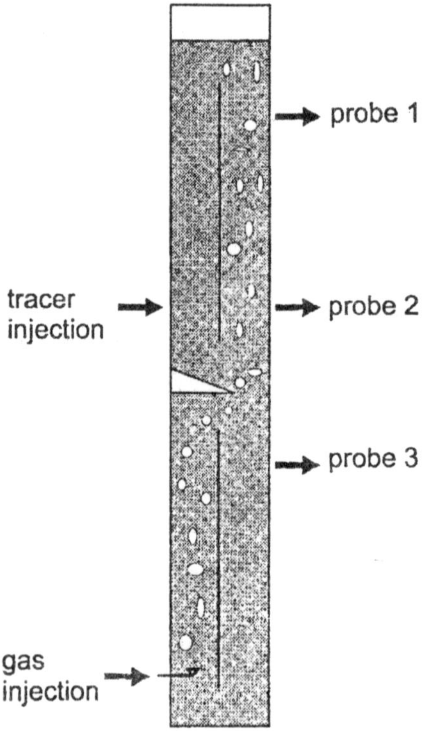

Fig. 6.19 Laboratory reactor representing a model of two modules of the BTR. It was filled with 0.1% ethanol in tap water, and air was injected through a sparger at the bottom to simulate biogas production (height: 6.5 m; diameter 0.4 m; volume 0.7 m³; height of a module 3.5 m; length of the baffle 2.89 m).

In contrast, if all collected gas is withdrawn, the circulation slows and good settling conditions for biomass set in. In the lower zones of the reactor it might be advantageous to support the mixing characteristics, in the higher zones good settling conditions should be established. As in mixing within one module, the mixing between two neighboring modules depends, as experiments show, on the gas flow rate through the open cross-sectional area (3) between the two modules. If gas rises through this area, turbulence is generated, causing a convective transport between the two modules. If the gas flow rate through the connecting area (3) is low, the mass transport between the modules decreases.

MIXING OF THE LIQUID PHASE

Reinhold et al. (1996) provided a theoretical and analytical analysis of the mixing behavior of a BTR. Experiments were performed on a laboratory (Fig. 6.19) and a pilot scale (Fig. 6.20)..

To study mixing, a saline solution was injected in the form of a Di-rac impulse as a tracer at positions indicated in Figures 6.19 and 6.20. The time course of the salt concentration was continuously monitored by conductivity probes at different positions. For the experiments the reactors were filled with tap water.

To reduce the coalescence of bubbles and to obtain small bubbles as observed in biogas reactors, 0.1% ethanol was added. Instead of biological gas production, air was injected at the bottom of the reactors. It was assumed that the dominating effect on the circulating flow was caused by gas coming from the lower module. The results of the experiments can be summarized as follows. The mixing times for a 95% homogeneity after a tracer impulse are

- mixing within one module: $(1–2) \cdot 10^2$ s
- mixing from one module to.a neighboring module: $(0.5–2) \cdot 10^3$ s

Because the heights of a module in the laboratory and in the pilot scale reactor do not differ much, the situation on the pilot scale is more or less the same as in the laboratory scale reactor.

Mixing within one module due to the axial dispersion in the circulating flow is shown in Figure 6.21, presenting laboratory scale experiments. The concentration profiles over time for the four modules of the pilot scale reactor after applying a Di-rac impulse in the third module are recorded in Figure 6.22. The experimental behavior is simulated very well by a mathematical model.

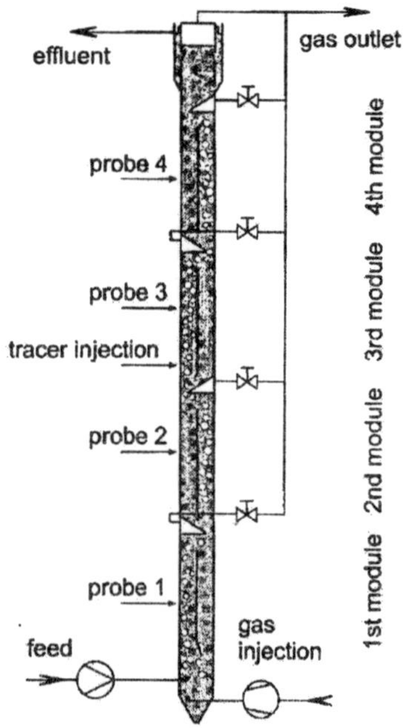

Fig. 6.20 Pilot scale BTR (height 20 m; diameter 1 m; volume 15 m³; height of a module 4 m; length of the baffle 3 m).

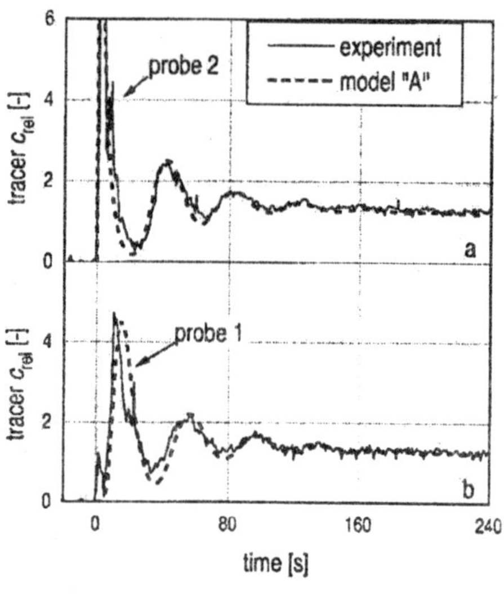

Fig. 6.21 Mixing of a Dirac impulse in the upper module of the laboratory scale reactor (Fig. 6.19).

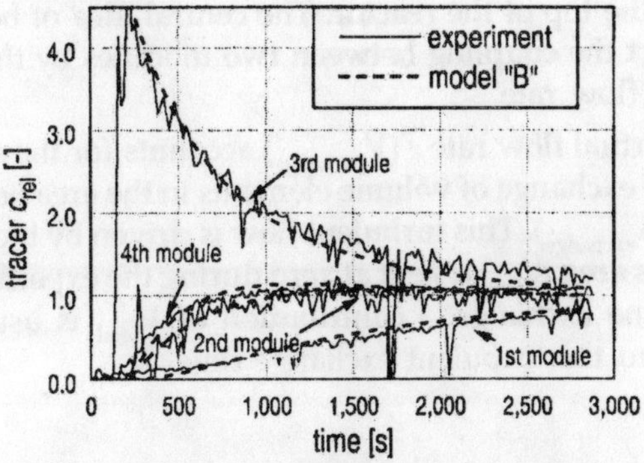

Fig. 6.22 Mixing of a Dirac impulse (3rd module) in the pilot scale BTR (Fig. 6.20).

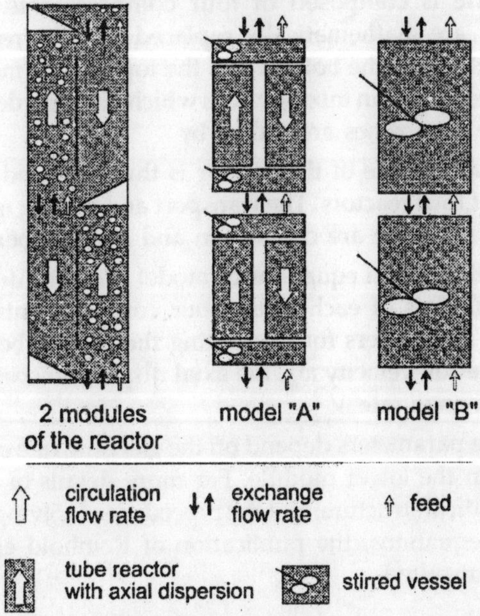

Fig. 6.23 Structure of models A and B as compared to the BTR for describing the mixing behavior of the liquid phase.

The structure of the mathematical model developed is shown in Figure 6.23. The structures of the two models A and B follow the modular structure of the reactor concept. Both models couple two neighboring modules by the flow of the feed $\cdot$ (V_{feed}), which is constant within the tower reactor and is directed from the bottom to the top of the reactor. The central ideə of both models is to predict the coupling between two modules by the so-called "exchange flow rate".

This virtual flow rate · ($V_{exchange}$) accounts for the situation of a turbulent exchange of volume elements in the area between two modules ($A_{exchange}$). This turbulent flow is driven by the bub- · bles passing this area. V_{feed} is kept at zero during the experiment. Also, in reality the exchange. · contribution of V_{feed} is usually small compared to the turbulent exchange flow

Model A

Model A, which is a more detailed one, is able to describe mixing within a module as well as intermixing between modules. Each module is composed of four compartments. Riser and downcomer are mathematically replaced by tube reactors with axial dispersion. At the bottom and the top of each module, riser and downcomer join in mixing zones which are regarded as stirred vessels. The four zones are linked by

Each real module of the reactor is thus replaced by a "ring structure" of four reactors. The transport and mixing mechanisms in this ring structure are convection and axial dispersion.

The mathematical equations of model A can be derived from the mass balances of each of the four compartments. Model A needs three parameters for calculating the mixing behavior: the liquid circulation velocity w_m, the axial dispersion coefficient D_{ax}, and the exchange rate $V_{exchange}$.

All these parameters depend on the gas flow rate entering the module from the lower module. For more details of the model, the mathematical structure, and the procedure of solving the partial differential equations, the publication of Reinhold et al. (1996) should be consulted.

Model B

Model B, which is simpler, consists of only one stirred vessel per module (Fig. 6.23). This model is able to describe the mixing behavior of the whole reactor if the mixing intensity within one module is high compared to the tracer transport from one module to another. This assumption holds true in the real situation, as shown earlier. Model B links the stirred vessels in the same way as model A. The intermixing between two neighboring modules is again modeled by an exchange flow rate V_{ex}change going up and down.

For describing the mixing of one compound in a BTR with model B, the number of ordinary differential equations is equal to the number of modules. It is an initial-value problem which can be solved by the Runge-Kutta method. The only necessary parameter for calculating the mixing behavior is the exchange flow rate · exchange.

Experiments in both laboratory and pilot scale reactors are carried out at different gas flow rates V_{gas} to investigate the dependence of the hydrodynamic parameters on the gas loading. Although there are many investigations on airlift loop reactors and bubble columns in general, the results cannot be applied to this type of reactor because the gas and liquid loading of the BTR are far below those of the airlift loop and bubble column reactors found in the literature.

Since the present BTR has unique characteristics, it was necessary to determine the exchange flow rates · change. Consequently, studies on the circulation velocity w_m and the axial dispersion D_{ax} were carried out.

The characteristic parameters D_{ax}, w_m, Vexchange, are a function of the gas loading of the system. The parameters can be obtained by using the least-squares method to fit the simulation to the experimental data. The results are shown in Figures 6.24-6.26.

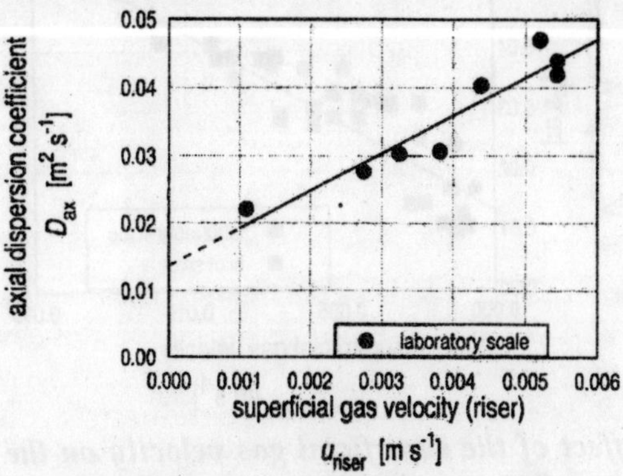

Fig. 6.24 Axial dispersion coefficient as a function of the superficial gas velocity in the riser.

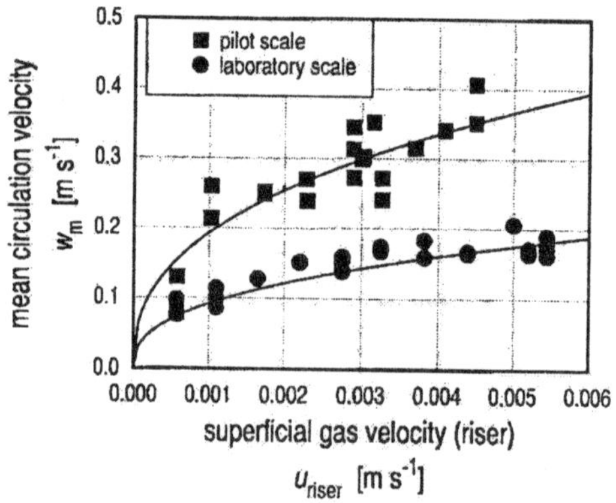

Fig. 6.25 Mean circulation velocity of the liquid as a function of the superficial gas velocity of the riser.

This coefficient was only determined on the laboratory scale. Figure 6.25 shows the mean circulation velocity w_m of the laboratory scale and the pilot scale reactors as a function of the superficial gas velocity of the riser M_{riser}. From a momentum balance the mean circulation velocity w_m can be calculated on the basis of the difference in gas holdup between riser and downcomer Ae and the knowledge of the total pressure loss (friction) coefficient <; according to Eq. 22.

1/2 g L

w_m = y As (22)

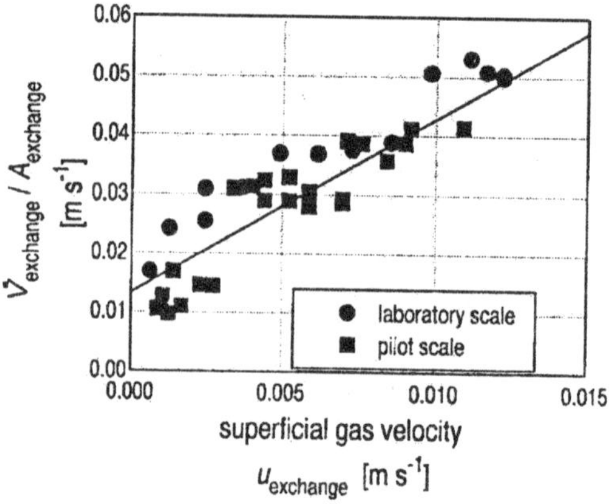

Fig. 6.26 Effect of the superficial gas velocity on the exchange flow rate between two modules.

L is the length of the baffle and *g* is the gravitational acceleration. The gas holdup can be correlated from the superficial gas velocity w_{riser} according to Weiland (1978). Due to experiments of Reinhold et al. (1996), it can be calculated according to Eqs. 23 and 24).

$$Ae = 0.27\ Mri_{s\ er}^{\cdot 8} \quad \text{(laboratory scale)} \tag{23}$$

$$Ae = 0.76\ Mri_{s\ er}^{\cdot 8} \quad \text{(pilot scale)} \tag{24}$$

The pressure loss coefficients were determined to be ^ = 6.9 on the laboratory scale and to be ^ = 4.8 on the pilot scale. As expected, the total friction coefficient i; slightly decreases during scale-up.

Figure 6.26 shows the exchange flow rate *V*exchange as a function of the superficial gas velocity M_{excha}nge, which can be calculated according to Eq. 25.

It is quite remarkable that the findings of Figure 6.26 are invariant with the scale of the reactor. Because *V*exchange dominates the mixing behavior of the system (indeed, it is the only experimental parameter necessary for model B) this result is very important for the scale-up of biogas tower reactors.

DISTRIBUTION OF BIOMASS WITHIN THE REACTOR

The wastewater is passing the BTR from the bottom to the top of the reactor. With this feeding procedure the upflow velocity due to the feed increases - at a constant mean residence time of wastewater in the reactor - linearly with the height of the reactor. Therefore, in high reactors it is essential to have reliable mechanisms to retain the active biomass. These mechanisms and the resulting distribution of biomass within the reactor were studied by Reinhold and Märkl (1997).

Experiments

Experiments were performed with a two-modular laboratory tower reactor (height 6.5 m) and in a pilot scale tower reactor (height 20 m) as shown in Figure 6.2 and described in Table 6.1. The laboratory tower reactor was filled with tap water and anaerobic pelletized sludge. The sludge was biologically, inactive, as no substrate was present in the tap water, i.e., it did not produce any fermentation gas. Air was injected at the bottom of the column instead of real biogas. As the reactor was built out of transparent material, visual observations were possible in addition to measurements from samples. The following observations were made during these experiments:

- The suspended solids concentration in the lower module is always higher than in the upper module.
- The macroscopic liquid turbulence backmixing flow ($V_{exchange}$), which causes the interaction between adjoining modules, was visualized through the movement of the sludge pellets as indicated by the arrows (7) in Figure 6.27.
- The most remarkable observation is also indicated in Figure 6.27: At the lower end of the baffle (4) the suspension turns 180° (6) and from this flow a continuously downward-directed solid mass flow (5) is observed, falling at the downward-sloping flat blade (1) and from there sliding to the module below. This may prove to be a very effective mechanism of retaining active sludge in the reactor.

Measurements of sludge distribution were also performed in the pilot scale tower reactor digesting wastewater of the bakers' yeast company.

The BTR was inoculated with pelletized sludge, and the space loading was increased in 75 d to 8.8 kg TOC m^{-3} d^{-1} with a TOC removal efficiency of 60%. The TOC conversion rate by the sludge was 1.2 kg TOC (kg SS)$^{-1}$ d^{-1}. The size of the pellets in the reactor ranged from 0.08 to 1 mm. Volatile suspended solids were about 50%–60% of the suspended solids. Elementary analysis showed that 50% of the dry matter was carbon. Two main observations concerning the sludge distribution were made during these experiments on the pilot scale:

- There is no difference in the concentration of suspended solids between riser and downcomer. Each module can be regarded as a completely mixed reactor.
- The concentration of suspended solids in the BTR decreases gradually in upward direction from module to module.

the modules; (3) upper end of the lower baffle; (4) lower end of the upper baffle; (5) sedimenting mass flow (M_{sedi}); (6) circulating flow (V_{circ}); (7) backmixing flow ($V_{exchange}$); (8) feed flow (V_{feed}).

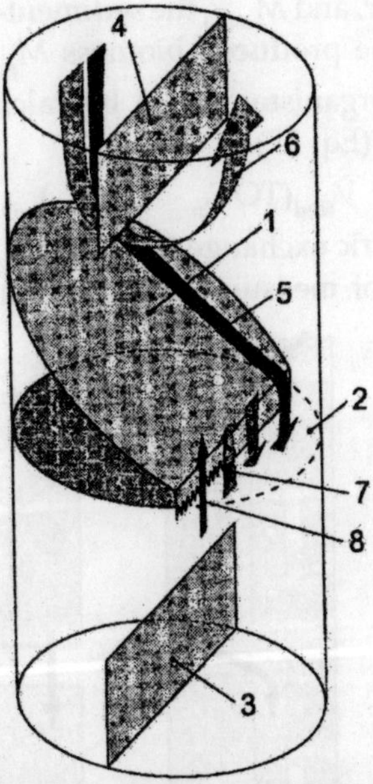

Fig. 6.27 Flows in the coupling zone of two adjacent modules: (1) gas collecting device; (2) connecting area between

Mathematical Modeling

The structure of the mathematical models is shown in Figure 6.28. The mass balance of one module (i), including the interaction with an upper (i+1) and a lower module (i–1), leads to Eq. 26.

$V_i \ SS_i$

prod $\quad n$

$\wedge \ V_k \cdot SS_k$

V_i

$dSS_i \ dt$

exchange,i–1

(SS*i*–1–SS*i*)+*V*exchange,*i* (SS*i*c1–SS*i*)

1 + *M* + *M*

+ *V*feed($SS_{i\ -1}$–SS_i) - M_{se} (26)

In this equation V_i denotes the volume of a module, SS_i the concentration of sus-·· pended solids, $V_{feed'}$ the volumetric feed rate of the reactor, and $M_{sedi,i}$ the sediment- ·ing mass flow between the modules. The produced biomass M_{prod} according to the

growth of organisms could be calculated according to the TOC consumed (Eq. 27).

$$M_{prod} = 0.1 \cdot V_{feed}(TOC_{in} - TOC_{out}) \qquad (27)$$

The volumetric exchange flow $V_{exchange,i}$ is calculated with Eq. 28 on the basis of measurements in Figure 6.26.

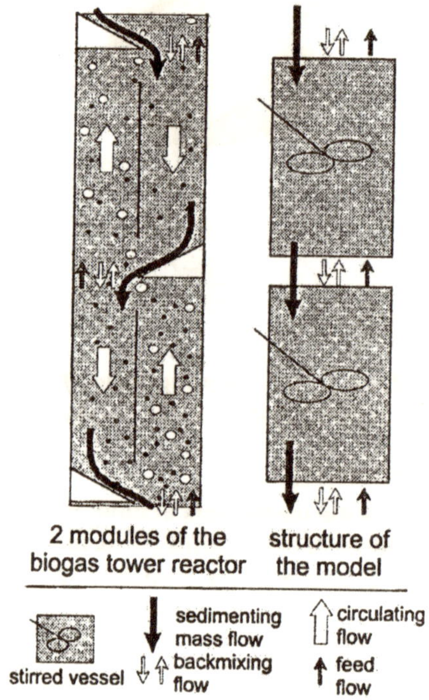

Fig. 6.28 Structure of the mathematical model compared to two modules of the BTR.

$$\frac{\dot{V}_{exchange}}{A_{exchange}} = 0.014\ m\ s^{-1} + 3.1 \cdot \frac{V_{gas}}{A_{exchange}} \qquad (28)$$

The only parameter that is not known a priori, is the sedimenting mass flow rate ·

M_{sedi}. This value was determined by regression analysis from the experiments performed as shown in Fig. 6.29. It can be clearly seen that the sedimentation capacity of active gassing sludge is much smaller compared to inactive (dead) sludge as used in the laboratory experiment. The sedimentation of active sludge follows Eqs. 29 and 30 where $A_{reactor}$ is the cross-sectional area of the reactor.

In Figure 6.30 results of experiments and the calculation on the basis of the mathematical model are compared. The agreement between simulated data and measured suspended solid concentration is quite good. The relative deviation between measured and calculated values increases with decreasing concentration of suspended solids. The relative deviation ranges from 10%–15% of the concentrations in the BTR. To investigate the scattering of the measured concentration of suspended solids, 10 samples were taken at one sampling point during a laboratory scale experiment. The detected suspended solid concentrations deviated by up to 8% from the average value. This shows that part of the deviation might be due to sampling errors.

Reinhold and Märkl (1997) also demonstrated that the mathematical model allows for realistic predictions of the dynamic behavior of the system, as was shown by simulating the start-up of a BTR.

·scale BTR. V_{feed} = 315 L h^{-1}; total gas production of the reactor 2.3 m^3 h^{-1}; gas recirculated 1.8 m^3

h^{-1}; ÄTOC = 7.3 kg m^{-3}; gas loading $V_{gas,\ i}$ of the connecting areas between the modules as indicated.

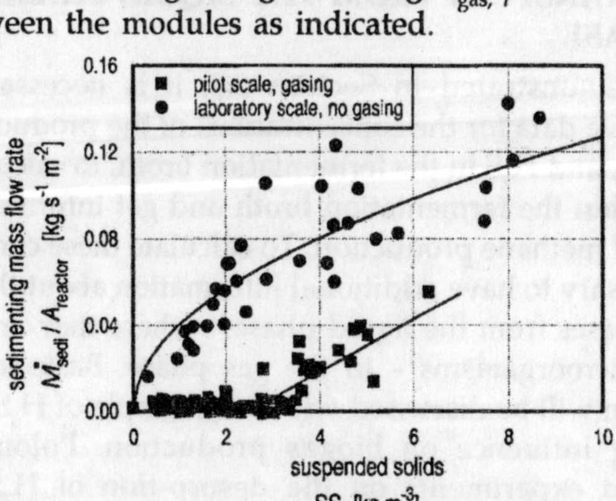

Fig. 6.29 Sedimenting mass flow rate between adjacent modules on the laboratory scale and pilot scale as a function of the suspended solid concentration in the upper module.

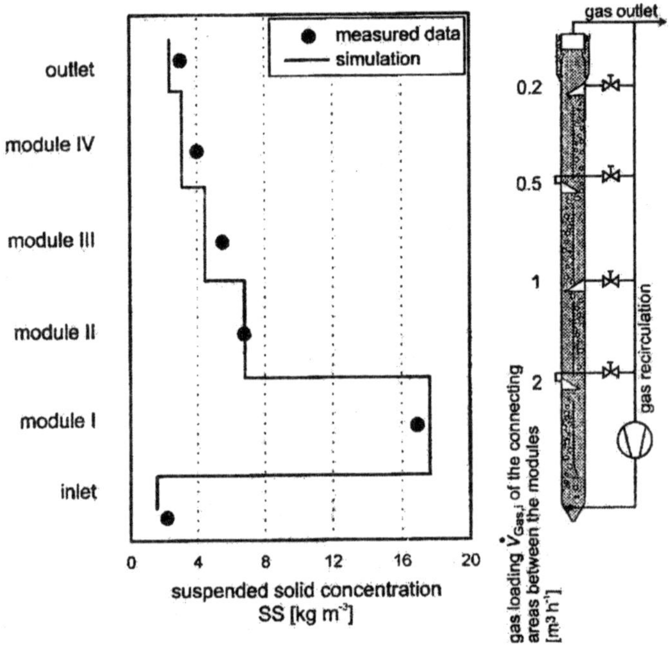

Fig. 6.30 Concentration of suspended solids as a function of reactor height in the 15 m³ pilot

MASS TRANSPORT FROM THE LIQUID PHASE TO THE GAS PHASE

As demonstrated in Section 6.3, it is necessary to have quantitative data for the concentrations of the product gases, like CO_2, NH_3, and H_2S in the fermentation broth, to calculate the pH value within the fermentation broth and get information on the kinetics of methane production. To calculate these concentrations it is necessary to have additional information about the transport of these gases from the liquid phase - where they are produced by the microorganisms - to the gas phase. Basic ideas of this calculation will be discussed with the example of H_2S because of its strong influence on biogas production. Polomski (1998) performed experiments on the desorp-tion of H_2S from the fermentation liquid broth in laboratory and pilot scale reactors. The experimental setup of the laboratory experiment is shown in Figure 6.31. The UASB reactor is supplied with wastewater at the bottom. A part of the generated bi-ogas is withdrawn at the top of the reactor and recycled to the bottom where it is injected by means of a perforated tube. The recycled biogas is either recycled directly or over a H_2S adsorber. The H_2S concentration in the fermentation liquid and the partial presure of H_2S in the gas were measured by means of a silicon membrane probe and the mass spectrometer (see also Section 6.2.1).

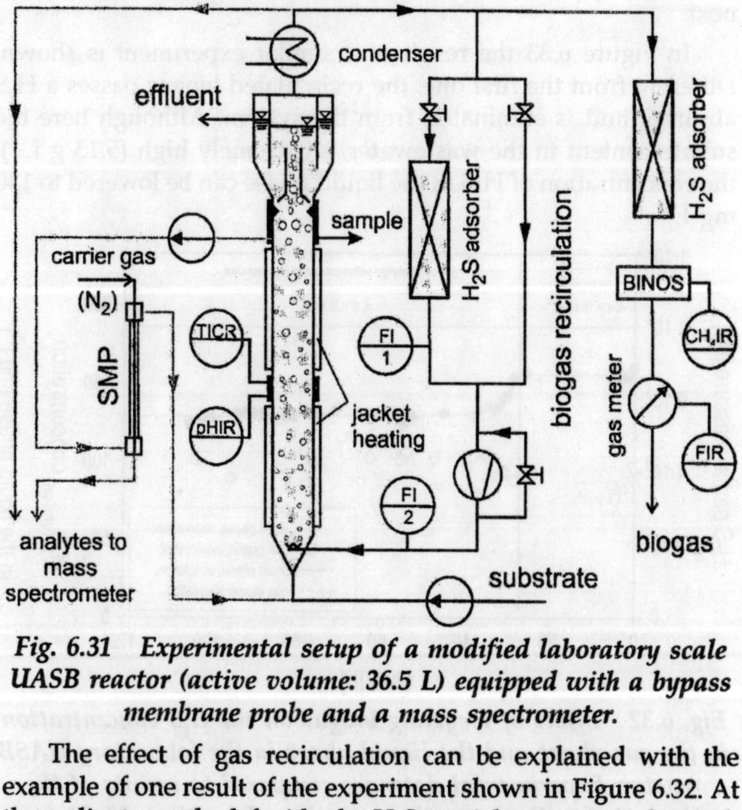

Fig. 6.31 Experimental setup of a modified laboratory scale UASB reactor (active volume: 36.5 L) equipped with a bypass membrane probe and a mass spectrometer.

The effect of gas recirculation can be explained with the example of one result of the experiment shown in Figure 6.32. At the ordinate on the left side the H_2S partial pressure is denoted; on the right side the H_2S concentration in the liquid phase is denoted which is in equilibrium with the partial pressure in the gas according to Eq. 31 and the Henry coefficient $H_{H2S} = 2.330 \cdot 10^{-2}$ mg L^{-1} Pa^{-1} (equal to $6.85 \cdot 10^{-4}$ mmol L^{-1} Pa^{-1}).

$$c_i = p_i \cdot H_i \tag{31}$$

It can be easily seen that in this type of reactor without gas recirculation (first 23 h of the experiment) H_2S in the liquid and the gas phases is far from equilibrium. The concentration in the liquid phase is overconcentrated by 75% compared to the gas phase.

After recirculating the gas and concurrently producing a larger interfacial area between the liquid and gas phases the overconcentration is diminished to 18%. After starting recirculation of biogas 8 h are required to come from one steady state to the next.

In Figure 6.33 the result of a similar experiment is shown. Different from the first one, the recirculated biogas passes a H_2S absorber and is eliminated from the system. Although here the sulfate content in the wastewater is extremely high (5.13 g L^{-1}), the concentration of H_2S in the liquid phase can be lowered to 130 mg L^{-1}.

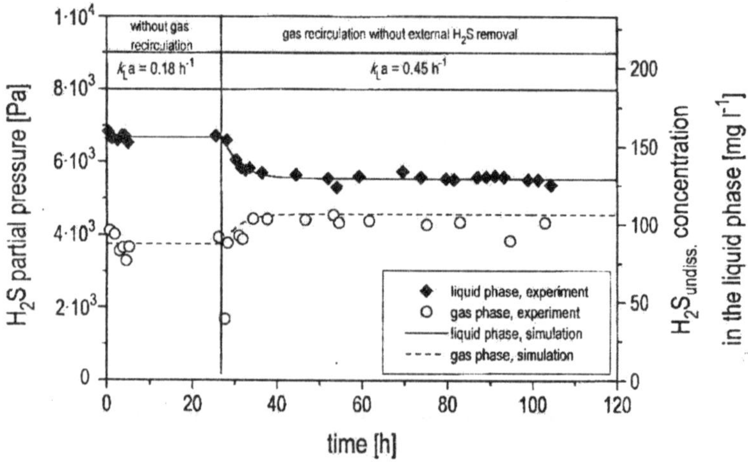

Fig. 6.32 Effect of recycling biogas on the H_2S concentration in the gas phase and the liquid phase in the laboratory UASB reactor. Experimental data are compared to results of the calculation with the mathematical model of Eqs. 32–34 (gas recirculation: 7.5 L h^{-1}; gas production: 7.45 L h^{-1}; pH value: 7.2 (constant); sulfate concentration in the wastewater: 3.85 g L^{-1}; residence time of wastewater: 2 d).

Figures 6.32 and 6.33 also demonstrate that model calculations fit well with the experimental data. The H_2S content in the liquid and the gas phases can be calculated by using H_2S balances for the different compartments.

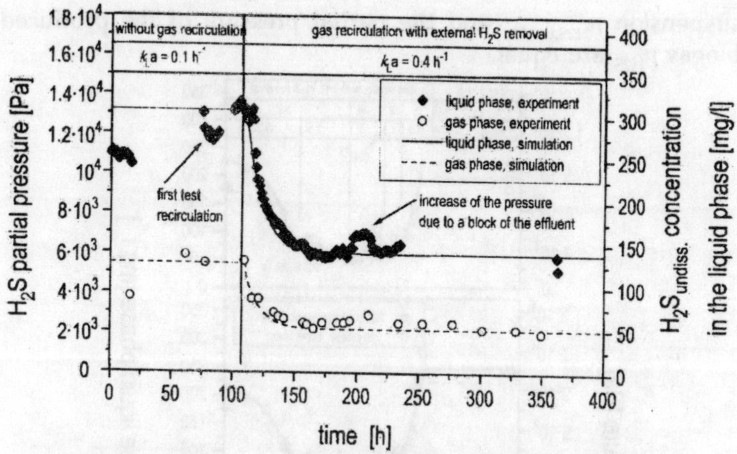

Fig. 6.33 Different from Figure 6.32 an H_2S absorber was integrated in the recycled biogas (gas recirculation 27 L^{-1}; gas production: 7.6–13.7 L h^{-1}; pH value: 7.1–7.3; sulfate concentration: 5.13 g L^{-1}; mean residence time of wastewater in reactor: 1 d).

LIQUID PHASE

In Eq. 32 $V_{reactor}$ is the volume of the liquid in the reactor, $c_{S,tot}$ the concentration of the total sulfur in the liquid according to Eq. 7, V_{feed} is the volumetric feed rate of the reactor and $c_{S,tot,e}$ the concentration of the total sulfur in the reactor feed.

k_La denotes the transport capacity between the liquid phase and the gas phase (*a*: interfacial area per volume m^2 m^{-3}), c_{H2S} is the concentration of the undissociated portion of the H_2S in the liquid, and $p_{H2S,bubble}$ the partial pressure of H_2S in the bubbles rising in the reactor liquid. H_{H2S} is the Henry coefficient for H_2S.

HEAD SPACE

Eq. 34 gives the H_2S (p_{H2S}) partial pressure in the head space located over the reactor liquid, which is equal to the partial pressure of H_2S in the biogas outlet of the reactor:

$$\frac{dp_{H2S}}{dt} = \frac{V_{bubble}}{V_{gas}} (pH_2S,bubble - pH_2S) \quad (34)$$

V_{gas} is the volume of the head space. Assuming steady state, the partial pressure of H_2S in the gas bubbles rising in the biogas suspension $p_{H2S,bubble}$ and the partial pressure of the produced biogas p_{H2S} are equal.

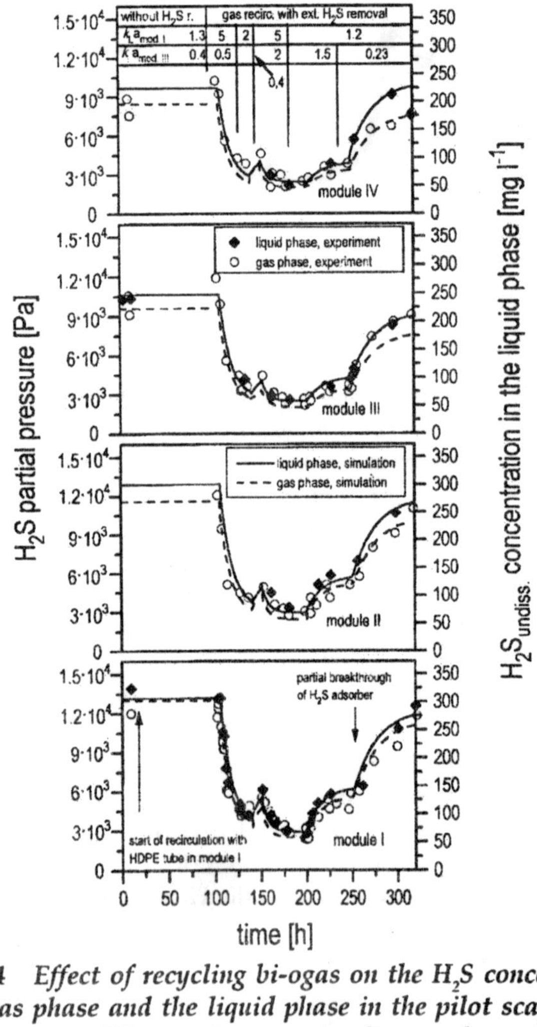

Fig. 6.34 Effect of recycling bi-ogas on the H_2S concentration in the gas phase and the liquid phase in the pilot scale biogas tower reactor. Wastewater was simultaneously supplied to modules I, II, and III. Gas was recycled to module I: 2.3, 13, 5, 13, 1.8, 1.8 $m^3 h^{-1}$ and to module II: 0, 0, 2, 2, 3, 0 $m^3 h^{-1}$ in the sequence of the experiment according to the denoted time intervals; sulfate content of wastewater: 3.4–4.5 g L^{-1}; mean residence time of waste-water in the reactor: 2.1 d), r., recirc. recirculation, ext. external, mod. module.

The k_La value in Eqs. 32 and 33 is not known a priori. It can be estimated by a regression analysis, fitting the model calculation to the experimental data. The resulting k_La values are denoted in the Figures 6.32 and 6.33. It can be seen that recircula-tion of biogas in the experimental reactor of Figure 6.31 increases the k_La value by a factor of 3–4 compared to the situation without gas recirculation. Applying Eqs. 32–34 to each module of the biogas tower reactor and paying additional regard to the liquid mixing, which is described in Section 6.4.1, the H_2S content in the liquid phase and the gas phase in the different sections of the reactor can be simulated as shown in Figure 6.34. It can be seen that the highest concentration of H_2S is found in the liquid phase at the bottom of the reactor (module I).

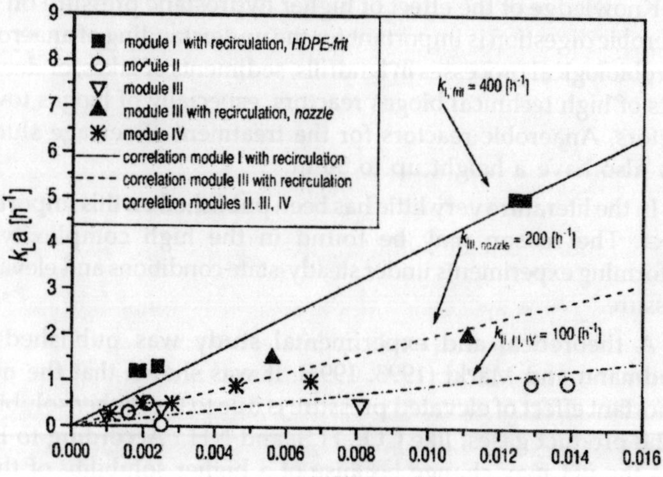

***Fig. 6.35** k_La values as a function of gas holdup in the different reactor modules of the pilot scale biogas tower reactor. Gas was supplied to module I by means of a HDPE frit and to module III by means of a simple nozzle.*

The cal- culated k_La values in the pilot scale biogas tower reactor are larger by a factor of about 5-10 than those in the UASB reactor. Therefore, the differences between the liquid and the gas phase concentrations are much smaller.

By recirculating biogas using an external H_2S adsorber, values as small as 50 mg L^{-1} undissociated H_2S in the reactor liquid can be realized. The k_La values identified are proportional to the gas holdup e_G in the reactor suspension according to Eq. 35 as shown in Figure 6.35.

$$fe_L a = k \ \% \ e_G \tag{35}$$

The proportional coefficient k depends largely on the size of the bubbles produced. The smallest interfacial area is found when bubbles are generated only by an overflow of the gas collection devices $k_{II} = k_{III} = k_{IV} = 100\ h^{-1}$. $k_L a$ is improved by using a nozzle for the gas injection $k_{III,nozzle} = 200\ h^{-1}$. In a gas injection over a frit made of high density polyethylene, $k_{I,frit} = 400\ h^{-1}$ is found.

INFLUENCE OF HYDROSTATIC PRESSURE ON BIOGAS PRODUCTION

Knowledge of the effect of higher hydrostatic pressure on the anaerobic digestion is important for the understanding of anaerobic microbiological processes in landfills, sediments of lakes, or deeper parts of high technical biogas reactors, especially of biogas tower reactors. Anaerobic reactors for the treatment of sewage sludge may also have a height up to 50 m.

In the literature very little has been published on this important effect. The reason may be found in the high complexity of performing experiments under steady-state conditions and elevated pressure.

A theoretical and experimental study was published by Friedmann and Märkl (1993, 1994). It was shown that the most important effect of elevated pressure is due to the higher solubility of the product gases, like CO_2, H_2S, and NH_3. According to Eqs. 3–14 the pH may change because of a higher solubility of these gases and, therefore, the equilibrium of dissociation of all the relevant substances will shift, with a significant effect on the kinetics of biogas production.

If a higher percentage of the produced gases is dissolved in the liquid phase of the reactor broth at higher pressures, a smaller amount of gas G will remain compared to the gas volume at a usual pressure of 10^5 Pa G_0. Because this effect is different for each gas component, the composition of the produced biogas will change when increasing hydrostatic pressure.

Altogether at a higher hydrostatic pressure the transport capacity of the product gases from the liquid phase to the gas phase (Section 6.5, Eqs. 32 and 33) decreases and, therefore, the concentration of these gases in the liquid phase will increase additionally. Friedmann and Märkl (1993) give a solution of this complex physicochemical system (39 nonlinear equations have to be solved simultaneously). Figure 6.36 gives an example of the results, showing the relative change in the composition of produced biogas as a function of pressure.

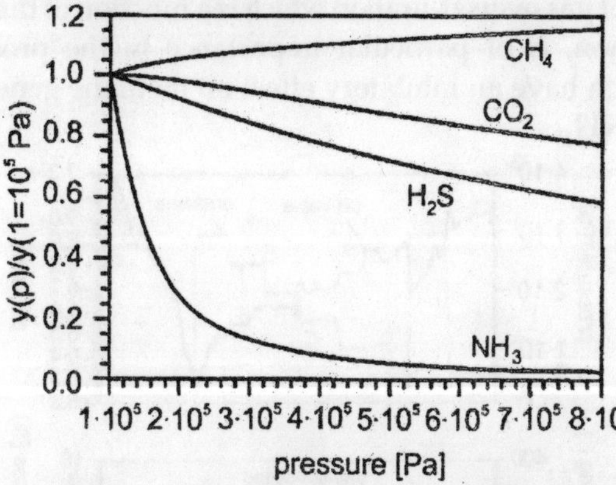

Fig. 6.36 Relative change in the composition of the produced biogas due to an alteration in the absolute pressure (model calculation for the digestion of wastewater of bakers' yeast production).

Experiments were performed in a 16 L stirred tank reactor. The reactor was equipped for continuous experiments under elevated pressures (up to $8 \cdot 10^5$ Pa). The pH value, the concentration of undissociated H_2S in the liquid, and the H_2S content in the gas were measured in situ and continuously. Concentrations of the undissociated acetic acid and propionic acid were also detected (Fig. 6.37).

A comparison of the total experimental data investigated with model calculations is given in Figure 6.38 showing a reasonable degree of agreement.

Outlook

The mathematical model was developed and its use was demonstrated with the example of a biogas tower reactor. The hydrodynamic and liquid mixing behavior (Section 6.4), as well as the application of the mathematical model for reactor control (Section 6.7) are directly attributed to this reactor type.

But it should also be stated that the structure of the model and the basic understanding of the system behavior are of a more general nature and can be applied to all reactor types. This holds especially true for the measuring techniques (Section 6.2) and the microbial kinetics (Section 6.3). In each biogas reactor the transport of the gas phase (Section 6.5) will plays an important role. The influence of gas oversat-uration which is a function of that transport phenomenon, is of particular importance in the production of gases which have an inhibitory effect on methane generation like H_2S and NH_3.

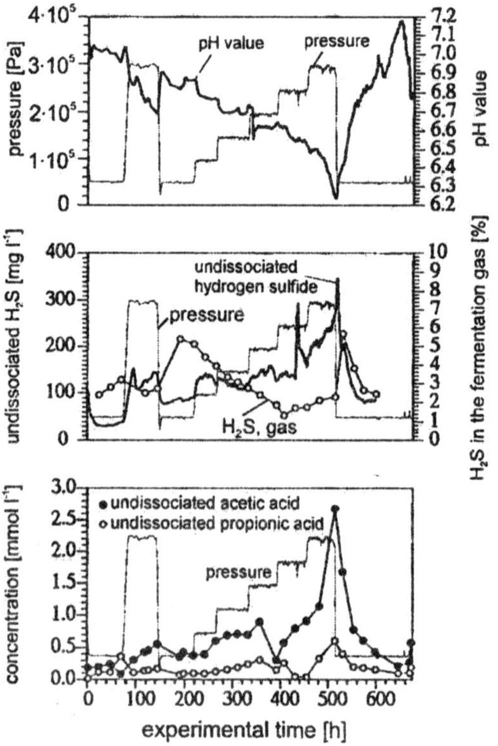

Fig. 6.37 Experiments digesting wastewater of bakers' yeast production at different pressures (pressure difference to normal pressure) in a stirred tank reactor (active volume 16 L). Continuous feeding of wastewater (TOC = 12 g L^{-1}, concentration of sulfate 2.8 g L^{-1}). Pressure was kept constant b 2500 Pa within a certain time interval to achieve steady state conditions.

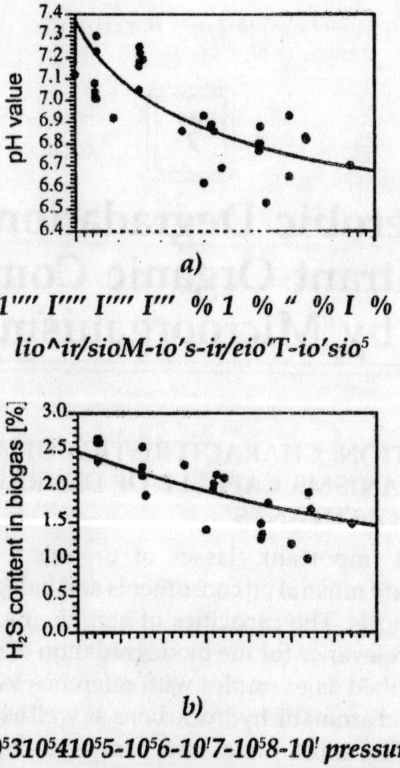

Fig. 6.38a, b Comparison between model calculation and experiment. a pH as a function of the absolute pressure, b H_2S content in the bio-gas as a function of the absolute pressure.

The influence of hydrostatic pressure on biogas production (Section 6.6) should be taken into consideration for most large technical scale bioreactors with a height of more than 5 m.

7

Aerobic Degradation of Recalcitrant Organic Compounds by Microorganisms

INTRODUCTION: CHARACTERISTICS OF AEROBIC MICROORGANISMS CAPABLE OF DEGRADING ORGANIC POLLUTANTS

The most important classes of organic pollutants in the environment are mineral oil constituents and halogenated products of petrochemicals. The capacities of aerobic microorganisms are of particular relevance for the biodegradation of such compounds and are described as examples with reference to the degradation of aliphatic and aromatic hydrocarbons as well as their chlorinated derivatives. The most rapid and complete degradation of the majority of pollutants is brought about under aerobic conditions.

The following are essential characteristics of aerobic microorganisms degrading organic pollutants (Fig. 7.1):

- Metabolic processes for optimizing the contact between the microbial cells and the organic pollutants. The chemicals must be accessible to the organisms having biodegrading activities. For example, hydrocarbons are water-insoluble and their degradation requires the production of biosurfactants.
- The initial intracellular attack on organic pollutants is an oxidative process; the activation and incorporation of oxygen is the enzymatic key reaction catalyzed by oxygenases and peroxidases.
- Peripheral degradation pathways convert the organic

pollutants step by step into intermediates of the central intermediary metabolism, e.g., the tricarboxylic acid cycle.

- Biosynthesis of cell biomass from the central precursor metabolites, e.g., acetyl-CoA, succinate, pyruvate. Sugars required for various biosyntheses and growth must be synthesized by gluconeogenesis.

A huge number of bacterial and fungal genera possess the ability to degrade organic pollutants. Biodegradation is defined as the biologically catalyzed reduction in complexity of chemical compounds (Alexander 1994). It is based on two processes: growth and cometabolism. In growth, an organic pollutant is used as sole source of carbon and energy. This process results in a complete degradation (mineralization) of organic pollutants, as demonstrated in Section 7.2.2. Cometabolism is defined as the metabolism of an organic compound in the presence of a growth substrate that is used as the primary carbon and energy source. The principle is explained in Section 7.2.4.

Key enzymatic reactions of aerobic biodegradation are oxidations catalyzed by oxy-genases and peroxidases. Oxygenases are oxidoreductases that use O_2 to incorporate oxygen into the substrate. Degradative organisms need oxygen at two metabolic sites - the initial attack on the substrate and the end of the respiratory chain (Fig. 7.1). Certain higher fungi have developed a unique oxidative system for the degradation of lignin based on extracellular ligninolytic peroxidases and laccases. This enzymatic system possesses increasing significance for the cometabolic degradation of persistent organopollutants. Thus, the basidiomycetous fungi require deeper insights and extensive consideration. Therefore, this chapter is divided into two sections: bacterial and fungal degradation.

PRINCIPLES OF BACTERIAL DEGRADATION

Typical Aerobic Degrading Bacteria

The predominant degraders of organopollutants in the oxic zone of contaminated areas are chemo-organotrophic species, which are able to use a huge number of natural and xenobiotic compounds as carbon sources and as electron donors for the generation of energy. Although many bacteria are able to metabolize organic pollutants, a single bacterial species does not possess the enzymatic capability to degrade all or even most of the organic compounds in a polluted soil. Mixed microbial communities have the most powerful biodegradative potential, because the genetic information of more than one organism is necessary to degrade the complex mixtures of organic compounds present in contaminated areas. The genetic potential and certain environmental factors such as temperature, pH, and available nitrogen and phosphorous sources, therefore, seem to determine the rate and the extend of degradation.

The predominant bacteria in polluted soils belong to a spectrum of genera and species (Table 7.1). The table lists only bacteria that can be cultured on nutrient-rich media. We have to consider that the majority of bacteria present in soils cannot yet be cultivated in the laboratory.

The pseudomonads, aerobic gram-negative rods that never show fermentative activity, seem to have the highest degradative potential, e.g., *Pseudomonas putida* and *P. fluorescens*. Further important degraders of organic pollutants are found within the genera *Comamonas*, *Burkholderia*, and *Xanthomonas*. Some species utilize >100 different organic compounds as carbon sources. The immense potential of the pseu-domonads does not solely depend on the catabolic enzymes, but also on their capability for metabolic regulation (Houghton and Shanley 1994). A second important group of degrading bacteria are the gram-positive rhodococci and coryneform bacteria. Many species, now classified as *Rhodococcus* spp., were originally described as *Nocardia* spp., *Mycobacterium* spp., and *Corynebacterium* spp.. Rhodococci are aero-Table 7.1 Predominant bacteria in soil samples polluted with aliphatic and aromatic hydrocarbons, polycyclic aromatic hydrocarbons and chlorinated compounds.[a]

Gram-negative bacteria	*Gram-positive bacteria*
Pseudomonas spp.	*Nocardia* spp.
Acinetobacter spp.	*Mycobacterium* spp.
Alcaligenes sp.	*Corynebacterium* spp.
Flavobacterium/Cytophaga group	*Arthrobacter* spp.
Xanthomonas spp.	*Bacillus* spp.

[a] Bacteria have been reclassified based on phylogenetic markers, resulting in changes in some genera and species; thus, the names

of species are not mentioned. Actinomycetes that show considerable morphological diversity. A certain group of these bacteria possesses mycolic acids on the external surface of the cell. These compounds are unusual long-chain alcohols and fatty acids, esterified to the pepti-doglycan of the cell wall. These lipophilic cell structures probably are important for the affinity of rhodococci to lipophilic pollutants. In general, rhodococci have high and diverse metabolic activities and can synthesize biosurfactants.

GROWTH-ASSOCIATED DEGRADATION OF ALIPHATICS

The aerobic initial attack on aliphatic and cycloaliphatic hydrocarbons requires molecular oxygen. Two types of enzymatic reactions are involved in these processes (Fig. 7.2); whether a monooxygenase or a dioxygenase reaction occurs depends on the nature of the substrate and the enzymes possessed by the microorganisms. The *n*-alkanes are the main constituents of mineral oil contaminations. Long-chain *n*-al-kanes (C_{10}–C_{24}) are degraded most rapidly by the pathways shown in Figure 7.3. Short-chain alkanes (less than C_9) are toxic to many microorganisms, but they evaporate rapidly from petroleum-contaminated sites.

Oxidation of alkanes is classified as terminal or diterminal. Monoterminal oxidation is the main pathway and proceeds by formation of the corresponding alcohol, aldehyde, and fatty acid. Beta oxidation of fatty acids results in the formation of acetyl-CoA. *n*-Alkanes having an odd number of carbon atoms are degraded to propionyl-CoA, which is in turn carboxylat-ed to methylmalonyl-CoA and further converted to succinyl-CoA.

Fatty acids having a physiological chain length may be directly incorporated into membrane lipids, but most degradation products are fed into the tricarboxylic acid cycle. Subterminal oxidation occurs with lower (C_3–C_6) and longer alkanes, with formation of a secondary alcohol and subsequently of a ketone. Unsaturated 1-alkenes are oxidized at the saturated end of the chains. A minor pathway proceeds via an epoxide, which is converted to a fatty acid. Branching generally reduces the rate of biodegradation. Methyl side groups do not noticeably decrease the biodegradability, whereas complex branched chains, e.g., the tertiary butyl group, hinder the action of the degradative enzymes.

Cyclic alkanes represent minor components of mineral oil and are relatively resistant to microbial attack. The absence of an exposed terminal methyl group complicates the primary attack. A few species can use cyclohexane as a sole carbon source, but it is more commonly cometabolized by mixed cultures. The pathway of cyclohexane degradation is shown in Figure 7.4. In general, the presence of alkyl sidechains on cycloalkanes facilitates their degradation.

Aliphatic hydrocarbons become less water soluble with increasing chain length; those with a chain length of C_{12} or more are virtually water-insoluble. Two mechanisms are involved in microbial uptake of these lipophilic substrates: attachment of microbial cells to oil droplets and production of biosurfactants. The uptake mechanism linked to attachment of the cells is still unknown, but the effect of biosurfactants has been studied well (Fig. 7.5). Biosurfactants are molecules consisting of a hydrophilic and a lipophilic moiety. They act as emulsifying agents by decreasing the surface tension and by forming micelles. The latter can be encapsulated by the hydrophobic microbial cell surface.

The products of hydrocarbon degradation that are fed into the central tricarboxyl-ic acid cycle have a dual function: as substrates of energy metabolism and building blocks for the biosynthesis of cell biomass (Fig. 7.1). Synthesis of amino acids and proteins requires nitrogen and sulfur sources, that of nucleotides and nucleic acids a phosphorous source. Biosynthesis of the bacterial cell wall requires activated sugars synthesized by gluconeogenesis. The cells act as complex biocatalysts of degradation.

Products of growth-associated degradation are CO_2, H_2O, and cell biomass. The cell biomass can be mineralized after exhaustion of degradable pollutants in a contaminated site.

DIVERSITY OF AROMATIC COMPOUNDS: UNITY OF CATABOLIC PROCESSES

Aromatic hydrocarbons, e.g., benzene, toluene, ethylbenzene and xylenes (BTEX compounds), and naphthalene, belong to the large-volume petrochemicals, which are widely used as fuels and industrial solvents. Phenols and chlorophenols are released into the environment as products and waste materials from industry. Aromatic compounds are formed in large amounts by all organisms, e.g., as aromatic ami-no acids, phenols, or hydroquinones/

quinones. Thus, it is not surprising that many microorganisms have evolved catabolic pathways to degrade aromatic compounds. In general, man-made organic chemicals (xenobiotics) can be degraded by microorganisms when they are similar to natural compounds. The range of man-made aro-matics shown in Figure 7.6 can be converted enzymatically to the natural intermediates of degradation: catechol and protecatechuate. In general, benzene and related compounds are characterized by greater thermodynamic stability than aliphatics are. The first step in benzene oxidation is a hydroxylation that is catalyzed by a dioxygenase (Fig. 7.2). The product, a diol, is then converted to catechol by a dehydroge-nase. These initial reactions, hydroxylation and dehydrogenation, are also common to pathways of degradation of other aromatic hydrocarbons, e.g., of 3- and 4-ring polycyclic aromatic hydrocarbons (PAHs; Kästner 2000).

The introduction of a substituent onto the benzene ring makes it possible to attack sidechains or to oxidize the aromatic ring by alternative mechanisms. The versatility and adaptability of bacteria are based on the existence of catabolic plasmids. Catabol-ic plasmids have been found that encode enzymes that degrade such naturally occurring aromatics as camphor, naphthalene, and salicylate. Most of the catabolic plas-mids are self-transmissible and have a broad host range. The majority of gram-negative soil bacteria isolated from polluted areas possess degradative plasmids, mainly the so-called TOL plasmids. These pseudomonads can grow on toluene, *m*- and *p*-xy-lene, and *m*-ethyltoluene. The main reaction involved in the oxidation of toluene and related arenes is methyl-group hydroxylation. The methyl group of toluene is oxidized stepwise to the corresponding alcohol, aldehyde, and carboxylic group. Ben-zoate formed or its alkylated derivatives are then oxidized by toluate dioxygenase and decarboxylated to catechol.

The oxygenolytic cleavage of the aromatic ring occurs via *ortho* or *meta* cleavage. The significance of the diversity of degradative pathways and of the few key intermediates is still under discussion. Both pathways may be present in one bacterial species. "Whenever an alternative mechanism for the dissimilation of any compound becomes available (*ortho* versus *meta* cleavage of ring structures, for example), control of each outcome must be imposed" (Houghton and Shanley 1994). The metabolism of a broad spectrum of aromatic compounds by one species requires the metabolic isolation of intermediates into distinct pathways. This kind of metabolic com-partmentation seems to be implemented by metabolic regulation. The key enzymes in the degradation of aromatic substrates are induced and synthesized in appreciable amounts only when the substrate or structurally related compounds are present. The enzyme induction depends on the concentration of the inducing molecules. The substrate-specific concentrations represent the threshold of utilization and growth and are in the micromolar range. A report on the regulation of TOL cat-abolic pathways was published by Ramos et al. (1997).

Figure 7.7 shows the pathways of oxygenolytic ring cleavage to intermediates of the central metabolism. At the branchpoint, catechol is oxidized by either intradiol *ortho* cleavage or extradiol *meta* cleavage. Both ring-cleavage reactions are catalyzed by specific dioxygenases.

The product of the *ortho* cleavage - *cis,cis*-muconate - is transformed into an unstable enol-lactone, which is in turn hydrolyzed to oxoadi-pate. This dicarboxylic acid is activated by transfer to CoA, followed by thiolytic cleavage to acetyl-CoA and succinate. Protocatechuate is metabolized by a homologous set of enzymes.

The additional carboxylic group is decarboxylated, and the double bond is simultaneously shifted to form oxiadipate enol-lactone. The oxygenolytic *meta* cleavage yields 2-hydroxymuconic semialdehyde, which is metabolized by hy-drolytic enzymes to formate, acetaldehyde, and pyruvate. These are then utilized in the central metabolism. In general, a wealth of aromatic substrates are degraded by a limited number of reactions: hydroxylation, oxygenolytic ring cleavage, isomeriza-tion, and hydrolysis. The inducible nature of the enzymes and their substrate specificity enable bacteria having high degradation potential, e.g., pseudomonads and rhodococci, to adapt their metabolism to the effective utilization of substrate mixtures in polluted soils and to grow at a high rate.

EXTENSION OF DEGRADATIVE CAPACITIES

Cometabolic Degradation of Organopollutants

Cometabolism, the transformation of a substance without nutritional benefit in the presence of a growth substrate, is a common phenomenon in microorganisms. It is the basis of biotransformations (bioconversions) used in biotechnology to convert a substance to a chemically modified form. Microorganisms growing on a particular substrate can gratuitously oxidize a second substrate (cosubstrate). The cosubstrate is not assimilated, but the product can be available as a substrate for other organisms in a mixed culture.

The prerequisites for cometabolic transformations are the enzymes of the growing cells and the synthesis of cofactors necessary for enzymatic reactions, e.g., of hydrogen donors (reducing equivalents, NAD(P)H) for oxygenases. For example, me-thanotrophic bacteria can use methane or other C_1 compounds as a sole source of carbon and energy. They oxidize methane to CO_2 via methanol, formaldehyde, and formate. The assimilation requires special pathways, and formaldehyde is the intermediate that is assimilated.

The first step in methane oxidation is catalyzed by methane monooxygenase, which attacks the inert CH_4 (Fig. 7.8). Methane monooxyge-nase is unspecific and also oxidizes various other compounds, e.g., alkanes, aromatic compounds, and trichloroethylene (TCE). The proposed mechanism of TCE transformation according to Henry and Grbic-Gallic (1994) is shown in Figure 7.8. TCE is oxidized to an epoxide that is excreted from the cell. The unstable oxidation product breaks down to compounds that can be used by other microorganisms.

Methanotrophic bacteria are indigenous aerobic bacteria in soils and aquifers, but methane has to be added as growth substrate and inducer for the development of methanotrophic biomass, which limits their usefulness in bioremediation.

Cometabolism of chloroaromatics is a widespread activity of bacteria in mixtures of industrial pollutants. Knackmuss (1997) demonstrated that the cometabolic transformation of 2-chlorophenol gives rise to dead-end metabolites, e.g., 3-chlorocatechol. This reaction product can be autoxidized or polymerized in soils to humic-like structures. Irreversible binding of dead-end metabolites may fulfill the function of detoxification. (The accumulation of dead-end products within microbial communities under selective pressure is the basis for the evolution of new catabolic traits (Reinecke 1994).)

OVERCOMING PERSISTENT POLLUTANTS BY COOPERATION BETWEEN ANAEROBIC AND AEROBIC BACTERIA

As a rule, the recalcitrance of organic pollutants increases with the degree of halog-enation. Substitution of halogen as well as nitro and sulfo groups on the aromatic ring is accompanied by increasing electrophilicity. These compounds resist electro-philic attack by oxygenases of aerobic bacteria. Compounds that persist under oxic conditions include PCBs (polychlorinated biphenyls), chlorinated dioxins, and some pesticides, e.g., DDT and lindane.

To overcome the relatively high persistance of halogenated xenobiotics, reductive attack by anaerobic bacteria is important. Degradation of environmental pollutants by anaerobic bacteria is the subject of Chapter 8 of this volume. Reductive dehalog-enation as the first step in the degradation of higher halogenated compounds by anaerobic bacteria is a significant finding, because it is either a gratuitous reaction or a new type of anaerobic respiration. The process reduces the degree of chlorination and thus makes the products more accessible to mineralization by aerobic bacteria.

A sequence of anaerobic and aerobic bacterial activities for the mineralization of chlorinated xenobiotics is shown in Figure 7.9. PCBs, which are selected as an example for the degradation of halogenated compounds, are well-studied substances. The implementation of the reactions depends on the structure of the chemical compounds as well as on the microorganisms and conditions in a polluted ecosystem. We have to distinguish between the general degradation potential and the actual conditions necessary for it to occur.

Reductive dehalogenation, the first step in PCBs degradation, requires anaerobic conditions and organic substrates acting as electron donors. The PCBs function as electron acceptors to allow the anaerobic bacteria to transfer electrons to these compounds. Anaerobic bacteria capable of catalyzing reductive dehalogenation seem to be relatively ubiquitous in nature. Most dechlorinat-ing cultures are mixed cultures (consortia). Anaerobic dechlorination is always incomplete; products are di- and monochlorinated biphenyls. These products can be metabolized further by aerobic microorganisms. The substantial decrease in concentration of PCBs by sequential anaerobic and aerobic treatment has been demonstrated in the laboratory (Abramowicz 1990).

The principles of aerobic dehalogenation reactions of chloroaromatics are illustrated in Figure 7.9. Hydrolytic dechlorination has been elucidated by using 4-chlo-robenzoate as the substrate for *Pseudomonas* and *Nocardia* spp.. A halidohydrolase is capable of replacing the halogen substituent by a hydroxy group originating from water. This type of reaction seems to be restricted to halobenzoates substituted in the *para* position. Dechlorination after ring cleavage is a common reaction in the *ortho* pathway of chlorocatechols, catalyzed by catechol 1,2-dioxygenases to produce chloromuconates. Oxygenolytic dechlorination is a rare fortuitous reaction catalyzed by mono- and dioxygenases. During this reaction, the halogen substituent is replaced by an oxygen of O_2.

Higher-chlorinated phenols, e.g., pentachlorophenol, have been widely used as biocides. Several aerobic bacteria that degrade chlorophenols have been isolated (*Flavobacterium*, *Rhodococcus*). The degradation mechanism has been elucidated in some instances (McAllister et al. 1996). For example, *Rhodococcus chlorophenolicus* degrades pentachlorophenol through a hydrolytic dechlorination and three reductive dechlorinations, producing trihydroxybenzene. The potential of these bacteria is limited to some specialists and to specific conditions. Therefore, the use of poly-chlorinated phenols has been banned in many countries.

DEGRADATIVE CAPACITIES OF FUNGI

As saprophytic decomposers, members of the fungal kingdom permeate the living scene. An enormous number of fungi exist, perhaps as many as 1.5 million species, a magnitude that is comparable only with the huge biodiversity of insects. Fungi exist in a wide range of habitats: in freshwater and the sea, in soil, litter, decaying remains of plants and animals, in dung, and in living organisms. Fungi have been estimated to account for more than 60% of the living microbial biomass in certain habitats (e.g., forest and other soils; Dix and Webster 1995). Last but not least, fungi possess important degradative capabilities that have implications for the recycling of recalcitrant polymers (e.g., lignin) and for the elimination of hazardous wastes from the environment. Below, some aspects of the fungal degradation of organopollu-tants are discussed.

METABOLISM OF ORGANOPOLLUTANTS BY MICROFUNGI

For practical reasons, yeasts and molds can be grouped together into the microfun-gi (Gravesen et al. 1994). Taxonomically, they belong to the ascomycetous, deutero-mycetous, and zygomycetous fungi.

Yeasts preferentially grow as single cells or form pseudomycelia, whereas molds typically grow as mycelia-forming real hyphae. Microfungi colonize various habitats, and some genera are typical soil microorganisms (*Aspergillus, Penicillium, Trichoderma, Candida, Trichosporon*).

Aliphatic Hydrocarbons

Biodegradation of aliphatic hydrocarbons occurring in crude oil and petroleum products has been investigated well, especially for yeasts. The *n*-alkanes are the most widely and readily utilized hydrocarbons, with those between C_{10} and C_{20} being most suitable as substrates for microfungi (Bartha 1986). However, the biodegrada-tion of *n*-alkanes having chain lengths up to *n*-C_{24} has also been demonstrated (Frit-sche and Hofrichter 2000). Typical representatives of alkane-utilizing yeasts include *Candida lipolytica, C. tropicalis, Rhodoturula rubra,* and *Aureobasidion* (*Trichosporon*) pullulans; examples of molds using *n*-alkanes as growth substrates are *Cunningha-mella blakesleeana, Aspergillus niger,* and *Penicillium frequentans* (Watkinson and Morgan 1990).

In this context, one should keep in mind that in the 1960s and 1970s British Petrol (BP) and other companies ran large plants for the production of single-cell protein (SCP) from the wax fraction of crude oil. BP used two yeasts, *Candida lipolytica* and *C. tropicalis* to produce a product called Toprina that was marketed as a replacement for fish meal in high-protein feeds.

Yeast and molds preferentially oxidize long-chain *n*-alkanes, because short-chain liquid alkanes (*n*-C_5–C_9) are toxic. The toxic effects of short-chain alkanes can be reversed by adding nontoxic long-chain hydrocarbons. Thus, *Candida* spp. grew on *n*-octane if 10% pristane was present (Britton 1984). The soil fungus *Penicillium fre-quentans* is capable of utilizing monohalogenated *n*-alkanes (e.g., 1-fluorotetrade-cane) and dehalogenates them completely. Since all aliphatic hydrocarbons are nearly insoluble in water, fungi produce biosurfactants, which disperse the substrates into oil-in-water emulsions, increasing the interfacial area and thereby enhancing the bioavailability of hydrocarbons (Hommel 1990).

In microfungi, the alkanes are mostly terminally oxidized to their corresponding primary alcohols (*n*-alkan-1-ols) by a monooxygenase enzyme complex containing cytochrome P450 and NAD(P)H–cytochrome P450 reductase (Britton 1984):

$R\text{-}CH_2\text{-}CH_3 + O_2 + NAD(P)H_2$ '! $R\text{-}CH_2\text{-}CH_2OH + NAD(P) + H_2O$

Subterminal oxidation yielding various secondary alcohols is a rarer type of primary attack on *n*-alkanes and has been documented in certain molds (*Aspergillus* spp., *Fusarium* spp.; Rehm and Reiff 1982). Peroxisomal enzymes carry out the remaining degradation of alkanols to intermediates that are transferable to the mitochondria (Britton 1984). After terminal oxidation, the alcohol produced is normally oxidized to the corresponding aldehyde and fatty acid by means of pyridine nucleo-tide-linked dehydrogenases. In some *Candida* spp. and several molds, alcohol oxi-dases have been shown to be present instead of dehydrogenases. Secondary alcohols resulting from subterminal oxidation systems are oxidized to the corresponding ester and hydrolytically cleaved to acetic acid and an alcohol, which is subsequently also converted to a fatty acid. The fatty acids produced are always further metabolized by â-oxidation and finally to CO_2 via the tricarboxylic acid cycle.

In contrast to *n*-alkanes, fungi cannot utilize branched alkanes or cycloaliphatic compounds as sole sources of carbon and energy (Britton 1984; Morgan and Wat-kinson 1994).

Aromatic Compounds

Several yeasts and molds can utilize aromatic compounds as growth substrates (Table 7.2), but more important is their ability to convert aromatic substances comet-abolically. Figure 7.10 illustrates this principle with the example of 3,4-dichlorophe-nol oxidation in the presence of phenol as the actual growth substrate in the soildwelling mold *Penicillium frequentans* (Hofrichter et al. 1994). Whereas phenol is completely converted into biomass, carbon dioxide, and water, the chlorinated phenol is only transformed to a catechol that cannot be further degraded and remains as a dead-end product. Table 7.2 is a partial list of microfungal species that have been shown to utilize aromatic compounds as sole sources of carbon and energy.

Some species - such as the soil yeast *Trichosporon cutaneum* - possess specific energy-dependent uptake systems for aromatic substrates (e.g., for phenol; Mörtberg and Neujahr 1985). They cleave aromatic rings exclusively via the *ortho* pathway analogously to many bacteria (Wright 1993; compare Figure 7.7). To this end, they first insert activating hydroxyl groups into the aromatic ring. Phenol hydroxylase, benzoate-4-hydroxylase, and 4-hydroxybenzoate-3-hydroxylase are examples of enzymes hydroxylating the aromatic ring in the *ortho* or *para* position. They are $NADPH_2$-dependent monooxygenases and have been described in both yeasts and molds (e.g., *Trichosporon cutaneum, Pen-icillium frequentans, Aspergillus fumigatus;* Fritsche and Hofrichter 2000). After activation, dioxygenases cleave the aromatic ring to form *cis,cis*-muconic acids. The latter are lactonized, isomerized, and hydrolyzed, resulting in the formation of â-ketoadi-pate, which is degraded to CO_2 via the tricarboxylic acid cycle.

Hydroxylating and ring-cleaving enzymes of yeasts and molds are relatively un-specific and usually convert also related compounds, including halogenated and ni-tro aromatics. Thus, depending on the substitution pattern, fluoro- and chlorophen-ols are converted to the corresponding catechols, cleaved to halogenated muconic acids, or dehalogenated. The alkane- and phenol-utilizing mold *Penicillium frequentans* has been shown to degrade a mixture of phenol, *p*-cresol, and two chlorophenols without additional growth substrate in soil. In addition to halogenated aromatic compounds, microfungi transform numerous other aromatic organopollutants cometabolically, including polycyclic aromatic hydrocarbons (PAHs) and biphenyls, dibenzofurans, nitro aromatics, various pesticides, and plasticizers (Fritsche and Hofrichter 2000). Typical fungal transformations are glycosylations, hydroxylations and ring cleavage, methoxylations, and the reduction of nitro groups to amino groups (Table 7.3). Hydroxylation reactions are particular important for elimination of organopollutants in soils, because they increase the reactivity of the molecules and make their subsequent covalent coupling to humus possible (Kästner 2000). The introduction of hydroxyl groups is often catalyzed by relatively unspecific cyto-chrome

P450-containing monooxygenases which, for example, oxidize benzo(a)py-rene in *Aspergillus ochraceus* (Dutta et al. 1983).

DEGRADATIVE CAPABILITIES OF BASIDIOMYCETOUS FUNGI

Basidiomycetous fungi form characteristic macroscopic fruiting bodies and belong, like certain ascomycetes, to the macrofungi (Dix and Webster 1995). Colloquially, many of these fungi (especially the edible ones) are called mushrooms or toadstools. They preferably colonize the litter layer in woodlands and pastures as well as ligno-cellulosic materials (wood, straw). From the ecophysiological point of view, they can be broadly classified into litter-decomposing, wood-decaying, and mycorrhizal fungi, although there is, inevitably, some overlap of roles. Basidiomycetes can form huge mycelial clones, and it has been estimated that they can extend over an area of several hectares while reaching an age of 1500 y and a mycelial biomass of 100 t (Dix and Webster 1995).

The Ligninolytic Enzyme System

Lignin, like cellulose, is a major component of plant materials and the most abundant form of aromatic carbon in the biosphere. It provides strength and rigidity to the cell walls of all vascular plants (club mosses, ferns, horsetails, seed plants) by acting as a glue between the cellulose and hemicellulose fibers. In addition, lignin forms a barrier against microbial destruction and protects the readily degradable carbohydrates. From the chemical point of view, lignin is a heterogeneous, optically inactive polymer consisting of phenylpropanoid subunits that are linked by various covalent bonds (e.g., aryl-ether, aryl-aryl, aliphatic carbon-aryl bonds; Fengel and Wegener 1989). The polymer arises from the enzyme-initiated polymerization of phenolic precursors (coniferyl, sinapyl, *p*-cumaryl alcohol) via the radical coupling of their corresponding phenoxy radicals. Because of the types of bonds and their heterogeneity, lignin cannot be degraded by hydrolytic mechanisms as most other natural polymers can.

During the course of evolution, only certain basidiomycetous fungi have developed an efficient enzyme system to mineralize lignin substantially, so these microorganisms play an important role in maintaining the global carbon cycle (Griffin 1994). Because of their ability to remove lignin selectively while leaving behind white cellulose fibers, these fungi are also called white-rot fungi. Typical representatives are the wood degraders *Trametes versicolor, Phanerochaete chrysosporium, Pleuro-tus ostreatus,* and *Nematoloma frowardii,* as well as the litter-decomposers *Agaricus bi-sporus, Agrocybe praecox,* and *Stropharia coronilla.* Lignin degradation does not provide a primary source of carbon and energy for fungal growth and is therefore a com-etabolic process in principle (mostly sugars released by hydrolases from hemicellu-loses are used as growth substrates).

Lignin degradation is thought to be brought about by the synergistic action of several oxidoreductases (ligninolytic enzymes). Two types of enzymes, namely perox-idases (manganese peroxidase, MnP, EC 1.11.1.13; lignin peroxidase, LiP, EC 1.11.1.14) and laccase (Lacc, EC 1.10.3.2), are the key biocatalysts and are responsible for the unspecific attack on lignin (Hatakka 2001). Both peroxidases are ferric-iron–containing heme proteins requiring peroxides (e.g., H_2O_2) for function, and laccase belongs to the copper-containing blue oxidases that use molecular oxygen (O_2). The enzymes have the common ability to catalyze one-electron oxidations, resulting in the formation of free-radical species inside the lignin polymer (Fernando and Aust 1990). Afterwards, the radicals undergo spontaneous reactions leading to the incorporation of oxygen (O_2), bond cleavages, and finally, to the breakdown of the lignin molecule (Kirk and Farrell 1987).

LiP and laccase react directly with aromatic lignin structures, whereas MnP works via chelated Mn^{3+} ions acting as low-molecular-weight redox mediators. Thus, the function of MnP is the generation of Mn^{3+} from Mn^{2+}, which is the actual substrate of the enzyme. Similar to the catalytic cycle of other peroxidases, including LiP, that of MnP involves the formation of peroxidase compounds I and II. The latter are highly reactive and abstract one electron from Mn^{2+} to form Mn^{3+} (Fig. 7.11).

MnP catalysis has an absolute requirement for Mn-chelating organic acids (i.e., oxalate, malate, or malonate), which both increase the affinity of Mn^{2+} to the enzyme and stabilize the reactive Mn^{3+} at high redox potentials (Wariishi et al. 1992). In contrast to the relatively large enzyme molecules, Mn^{3+} chelates are small enough to diffuse into the compact lignocellulosic complex, where they preferably react with phenolic lignin structures. Therefore, it is supposed that – in most white-rot fungi – the primary attack on lignin is brought about by the MnP system (Wariishi et al. 1992, Hofrichter 2002). As the result of MnP-catalyzed primary attack, water-soluble lignin fragments are formed, which are accessible for the further conversion by ligninolytic enzymes.

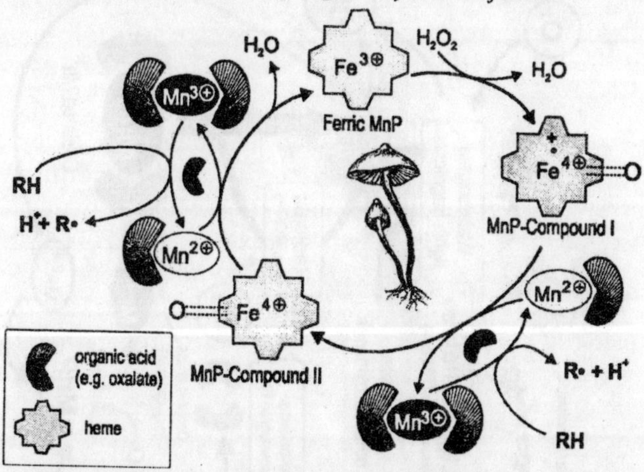

Catalytic cycle of manganese peroxidase (according to Wariishi et al. 1992; Hofrichter 2002).

Laccase oxidizes phenolic structures, whereas LiP preferentially cleaves recalcitrant nonphenolic lignin moieties (e.g., â-O-4 ethers). MnP is also involved in further degradation of the lignin fragments. Thus, there are indications that the MnP system even mineralizes aromatic lignin structures directly. It is the only enzyme – as far as known – that converts aromatic compounds, including lignin, partly to carbon dioxide (CO_2). This means that lignin can be mineralized – at least in part – outside the fungal hyphae (Hofrichter 2002). The reactions underlying the MnP-catalyzed mineralization are not yet completely understood, but it is certain that decarboxylation reactions involving Mn^{3+} are the final step in this process. Furthermore, certain radicals (carbon-centered radicals, peroxyl radicals, superoxide) that derive from the au-tocatalytic decomposition of organic acids in the presence of Mn^{3+} may also be involved in the mineralization process.

The oxidative strength of the MnP system can be enhanced in the presence of co-oxidants such as unsaturated fatty acids or thiols. These are first oxidized by Mn^{3+} and form – in the presence of O_2 – highly reactive radical species (peroxyl and alkoxy radicals of fatty acids, thioxyl radicals), which enhance lignin mineralization and make possible the cleavage of structures that are normally not attacked by the MnP system (e.g., nonphenolic aromatic aryl ethers; Hofrichter 2002).

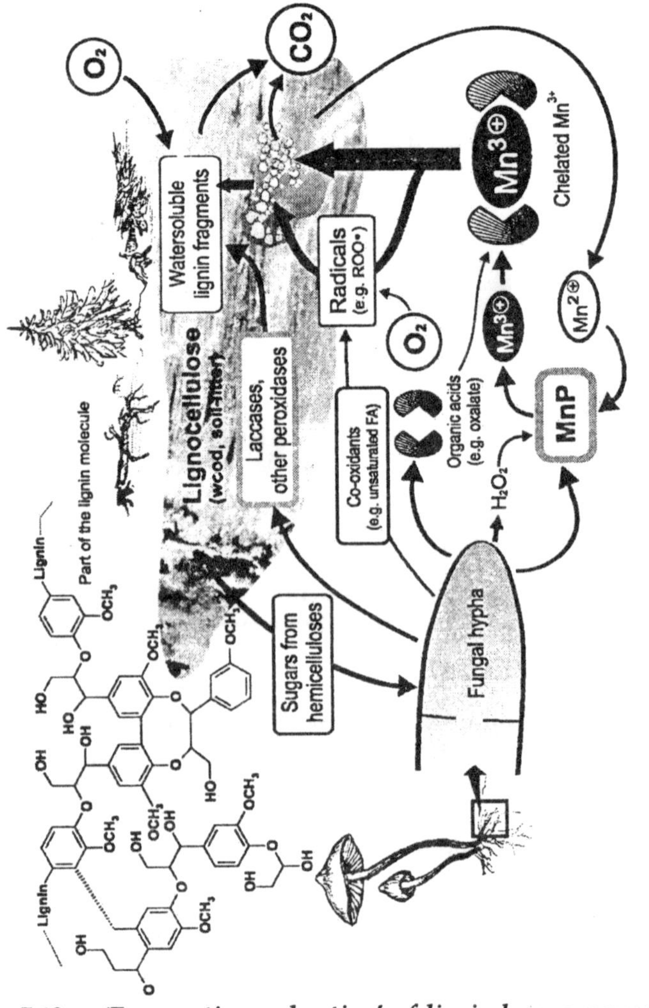

Fig. 7.12 'Enzymatic combustion' of lignin by manganese-peroxidase-producing basidiomy-cetes. The degradation of lignin is a generally aerobic, cometabolic process. Sugars and acetate derived from hemicelluloses and glucose from cellulose serve as the actual growth substrates.

According to a concept of Kirk and Frarrell (1987), the process of MnP-catalyzed degradation of lignin and other substances has been described as 'enzymatic combustion', in the course of which MnP acts as a 'radical pump' (Fig. 7.12, Hof-richter 2002).

Finally, we should mention that recent studies have indicated that alternative lig-ninolytic systems may exist that use chloroperoxidases (CPOs) as key enzymes. Examples are the ascomycete Leptoxyphium (*Caldariomyces*) *fumago* and the basidiom-ycete *Agrocybe aegerita*. Both fungi colonize plant debris and produce heme-thiolate CPOs that oxidize various aromatic substrates, including aryl alcohols, nonphenolic lignin model compounds, and synthetic lignin preparations (Ortiz-Bermúdez et al. 2003; Ullrich et al. 2004).

DEGRADATION OF ORGANOPOLLUTANTS

The unique ligninolytic enzyme system of basidiomycetous fungi, being based on a highly reactive free-radical depolymerization mechanism, should be ideal for the bi-odegradation of organopollutants in the environment (Fernando and Aust 1990). An excellent review of the feasibility of bioremediation with white-rot fungi was published by Pointing in 2001.

Compared with other potential bioremediation systems, the extracellular, nonspecific, nonstereoselective lignin-degrading system of basidiomycetous fungi has the advantage of being applicable to a variety of recalcitrant and toxic chemicals. Examples of such chemicals and selected fungi responsible for their biodegradation are given in Table 7.4. These substances include such hazardous xenobiotic compounds as polychlorinated dibenzodioxines and dibenzofurans, other chlorinated aromatics, nitroaromatic compounds (explosives), and carcinogenic organopollutants belonging to the polycyclic aromatic hydrocarbons (Hofrichter and Fritsche 2000, Manji and Ishihara 2003). MnP, LiP, and laccase have all been shown to be involved in the oxidation of organopollutants (Bollag 1988, Barr and Aust 1994). As a result of the attack on organopollutants by ligninolytic enzymes, various metabolites are formed that either can be further degraded intracellularly, coupled to the humus, or mineralized by the MnP system. The latter has been shown to mineralize several organo-pollutants partly in cell-free systems, indicating that an extracellular 'enzymatic combustion' of hazardous chemicals is possible in principle (Hofrichter 2002).

Over the last decade, efforts have been made to use ligninolytic basidiomycetes in bioremediation technologies. Laboratory experiments have shown that degradation of certain organopollutants (e.g., PAHs, PCP, TNT) is stimulated by wood-inhabiting white-rot fungi in contaminated soils (*Phanerochaete chrysosporium, Lentinus edodes, Kuehneromyces mutabilis*; Rajarathnam et al. 1998). However, a disadvantage of these fungi is their small competitive potential in soil. Therefore, recent research has focused on litter-decomposing basidiomycetes, which naturally colonize the upper-most portion of the soil and the humus layers of forests and grasslands. *Stro-pharia rugosoannulata, S. coronilla, Agrocybe praecox,* and *Collybia dryophila* are examples of such fungi. *Stropharia rugosoannulata* has already been successfully tested for decontamination of soils containing TNT as well as for PAH removal (Fritsche et al. 2000, Steffen et al. 2003).

CONCLUSIONS

It has been said that without microorganisms and their degradative capabilities animal life, including human life, on the earth would cease to exist within about five years. Whether or not this is an exaggeration as to the time scale, it is true in principle that we absolutely depend on microbial activities for the renewal of our environment and maintenance of the global carbon cycle (Ratledge 1991).

Among the substances that can be degraded or transformed by microorganisms are a huge number of synthetic compounds (xenobiotics) and other chemicals having environmental relevance (e.g., mineral oil components). However, it has to be considered that this statement concerns potential degradabilities which - in most instances - were estimated in the laboratory by using pure cultures and ideal growth conditions.

Under natural conditions in soil, the actual degradability of organopollutants is lower, due to a whole range of factors: competition with other microorganisms, insufficient supply with essential substrates (C, N, P, S sources), unfavorable external conditions (O_2, H_2O, pH, temperature), and low bioavailability of the pollutant that is to be degraded. Thus, environmental biotechnology has the important assignment of tackling and solving these problems so as to permit the use of microorganism in bioremediation technologies.

For this purpose, it is necessary to support the activities of the indigenous microorganisms in polluted soils and to enhance their degradative potential by bioaugmentation. The former measure particularly applies to bacteria, whereas bioaugmentation mainly concerns basidiomycetous fungi. In this context, we should point out that neither bacteria nor fungi are 'better' degraders. In nature, both groups of microorganisms work together of course, and complement one another in their degradative capabilities.

8

Principles of Anaerobic Degradation of Organic Compounds

GENERAL ASPECTS OF ANAEROBIC DEGRADATION PROCESSES

The vast majority of organic compounds produced in nature or through human manufacture is degraded aerobically, with molecular oxygen as terminal electron acceptor. As long as oxygen is available, it is the preferred electron acceptor for microbial degradation processes in nature.

Anaerobic degradation processes have always been considered inferior to aerobic degradation in their kinetics and capacities. They are thought to be slow and inefficient, especially with certain comparably stable types of substrates. Nonetheless, in certain anoxic environments, such as the cow's rumen, the turnover of, e.g., cellulose is much faster than in the presence of oxygen, with average half-life times in the range of one day. Fermentative degradation of fibers in the rumen reaches its limit with plant tissues rich in lignin which largely withstands degradation in the absence of oxygen.

Also in waste treatment, especially with high loads of easy-to-degrade organic material, anaerobic processes have proved to be efficient and far less expensive than aerobic treatment: they require only small amounts of energy input, in contrast to treatment in aeration basins, and can produce a mixture of methane and CO_2 ('bio-gas'), which can be used efficiently for energy generation. This holds true for most waste materials that are easily accessible to degradation without the participation of oxygen, such as polysaccharides, proteins, fats, nucleic acids, etc. These polymers are hydrolyzed through specific extracellular enzymes, and the oligo- and monomers can be degraded inside the cell through enzyme reactions similar to those known in aerobic metabolism. The specific activities of such enzymes in anaerobic cultures are in the same range (0.1–1 μmol substrate per min and mg cell protein) as those of aerobic bacteria, and thus the transformation rates per unit bio-mass should be equivalent.

Nonetheless, anaerobic bacteria obtain far less energy from substrate turnover than their aerobic counterparts. Whereas aerobic oxidation of hexose to six CO_2 yields 2870 kJ per mol, dismutation of hexose to three CH_4 and three CO_2 yields only 390 kJ per mol, about 15% of the aerobic process, and this small amount of energy has to be shared by at least three different metabolic groups of bacteria (see Schink, 1997). As a consequence, they can produce far less biomass per substrate molecule than aerobes can. Their growth yields are low, and most often growth is slower than that of aerobes. Maintaining the biomass inside specifically designed reactors (fixed bed, fluidized bed reactors, Upflow Anaerobic Sludge Blanket reactors) helps to overcome the problem of low and slow biomass production in anaerobic degradation and largely uncouples substrate turnover from biomass growth (for an overview, see, e.g., Schink, 1988). These systems allow anaerobic wastewater treatment to be nearly as efficient as and less expensive than the aerobic process, with methane as a useful product; but the microbial communities in these advanced anaerobic reactors still are comparably sluggish in reacting to changes in substrate composition or in their reestablishment after accidental population losses due to toxic ingredients in the feeding waste.

Degradation of organic matter in the absence of oxygen can be coupled to the reduction of alternative electron acceptors following a certain sequence that appears to be determined by the respective redox potentials. Molecular oxygen (O_2/H_2O E_h = +810 mV; E_h values calculated for pH 7.0) is followed by nitrate (NO_3^-/NO_2^- E_h = +430 mV), manganese(IV) oxide (MnO_2/Mn^{2+} E_h = +400 mV), iron(III) hydroxides ($FeOOH/Fe^{2+}$ E_h = +150 mV), sulfate (SO_4^{2-}/HS^- E_h = –218 mV), and finally CO_2 (CO_2/CH_4 E_h = –244 mV), with the release of nitrite, ammonia, dinitrogen, manganese(II) and iron(II) carbonates, sulfides, and finally methane as products (Zehnder and Stumm, 1988). Reduction of these acceptors with electrons from organic matter (average redox potential for glucose '! 6 CO_2 is –0.434 V; calculated after data of Thauer et al., 1977) provides metabolic energy in the mentioned sequence. Thus, the energy yields of the various anaerobes mentioned differ, and the availability of either high- or low-potential electron acceptors may also influence the biochemistry of anaerobic degradation processes.

Limits of anaerobic degradation become obvious with those organic compounds that accumulate in anoxic sediments or that persist in anoxic soil compartments contaminated with mineral oil or other rather recalcitrant compounds. Mineral oil consists mainly of aliphatic and aromatic hydrocarbons which, in the presence of molecular oxygen, are attacked biochemically through oxygenase reactions, which introduce molecular oxygen into the respective molecule (Lengeler et al., 1999; see also Chapter 7). Oxygenase reactions cannot be employed in the absence of oxygen, and, in particular, compounds that require oxygenases for aerobic breakdown might resist degradation under anoxic conditions. Alternatives usually exist in the anoxic world that also allow oxygen-independent degradation of such compounds.

Oxygen is not always advantageous in degradation processes. Oxygenases introduce hydroxyl groups into aromatics, and further oxygen may cause formation of phenol radicals that initiate uncontrolled polymerization and condensation to polymeric derivatives, similar to humic compounds in soil, which are very difficult to degrade further, whether anaerobically or aerobically. Therefore, anaerobic degradation processes may be used for treatment of specific wastewaters rich in phenolic compounds, e.g., from the chemical industry, to avoid formation of unwanted side products such as condensed polyphenols.

In other situations, aerobic treatment may cause technical problems, e.g., by extensive foam formation during aerobic treatment of surface-active compounds such as tensides. Thus, knowledge of the limits and principles of anaerobic degradation processes under the various conditions prevailing in natural habitats might help to design suitable alternative techniques for cleanup of contaminated soils or for treatment of specific wastewaters that have so far been applied only insufficiently.

The following survey gives an overview of our present knowledge of the limits and principles of anaerobic degradation of organic compounds. The focus is on those compounds that were for long times considered to be stable in the absence of oxygen.

KEY REACTIONS IN ANAEROBIC DEGRADATION OF CERTAIN ORGANIC COMPOUNDS

Degradation of Hydrocarbons

Saturated aliphatic hydrocarbons are attacked only slowly in the absence of oxygen, and the first reliable proof of such a process was provided only about eight years ago for a culture of sulfate-reducing bacteria (Aeckersberg et al., 1991). Growth of this culture with hexadecane was very slow, with doubling times of more than one week under optimal conditions. In the meantime, several strains of alkane-oxidizing anaerobes were isolated (Aeckersberg et al., 1998; Rueter et al., 1994), which are specialized for either long-chain (C_{12}–C_{20}) or medium-chain (C_{6-16}) alkanes and use either sulfate or nitrate as electron acceptor.

Insight into the biochemistry of alkane activation in the absence of oxygen has been obtained only recently. The initial activation is basically similar to the corresponding reaction involved in anaerobic oxidation of toluene (see Section 8.2.6.8): the hydrocarbon is added with its subterminal carbon atom to fumarate through a radical reaction, to form an alkyl succinate derivative (Rabus et al., 2001). This strategy is used in a basically similar manner by nitrate-reducing and sulfate-reducing bacteria (Wilkes et al., 2002). In either case, anaerobic hydrocarbon degradation is very slow, but may play a role in, e.g., natural attenuation of soil sites polluted with petroleum or diesel fuel.

A special example, although not of technical interest, is the anaerobic degradation of methane, e.g., with sulfate as electron acceptor, a process that is of major importance in global carbon transformations. No bacterium that catalyzes this reaction has been isolated so far, although it is thermodynamically feasible (see Schink, 1997). Recent evidence has shown that this reaction is most probably carried out by archaea similar to methanogens, which operate methane formation in the backwards reaction, most often in syntrophic association with sulfate-reducing partner organisms (Boetius et al., 2000). Although this concept was suggested many years ago (Zehnder and Brock, 1980), experimental evidence has been obtained only recently with samples from deep-sea sources, and efficient methane oxidation requires enhanced methane pressure (Nauhaus et al., 2002).

Unsaturated long-chain hydrocarbons with terminal double bonds can be hydrat-ed to the corresponding primary alcohols (although against the Markownikoff rule) and completely degraded (Schink, 1985a). A branched-chain unsaturated hydrocarbon such as squalene was degraded in methanogenic enrichment cultures (Schink, 1985a); however, degradation was incomplete, probably due to the formation of saturated branched derivatives. Other unsaturated isoprene derivatives such as ter-penes have been shown recently to be completely degraded, with nitrate as electron acceptor (Harder and Probian, 1995; Foß and Harder, 1998; Foß et al., 1998). Although the structures of terpenes differ substantially with respect to the way of possible attack, an amazingly broad variety of terpenes was completely degraded. Some concepts of the biochemistry of degradation of these compounds have been developed (Hylemon and Harder, 1999),but experimental evidence is still lacking. Acetylene, a highly unsaturated hydrocarbon, is fermented comparably rapidly to acetate and ethanol through acetaldehyde (Schink, 1985b), which is formed by a hydratase enzyme (Rosner and Schink, 1995). Acetylene hydratase is an iron-sulfur protein containing a tungsten cofactor (Meckenstock et al., 1999); it is active only in the reduced state, but the reaction mechanism is still unknown. No anaerobic degradation has been documented so far for ethylene, propylene, propine, and higher homologs having up to six carbon atoms.

Degradation of Ether Compounds and Nonionic Surfactants

Ether linkages are rather stable, and their chemical cleavage requires severe conditions, e.g., boiling at strongly alkaline or acidic pH. Biological ether cleavage in the presence of oxygen employs oxygen as cosubstrate in an oxygenase reaction, which transforms the ether into an unstable hemiacetal (Bernhardt et al., 1970). Thus, methyl groups of lignin monomers are released as formaldehyde, not as methanol.

Anaerobic demethylation of lignin monomers by the homoacetogen *Acetobacteri-um woodii* was first described by Bache and Pfennig (1981) and later was repeatedly observed with several other homoacetogens. The mechanism of this phenyl methyl ether cleavage were only recently elucidated. Studies with the homoacetogen *Ho-lophaga foetida* showed that the methyl group is first transferred as a methyl cation to a fully reduced cob(I)alamin carrier, which later methylates the coenzyme tetrahy-drofolate (Fig. 8.1; Kreft and Schink, 1993, 1994). Similar studies with *Acetobacteri-um woodii, Sporomusa ovata,* or *Acetobacterium dehalogenans* revealed that also in these species, the methyl group is transferred as a methyl cation, but that the details of further methyl transfer to coenzymes may differ with the strain studied (Berman and Frazer, 1992; Stupperich and Konle, 1993; Kaufmann et al., 1997; Kaufmann et al., 1998; Engelmann et al., 2001).

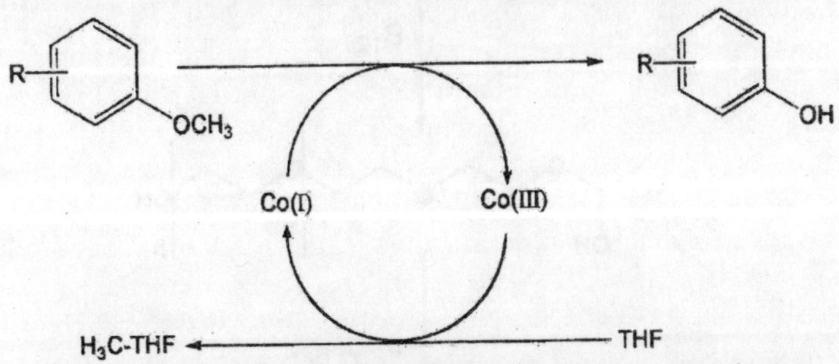

Fig. 8.1 ***Anaerobic demethylation of phenyl methyl ethers. Co(I), Co(III), cobalamin in different redox states; THF, tetrahydrofolate.***

A different type of anaerobic ether cleavage was observed with the synthetic poly-ether polyethylene glycol (PEG). Formation of acetaldehyde as the first cleavage product, extreme oxygen sensitivity of the ether-cleaving enzyme in cell-free extracts, and interference with cobalamins strongly suggest that the first step in this degradation is a cobalamin-dependent shift of the terminal hydroxyl group to the subterminal C atom, analogous to a diol dehydratase reaction (Fig. 8.2; Schramm and Schink, 1991; Frings et al., 1992). This reaction again transforms the ether into a hemiacetal derivative that decomposes spontaneously. Since the ether-cleaving enzyme is located in the cytoplasmic space, the polymeric PEG (which has molecular mass up to 40 kDa) has to cross the cell membrane(s) before it is cleaved inside, and the same is true for PEG-containing nonionic surfactants. Since the bacterial strains studied so far are specialized only for the degradation of the PEG chain, the lipophilic residues of the surfactants have to cross the membrane(s) again on their way back out. It is obvious that these transport steps considerably limit the applicability of such degradation capacities to treatment of, e.g., wastewaters rich in such surfactants. Nonetheless, the applicability of anaerobic fixed-bed reactors for treatment of nonionic surfactants of various types to methane, CO_2, and mixtures of fatty acids has been demonstrated (Wagner and Schink, 1987, 1988).

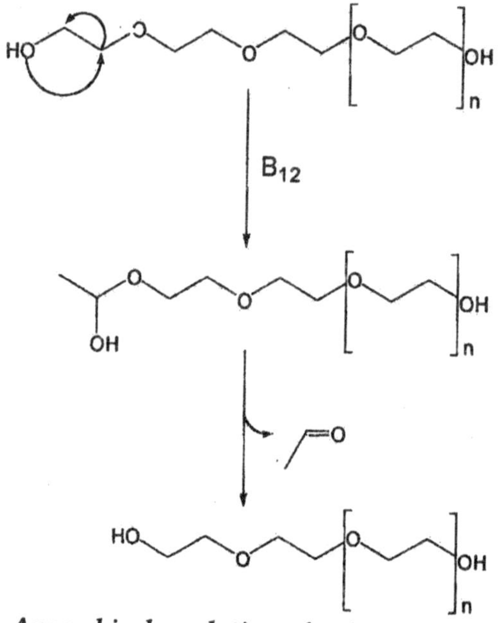

Fig. 8.2 Anaerobic degradation of polyethylene glycol by fermenting bacteria. B_{12}, coenzyme B_{12}.

The anaerobic ether cleavage reactions described here proceed only inside the bacterial cell. In this, they differ from the corresponding reactions reported for certain basidiomycetes (Kerem et al., 1998), which use these cleavage capacities, e.g., in lig-nin degradation. It is not surprising, therefore, that highly polymeric, condensed-ether compounds such as lignin are not degraded to any significant extent in the absence of molecular oxygen.

DEGRADATION OF N-ALKYL COMPOUNDS AND NITRILOTRIACETATE

Among the natural *N*-alkyl compounds are, in addition to t he amino acids, several methylated amines such as trimethylamine, which is formed during the initial decay of fish tissue through reduction of trimethylamine-*N*-oxide by several enterobacteria and others. Under strictly anoxic conditions, methanogenic archaea have been fcund to efficiently demethylate trimethylamine via dimethylamine to monomethyl-amine and to ferment the methyl moieties by dismutation to methane and CO_2 (Hippe et al., 1979). The cleavage between the nitrogen and the neighboring carbon atom is accomplished by a nucleophilic attack by a cob(I)alamin, analogous to the demethylation of phenyl methyl ethers by homoacetogenic bacteria (see above). So far, only methanogens have been found to demethylate methylamines, whereas homoacetogens appear to be specialists for demethylation of phenyl methyl ethers which, in turn, are not attacked by methanogens. It should be emphasized at this point that the strategy of methyl cation removal by cob(I)alamin derivatives is applicable only to these one-carbon compounds. Ethyl or higher homologs cannot be cleaved this way.

N-alkyl compounds of technical and environmental concern include ethylenedi-aminetetraacetate (EDTA) and nitrilotriacetate (NTA); the latter has largely replaced polyphosphates as a calcium chelator in most commercial washing detergents. The main problem in degrading EDTA is the formation of strong complexes of EDTA with metal ions, which make this substrate very difficult to attack. Nonetheless, mi-crobial EDTA degradation in the presence of oxygen has been documented (-Nörtemann, 1992), but no reports exist on possible anaerobic degradation of EDTA. NTA is degraded aerobically through oxygenase-dependent hydroxylation of one methylene carbon. The resulting hydroxy compound is unstable and releases glyox-ylic acid. Removal of an additional carboxymethylene residue produces glycine as co-product. Anaerobic degradation of NTA is possible with nitrate as electron acceptor. The first degradation step is dehydrogenation to an unsaturated iminium derivative which, upon hydration, can again release glyoxylic acid to form the iminodiacetate derivative (Egli et al., 1990). Since oxidation of NTA to the unsaturated derivative has a rather high redox potential (> +100 mV), it is not surprising that so far, only nitrate reducers have been found to be able to degrade NTA. We have to assume that, under strictly reducing conditions, i.e., in deeper sediment layers, NTA is stable to microbial attack, because neither sulfate-reducing nor fermenting bacteria can release electrons arising at this high redox potential.

DEGRADATION OF S-ALKYL COMPOUNDS

Dimethylsulfoniopropionate is an osmoprotectant found in several green algae and seaweeds. Its cleavage by anaerobic bacteria leads to acrylate and dimethylsulfide, which can escape into the atmosphere. The thioether dimethylsulfide can also be degraded anaerobically by methanogenic archaea (Kiene et al., 1986; Oremland et al., 1989). The carbon-sulfur linkage is cleaved by methyl cation removal, analogous to the demethylation reactions described above (Keltjens and Vogels, 1993).

Degradation of Ketones

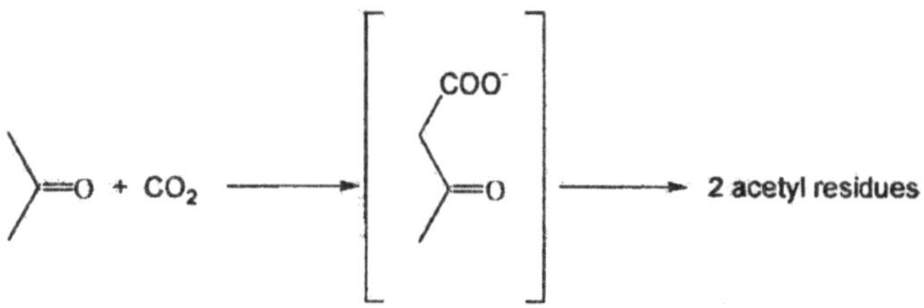

Fig. 8.3 Anaerobic degradation of acetone through carboxylation.

Aerobic degradation of ketones appeared to be well established. Indications of an oxygenase-catalyzed hydroxylation of acetone to acetol by aerobic bacteria were provided early (Lukins and Foster, 1963; Taylor et al., 1980), but this type of reaction was never confirmed unequivocally. Anaerobic degradation of acetone by nitrate-reducing, sulfate-reducing, or fermenting bacteria cooperating with methanogenic partners uses a carboxylation reaction as primary step of activation, leading to an acetoa-cetyl derivative that undergoes subsequent cleavage to two acetate moieties (Fig. 8.3; Platen and Schink, 1987, 1989; Bonnet-Smits et al., 1988; Platen et al., 1990). Unfortunately, the primary carboxylation reaction was never convincingly proved with these cultures. Very little acetone carboxylation activity was observed in enzyme assays (Platen and Schink, 1991) or in radiotracer experiments using suspensions of intact cells (Janssen and Schink, 1995). Acetone carboxylation activity in the photo-trophic anaerobe *Rhodobacter capsulatus* was also very weak in vitro (Birks and Kelly, 1997). An acetone-carboxylating enzyme complex of high activity has been found in an aerobic *Xanthobacter* strain (Sluis et al., 1996) and was purified and characterized (Sluis and Ensign, 1997; Sluis et al., 2002). The reaction requires as energy source for the acetone carboxylation reaction one ATP, which is hydrolyzed to AMP plus two P_i. Whether sulfate-reducing or fermenting bacteria provide the necessary energy for carboxylation in different ways still has to be examined. The fermenting bacteria especially cannot afford to spend the equivalent of two ATP molecules on this carboxylation reaction. To our surprise, all aerobic bacteria enriched with acetone also used a carboxylation step rather than an oxygenase reaction in acetone activation, even if CO_2 was trapped during the enrichment process (Schink, unpublished data). Thus, the original reports of oxygenase-dependent acetone activation may describe an exceptional situation with one single strain, which is not representative of the majority of aerobic acetone degraders.

Higher homologs of acetone appear to be attacked in a similar manner by carbox-ylations. This applies also to acetophenone, the phenyl-substituted analog of acetone (Schink, unpublished data).

DEGRADATION OF AROMATIC COMPOUNDS

In aerobic degradation of aromatic compounds, oxygenases activate the comparably stable oxygen molecule in such a way as to produce highly electrophilic species, which add to a comparably inert aromatic compound to form hydroxylated products such as catechol (Dagley, 1971; Schlegel, 1992). A further oxygenase-dependent step opens the aromatic ring, either between or vicinal to the two hydroxyl groups of cate-chol, thus forming an unsaturated, open-chain carboxylic acid which undergoes further degradation, typically to an acetyl and a succinyl derivative.

That aromatic compounds can also be degraded anaerobically was documented as early as 1934: a broad variety of mononuclear aromatic compounds, such as ben-zoate, phenols, and several lignin monomers, was converted stoichiometrically to methane and CO_2 (Tarvin and Buswell, 1934). Later these observations were forgotten, and some textbooks maintained even into the 1980s the dogma that aromatics can be attacked only with oxygen as cosubstrate. During the 1970s, Evans (1977) developed the concept that destabilization of the aromatic nucleus in the absence of oxygen could proceed through a reductive rather than an oxidative reaction. Today we know at least three different pathways of anaerobic degradation of mononuclear compounds, i.e., the benzoyl-CoA pathway, the resorcinol pathway, and the phloroglucinol pathway (Evans and Fuchs, 1988; Schink et al., 1992; Fuchs et al., 1994; Hei-der and Fuchs, 1997; Schink et al., 2000). In all these pathways, a 1,3-dioxo structure is formed through a reduction step, either inside the ring itself or in combination with a carboxyl coenzyme A moiety. This structure allows a nucleophilic attack on one of the ring ketone carbon atoms and subsequent ring fission. Depending on the aromatic substrate, either a pimelic (C_7-dicarboxylic) residue bound to coenzyme A or a partly oxidized caproic (C_6-monocarboxylic) acid is formed, which undergoes subsequent beta oxidation to three acetyl moieties. Formation of other products in fermentative benzoate degradation, such as succinate or propionate as claimed in earlier papers, could never be reproduced with defined cultures and may have been due to uncontrolled side reactions or misinterpretations of insufficient chemical analyses.

BENZOATE AND THE BENZOYL-COA PATHWAY

The benzoyl-CoA pathway appears to be the most important one in anaerobic degradation of aromatics, because a broad variety of compounds enter this path, including phenol, various hydroxybenzoates, phenylacetate, aniline, certain cresols, and even the hydrocarbon toluene (Fig. 8.4; Schink et al., 1992; Heider and Fuchs, 1997; Har-wood et al., 1999). Once benzoyl-CoA is formed, the stability of the aromatic ring structure is overcome by a reductive step that introduces two single electrons and protons, through radical intermediates, to form cyclohexadiene carboxyl-CoA as the first identifiable product (Fig. 8.5; Koch et al., 1993; Boll and Fuchs, 1995; Boll et al. 2000a). Because reduction of the benzene ring to a cyclohexadiene derivative, even with electrons at the ferredoxin level (Boll et al., 2000b) is endergonic, it requires the investment of energy in the form of two ATP molecules (Boll and Fuchs, 1995; Har-wood et al., 1999). Nitrate-reducing bacteria can recover this energy investment through the further breakdown of the C_7-dicarboxylic acid derivative produced upon ring cleavage, via beta oxidation to three acetyl-CoA residues that are finally oxidized in the citric acid cycle. Fermenting bacteria and sulfate-reducing bacteria recover only a little energy in the further breakdown of the open-chain intermediate. They may use a different type of reaction for benzoyl-CoA dearomatization that leads to a cy-clohexene carboxyl derivative (Schöcke and Schink, 1999; Harwood et al., 1999) or to a hydroxylated derivative through hydroxylations catalyzed by selenium- or molybdenum-containing enzymes (Peters et al. 2004).

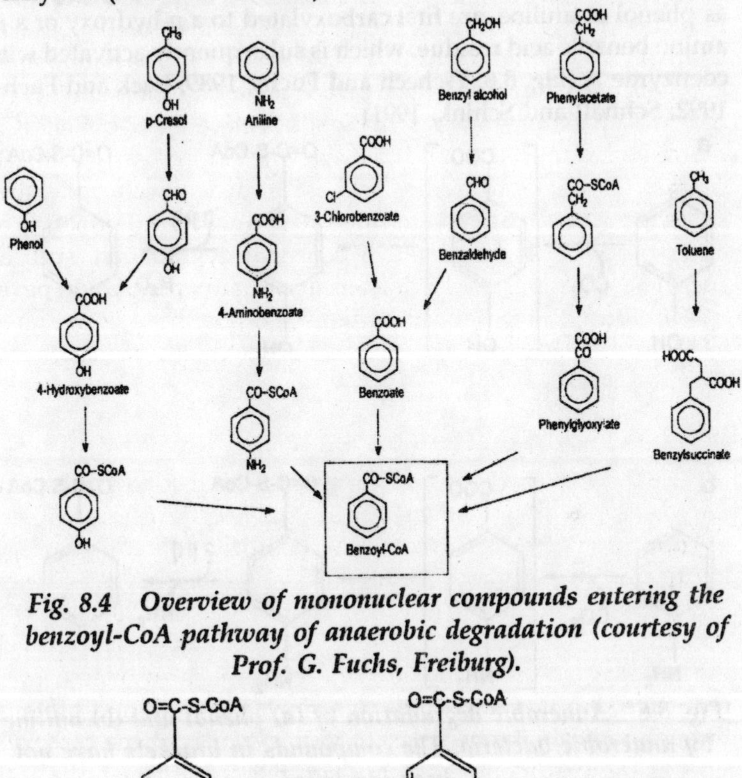

Fig. 8.4 Overview of mononuclear compounds entering the benzoyl-CoA pathway of anaerobic degradation (courtesy of Prof. G. Fuchs, Freiburg).

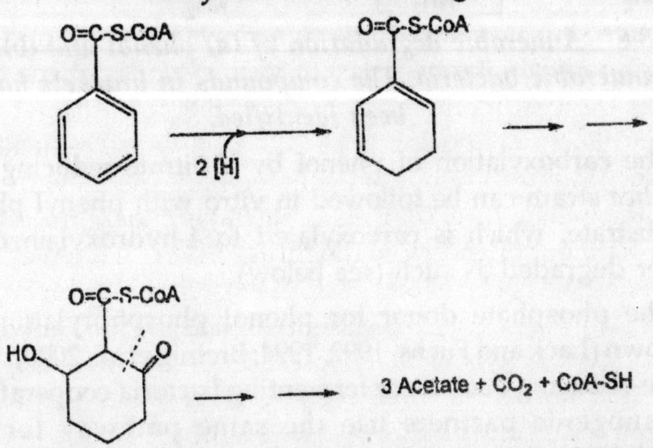

Fig. 8.5 Initial steps in anaerobic degradation of benzoate by the nitrate-reducing bacterium Thauera aromatica.

However, the biochemistry of these new reactions still needs to be elucidated.

PHENOL, HYDROXYBENZOATES, AND ANILINE

Aromatic compounds that do not carry a carboxyl group, such as phenol or aniline, are first carboxylated to a *p*-hydroxy or a *p*-amino benzoic acid residue, which is subsequently activated with coenzyme A (Fig. 8.6; Tschech and Fuchs, 1989; Lack and Fuchs, 1992; Schnell and Schink, 1991).

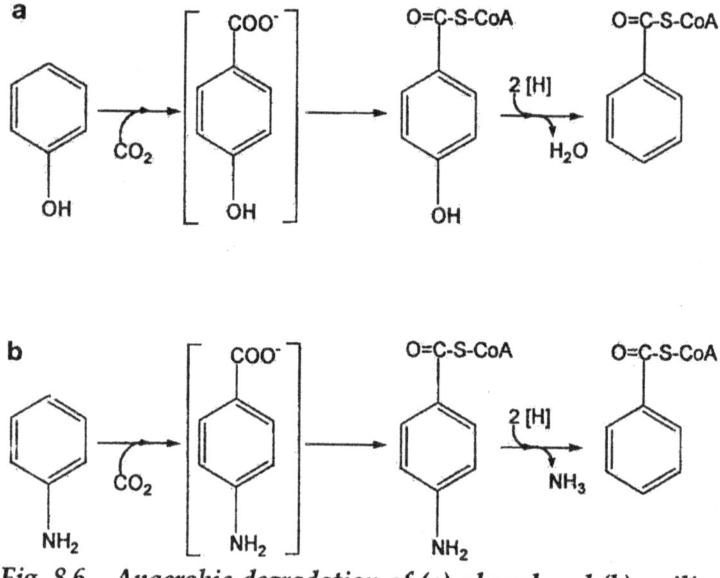

Fig. 8.6 Anaerobic degradation of (a) phenol and (b) aniline by anaerobic bacteria. The compounds in brackets have not been identified.

The carboxylation of phenol by a nitrate-reducing *Thauera aromatica* strain can be followed in vitro with phenyl phosphate as substrate, which is carboxylated to 4-hydroxybenzoate and further degraded as such (see below).

The phosphate donor for phenol phosphorylation is still unknown (Lack and Fuchs, 1992, 1994; Breinig et al., 2000). Whether sulfate-reducing bacteria or fermenting bacteria cooperating with methanogenic partners use the same pathway for phenol degradation also remains to be examined. An H/D exchange at carbon atom 4 of phenol by cell suspensions of a methanogenic phenol-degrading enrichment culture indicates that these cultures also activate phenol through carboxylation at this position (Gallert et al., 1991). Whether the carboxylation reaction in these fermentative bacteria is also initiated by phenol phosphorylation is still an open question.

The overall energy budget of fermentative phenol degradation is very tight and hardly allows spending a full ATP equivalent or even more on this carboxylation reaction.

The biochemistry of phenol degradation by sulfate-reducing bacteria has not been studied so far, but it is likely to proceed basically through the same pathway.The 4-hydroxybenzoate formed is activated through a ligase reaction, analogous to benzoyl-CoA formation from benzoate, to form 4-hydroxybenzoyl-CoA, which is subsequently reductively dehydroxylated to benzoyl-CoA (Fig. 8.6a).

4-Hydroxybenzoate may be degraded anaerobically through the same pathway. However, in cultures 4-hydroxybenzoate is not stable but is slowly decarboxylated to phenol, perhaps by an enzyme activity related to phenyl phosphate carboxylase.

3-Hydroxybenzoate is comparably stable and does not decarboxylate spontaneously. Instead, the hydroxyl group is reductively eliminated by fermenting bacteria to allow further degradation through the benzoyl-CoA pathway, as shown with *Sporoto-maculum hydroxybenzoicum* (Müller and Schink, 2000).

Aniline is degraded anaerobically through a pathway analogous to that for phenol degradation.

The initial activation is accomplished through carboxylation to 4-ami-nobenzoate, which is subsequently activated to 4-aminobenzoyl-CoA and undergoes reductive deamination to benzoyl-CoA (Fig. 8.6b; Schnell and Schink, 1991).

The initial carboxylation reaction has not been studied in cell-free extracts so far, and nothing is known about an activated intermediate that can provide the carboxylation reaction with the necessary energy.

Aminobenzoates, diaminobenzenes, and amino-hydroxybenzenes are degraded very slowly in anaerobic enrichment cultures, and nothing is known about the degradation pathways (Schnell and Schink, unpublished data).

Cresols

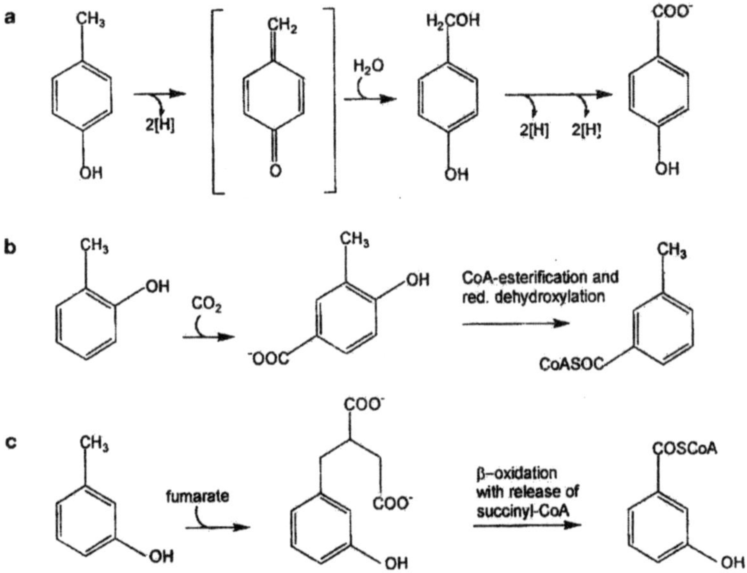

Fig. 8.7** **Anaerobic degradation of cresols. (a) Degradation of p-cresol, (b) degradation of o-cresol, (c) degradation of m-cresol.

Cresols (methylphenols) are anaerobically degraded through three different pathways, depending on the type of substitution. *p*-Cresol is hydroxylated at the methyl group by an oxygen-independent reaction, probably through a quinomethide intermediate as suggested earlier for an aerobic *Pseudomonas* strain (Fig. 8.7a; Hopper, 1978). The redox potential of this oxidation reaction is in the range of +100 mV (calculated after Thauer et al., 1977), and the reaction is therefore easy to do for a nitrate-reducing bacterium that couples this oxidation, e.g., with the reduction of a *c*-type cytochrome at +235 mV (Hopper et al., 1991). Sulfate-reducing or fermenting bacteria, on the other hand, have difficulty in disposing of these electrons. *o*-Cresol can be carboxylated to 3-methyl-4-hydroxybenzoate and further degraded as such (Fig. 8.7b; Bisaillon et al., 1991; Rudolphi et al., 1991). An alternative pathway could lead through methyl group hydroxylation, analogous to *p*-cresol, to form salicylic acid as an intermediate (Suflita et al., 1989; Schink et al., 1992), but this pathway has only been hypothesized so far. The pathway of anaerobic *m*-cresol degradation has been elucidated recently in the sulfate-reducing bacterium *Desulfobacterium cetonicum*. This degradation follows a strategy analogous to anaerobic toluene degradation by nitrate-reducing bacteria (Müller et al., 1999): the methyl group of *m*-cresol adds to fumarate to form 3-hydroxybenzylsuccinate. Activation and beta oxidation lead to succinyl-CoA and benzoyl-CoA (Fig. 8.7c). Thus, the new type of methyl group activation by addition to fumarate appears not to be restricted to the activation of hydrocarbons (see below).

Hydroquinone and Catechol

Hydroquinone is degraded by sulfate-reducing and fermenting bacteria. The degradation pathway has been studied in a sulfate-reducing *Desulfococcus* strain (Gorny and Schink, 1994a) and a fermenting bacterium that was later described as *Syntro-phus gentianae* (Gorny and Schink, 1994b). In both species, hydroquinone is carbox-ylated to gentisic acid; again, this carboxylation could not be studied in cell-free extracts and the way of energization of this reaction is unknown. Gentisate is activated to gentisyl-CoA through a CoA-ligase reaction and reductively dehydroxylated to benzoyl-CoA, which enters the modified benzoyl-CoA pathway. The dehydroxylation of both hydroxyl groups appears to proceed in a single step. Alternatively, gentisic acid is utilized by the fermenting bacterium.

Catechol, the key intermediate in aerobic breakdown of aromatic compounds, is by far the slowest phenolic compound to be degraded under anoxic conditions. The biochemistry of catechol degradation has been studied so far only in a sulfate-reduc-ing *Desulfobacterium* strain, which carboxylates catechol to protocatechuate (Gorny and Schink, 1994c). Protocatechuate is activated to form protocatechuyl-CoA, which is subsequently dehydroxylated to benzoyl-CoA. Efforts to isolate nitrate-reducing or fermenting bacteria with hydroquinone or catechol as substrate have failed so far.

Resorcinol

An entirely different strategy is used in the anaerobic degradation of resorcinol and its derivatives. The two hydroxyl groups in resorcinol are in positions relative to each other that allow tautomerization to a cyclohexene dione derivative having three isolated double bonds (Fig. 8.8a). Cell-free extracts of a fermenting *Clostridium* strain convert resorcinol to dihydroresorcinol (cyclohexanedione; Tschech and Schink, 1985; Kluge et al., 1990), which is further hydrolyzed to 5-oxohexanoate, probably through a nucleophilic attack on one of the carbonyl carbon atoms (Fig. 8.8a).

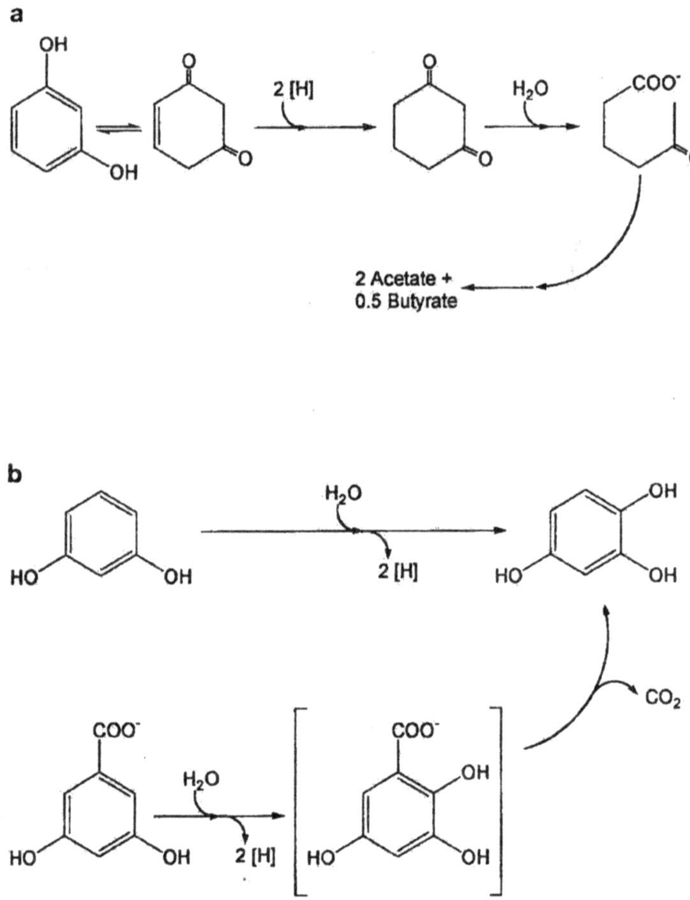

Fig. 8.8 Anaerobic degradation of resorcinol and á-resorcylate. (a) Resorcinol degradation by a fermenting bacterium, Clostridium *strain KN245, (b) degradation of resorcinol and á-resorcylate by nitrate-reducing bacteria.*

The resorcinol carboxylates â- and ã-resorcylate are degraded by the same fermenting bacterium after decarboxylation to resorcinol. These decarboxylations are chemically easy, because in these compounds the carboxylic group is located ortho or para to electron-withdrawing hydroxyl groups.

In cultures of nitrate-reducing bacteria growing with resorcinol as the sole substrate, no resorcinol-reducing activity could be identified (Kluge et al., 1990; Gorny et al., 1992). The nitrate reducer *Azoarcus anaerobius* destabilizes the ring by introducing an additional hydroxyl group to form hydroxyhydroquinone (Fig. 8.8b; Phi-lipp and Schink, 1998). The enzyme involved is membrane-bound, and the hydrox-ylation is coupled to reduction of nitrate to nitrite. In a later oxidation step, hydroxy-hydroquinone is oxidized to hydroxybenzoquinone (Philipp and Schink, 1998). The ring fission reaction has not been resolved yet.

Trihydroxybenzenes and Trihydroxybenzoates

Among the three trihydroxybenzene isomers, pyrogallol and phloroglucinol are degraded quickly by fermenting bacteria (Schink and Pfennig, 1982). Phloroglucinol degradation has been studied in detail with *Eubacterium oxidoreducens* and *Pelobac-ter acidigallici*. Phloroglucinol is reduced by an NADPH-dependent reductase to di-hydrophloroglucinol (Fig. 8.9; Haddock and Ferry, 1989; Brune and Schink, 1992), and the same strategy is followed by *Holophaga foetida* strain TMBS4 (Kreft and Schink, 1993). Hydrolytic ring cleavage leads to 3-hydroxy-5-oxohexanoic acid, which is thiolytically cleaved to three acetate residues (Brune and Schink, 1992). This pathway is easy to conceive, because the 1,3,5 arrangement of three hydroxyl groups on the aromatic ring allows tautomerization to 1,3,5-trioxocyclohexane to an extent that makes the molecule susceptible to a nucleophilic attack on the oxocarbon groups. The second trihydroxybenzene isomer, pyrogallol, cannot be hydrolyzed directly but is isomerized to phloroglucinol through a transhydroxylation reaction (Fig. 8.9; Krumholz and Bryant, 1988; Brune and Schink, 1990). The reaction requires 1,3,4,5-tetrahydroxybenzene as a cosubstrate, and the enzyme transfers a hydroxyl group from the tetrahydroxybenzene to pyrogallol, thus releasing phloroglucinol as product and the tetrahydroxybenzene as coproduct (Brune and Schink, 1990; Reichen-becher et al., 1996).

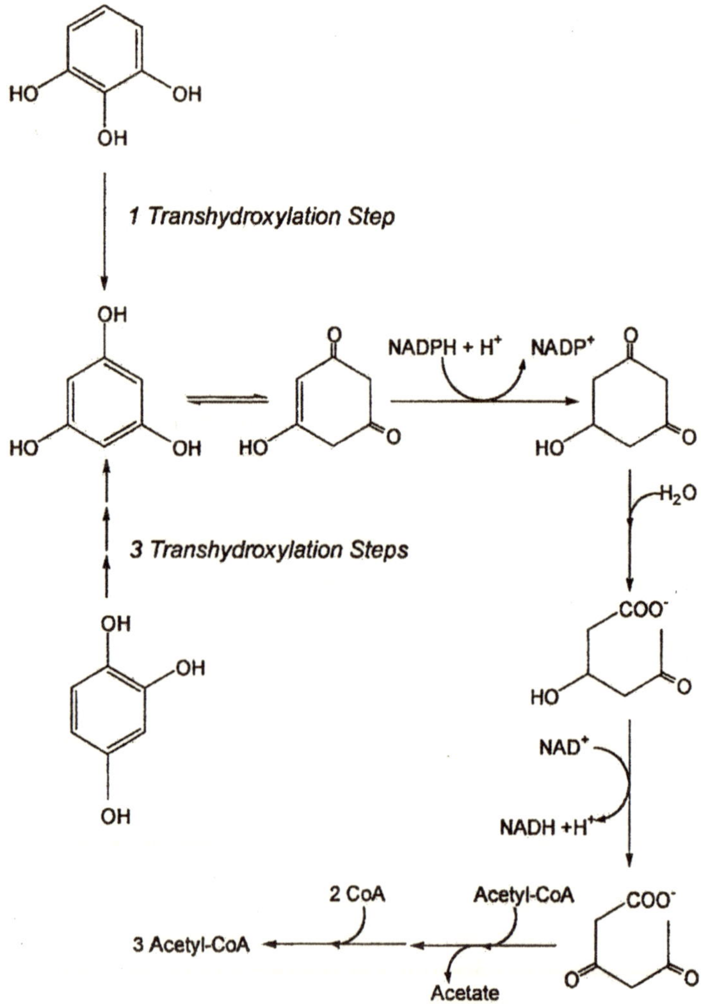

Fig. 8.9 Degradation of trihydroxybenzenes by fermenting bacteria.

Hydroxyhydroquinone, a New Important Intermediate

The third trihydroxybenzene isomer, hydroxyhydroquinone, is converted by the fermenting bacterium *Pelobacter massiliensis* to three acetates via three subsequent transhydroxylation reactions, analogous to the pyrogallol–phloroglucinol transhy-droxylation (Schnell et al., 1991; Brune et al., 1992). Alternative pathways of hydrox-yhydroquinone degradation were found in nitrate-reducing and sulfate-reducing bacteria. Hydroxyhydroquinone degradation by nitrate-reducing bacteria was mentioned above in the context of nitrate-dependent resorcinol degradation (Philipp and Schink, 1998).

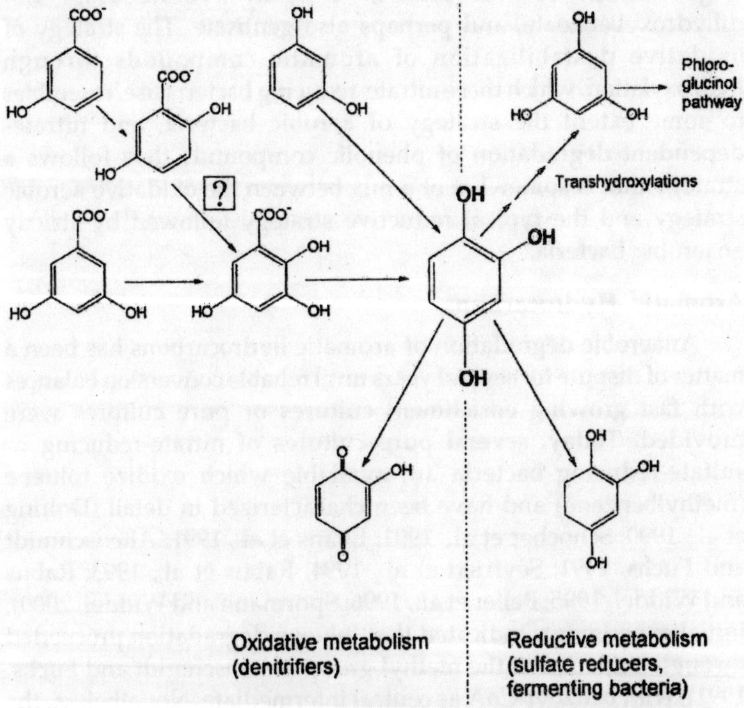

Fig. 8.10 Hydroxyhydroquinone as a new intermediate in anaerobic degradation of various aromatic compounds.

The reaction sequence leads to an acetate and a succinate residue, suggesting that the hydroxyhydroquinone intermediate is cleaved between carbon atoms 1 and 2 and between 3 and 4 (Fig. 8.10). Another alternative pathway of hy-droxyhydroquinone degradation was found in the sulfate-reducing bacterium *Desulfovibrio inopinatus*.

This bacterium destabilizes hydroxyhydroquinone by reduction to dihydrohydroxyhydroquinone, to form acetate and an as-yet unidentified 4-carbon derivative (Reichenbecher et al., unpublished data). Since *D. inopinatus* is unable to oxidize acetate, the final products are two acetate and two CO_2, and one mole of sul-fate is reduced concomitantly to sulfide.

Hydroxyhydroquinone has gained additional interest recently because it was found to be an intermediate in the nitrate-dependent degradation of resorcinol, 3-hy-droxybenzoate, 3,5-dihydroxybenzoate, and perhaps also gentisate. The strategy of oxidative destabilization of aromatic compounds through hydroxylation, which these nitrate-reducing bacteria use, resembles to some extent the strategy of aerobic bacteria, and nitrate-dependent degradation of phenolic compounds thus follows a strategy that is somewhat of a mix between the oxidative aerobic strategy and the typical reductive strategy followed by strictly anaerobic bacteria.

Aromatic Hydrocarbons

Anaerobic degradation of aromatic hydrocarbons has been a matter of dispute for several years until reliable conversion balances with fast growing enrichment cultures or pure cultures were provided. Today, several pure cultures of nitrate-reducing or sulfate-reducing bacteria are available which oxidize toluene (methylbenzene) and have been characterized in detail (Dolfing et al., 1990; Schocher et al., 1991; Evans et al., 1991; Altenschmidt and Fuchs, 1991; Seyfried et al., 1994; Rabus et al., 1993; Rabus and Widdel, 1995; Beller et al., 1996; Spormann and Widdel, 2000). Initial experiments indicated that toluene degradation proceeded through oxidation of the methyl group (Altenschmidt and Fuchs, 1991), with benzoyl-CoA as central intermediate. Nonetheless, the anticipated methyl hydroxylation reaction transforming toluene to benzylalcohol could never be observed in vitro. Labeling experiments with intact cells provided evidence that toluene was activated by addition of fumar-ate, through a radical intermediate, to form benzyl succinate (Fig. 8.11a; Biegert et al., 1996), and this mechanism was confirmed in nitrate-reducing and sulfate-reducing bacteria (Beller and Spormann, 1997a, b, 1998). Benzylsuccinate synthase has been characterized in great detail in the meantime (Achong et al., 2001; Verfurth et al., 2004). Benzylsuccinate releases succinyl-CoA through beta oxidation, leading again to benzoyl-CoA as key intermediate. This new type of methyl group activation is also employed in anaerobic degradation of alkanes and of *m*-cresol (see above).

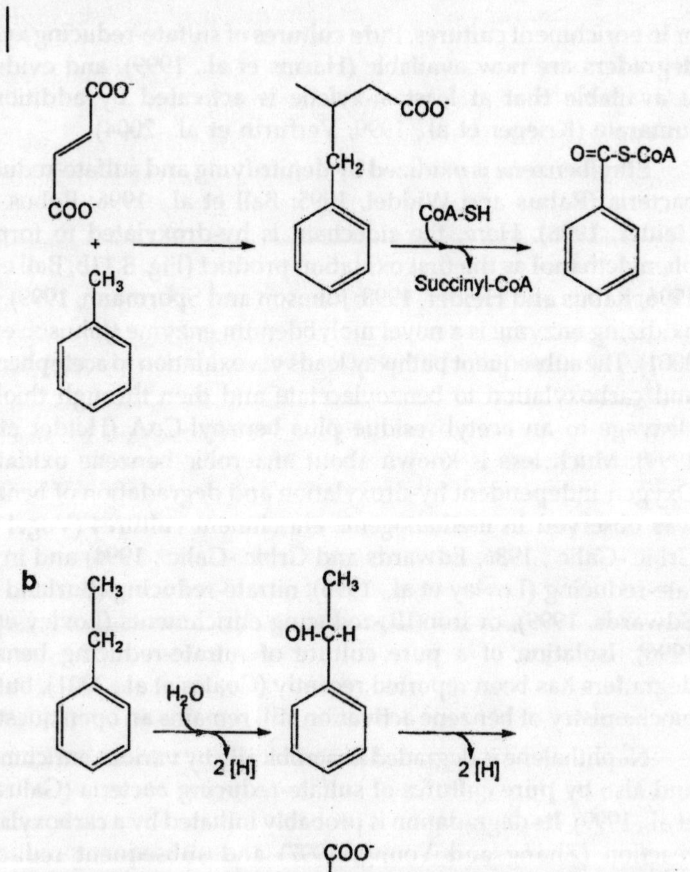

Fig. 8.11 Anaerobic degradation of (a) toluene and (b) ethylbenzene by nitrate-reducing or sul-fate-reducing bacteria.

Anaerobic degradation of *o*-, *m*-, and *p*-xylene has been documented mostly by tracer experiments with sediment samples or in enrichment cultures. Pure cultures of sulfate-reducing xylene degraders are now available (Harms et al., 1999), and evidence is available that at least *m*-xylene is activated by addition to fumarate (Krieger et al., 1999; Verfurth et al., 2004).

Ethylbenzene is oxidized by denitrifying and sulfate-reducing bacteria (Rabus and Widdel, 1995; Ball et al., 1996; Rabus and Heider, 1998). Here, the sidechain is hy-droxylated to form 1-phenylethanol as the first oxidation product (Fig. 8.11b; Ball et al., 1996; Rabus and Heider, 1998; Johnson and Spormann, 1999). The oxidizing enzyme is a novel molybdenum enzyme (Johnson et al., 2001). The subsequent pathway leads via oxidation to acetophenone and carboxylation to benzoylacetate and then through thiolytic cleavage to an acetyl residue plus benzoyl-CoA (Heider et al., 1999). Much less is known about anaerobic benzene oxidation. Oxygen-independent hy-droxylation and degradation of benzene was observed in methanogenic enrichment cultures (Vogel and Grbic´-Galic´, 1986; Edwards and Grbic´-Galic´, 1994) and in sulfate-reducing (Lovley et al., 1995), nitrate-reducing (Burland and Edwards, 1999), or iron(III)-reducing enrichments (Lovley et al., 1996). Isolation of a pure culture of nitrate-reducing benzene degraders has been reported recently (Coates et al., 2001), but the biochemistry of benzene activation still remains an open question.

Naphthalene is degraded anaerobically by various enrichments and also by pure cultures of sulfate-reducing bacteria (Galushko et al., 1999). Its degradation is probably initiated by a carboxylation reaction (Zhang and Young, 1997) and subsequent reductive dearomatization (Annweiler et al., 2002), but the details of this pathway have still to be worked out.

DEGRADATION OF HALOGENATED ORGANICS

Halogenated organics are widespread in nature and are formed especially as secondary metabolites by plants, marine algae, fungi, and certain bacteria at low rates (for a review, see Hutzinger, 1982). It is not surprising, therefore, that a broad variety of bacteria and fungi can degrade such compounds and that this capacity has grown in the past to include also the majority of synthetic halogenated compounds. Dehalog-enation can proceed basically through an oxidative, a hydrolytic, or a reductive reaction (Fetzner and Lingens, 1994; El Fantroussi et al., 1998). Among anaerobic bacteria, the reductive elimination of halogen substituents is the most common type of reaction and was first observed in enrichment cultures with 3,5-dihydroxybenzoate (Suflita et al., 1982). Later, several other aliphatic and aromatic compounds were found to be dehalogenated (mainly dechlorinated) in anoxic incubation experiments (Bouwer and McCarty, 1983), and today nearly all chlorinated organics can be deha-logenated and further degraded in strictly anaerobic microbial cultures. As a rule, reductive dechlorination is the preferred process for degradation of compounds with higher degrees of halogenation. The reaction is an excellent electron sink (E_h +250 to +580 mV), and highly halogenated compounds are much more amenable to a nucleophilic attack on the respective carbon atom than to an oxidative reaction.

The overall reaction of reductive dehalogenation can be diagrammed as in Figure 8.12 for a chlorinated compound: electrons derived from molecular hydrogen, formate, or more complex organic compounds are transferred to the halogenated substrate to release the organic residue in a reduced form, together with chloride. It has been shown in several instances that this redox process can yield metabolic energy through a respiratory mechanism, which implies that the process may establish a net translocation of protons across the cytoplasmic membrane and that the proton gradient drives ATP synthesis through a membrane-bound ATP synthase complex. The biochemistry of the dechlorination reaction has been studied best with bacteria converting tetrachloroethene via trichloroethene to dichloroethene (Holliger et al., 1999). The dechlorination reaction employs a corrinoid as cofactor, which attacks the carbon-chlorine linkage in its reduced Co(I) form and converts it to the Co(III) form, probably through two subsequent one-electron transfer reactions (Schumacher et al., 1997; Neumann et al., 1998; Neumann et al., 2002; Maillard et al., 2003). Whether this reaction mechanism is used also in the dehalogenation of aromatic compounds has still to be elucidated. There appear to be numerous differences with respect to the electron carriers involved and the spatial arrangement of the enzyme components in the cytoplasmic membrane.

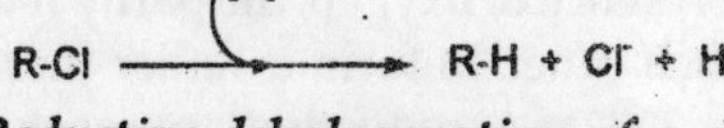

Fig. 8.12 Reductive dehalogenation of a chloro-organic compound.

Halo-organics can also be reductively dehalogenated by reduced Fe(II) phases (Pecher et al., 2002; Elsner et al., 2004) that are formed on the surface of Fe(III) minerals.

DEGRADATION OF SULFONATES

Sulfonated organics are rare in nature: only taurine, coenzyme M, cysteate, and a few secondary metabolites are known to contain sulfonate substituents. Aerobic degradation of such compounds typically requires an oxygenase reaction, which hy-droxylates the neighboring carbon atom and releases sulfite (Cook et al., 1999). Some sulfonates can also be partly degraded in the absence of molecular oxygen and can serve as sulfur sources under conditions of sulfur limitation (Chien et al., 1995; Cook et al., 1999). The biochemistry of anaerobic sulfur release from sulfonates has been studied extensively with taurine and related compounds, which are metabolized through sulfoacetaldehyde as key intermediate (Laue et al., 1997a, b). The sul-fono group is released from sulfoacetaldehyde probably through a thiamine pyro-phosphate-dependent reaction that forms sulfite and an acetyl residue, analogous to the reaction elucidated earlier with an aerobic bacterium (Kondo and Ishimoto, 1975). Since this desulfonation reaction requires an oxo group positioned â to the sulfur atom for linkage to the coenzyme, it remains questionable whether this concept can also be applied to desulfonation of commercial sulfonates, such as alkyl sul-fonates or alkylbenzene sulfonates, which so far resist anaerobic degradation.

DEGRADATION OF NITROORGANICS

Among the nitroaromatic compounds, trinitrotoluene (TNT) is of major importance as a soil pollutant because it has accumulated at old ammunition factory sites over several decades. The electron-withdrawing effect of the nitro substituents makes an oxidative attack on nitroaromatics rather difficult. Indeed, trinitrotoluene is attacked by aerobic bacteria primarily through a reductive reaction that transforms nitroaro-matics to the corresponding amino derivatives (Naumova et al., 1989) or reductively eliminates the nitro groups via a so-called Meisenheimer complex (Vorbeck et al., 1994). In the presence of oxygen, the partly reduced derivatives can react with each other to form a rather inert polymer (Heiss and Knackmuss, 2002). A reductive approach is taken also by strictly anaerobic bacteria, e.g., sulfate-reducing bacteria: trinitrotoluene is converted via diaminonitrotoluene to triaminotoluene. Whereas the first step can also be catalyzed purely chemically without the participation of micro-bial cells or enzymes, reduction of diaminonitrotoluene to triaminotoluene requires the participation of microbial cells or enzyme fractions (Preuss et al., 1993). The further fate of triaminotoluene is unclear. It is partly utilized as a nitrogen source by a sulfate-reducing bacterium; the remnant product possibly polymerizes, especially in the presence of traces of oxygen (Preuss et al., 1993). The same is likely to happen in contaminated soils; so far, there is no reliable proof of complete degradation of TNT by anaerobic bacteria or by anaerobic and aerobic bacteria cooperating in a two-step process (see Chapter 11, this volume).

CONCLUDING REMARKS

Anaerobic degradation can be applied in technical devices for treatment of waste material, often leading to CH_4 and CO_2 as products, which can be exploited as energy source or as a basis for biosynthetic processes. Moreover, anaerobic degradation proceeds in many anoxic habitats such as the intestinal tracts of humans and animals, sediments, and oxygen-deprived microenvironments in soil, sewage sludge, etc. Knowledge of the capacities, strategies, and limits of anaerobic degradation processes is therefore needed to assess the potential risk of synthetic compounds to health or to the environment, no matter whether such synthetics are released intentionally (as with plant protection agents), inadvertently through wastewater treatment, or accidentally through spills.

This overview shows that the degradative potential of anaerobic microbial communities is much greater than assumed only a few years ago: a broad variety of compounds can be subject to anaerobic degradation, most often down to methane and carbon dioxide as final products. Aliphatic hydrocarbons are degraded if they contain unsaturated bonds, preferentially if these are located terminally, but saturated long-chain aliphatic hydrocarbons are also anaerobically degradable. These processes are slow and can be applied only in long-term incubations, if at all. Ether compounds are degraded anaerobically if they are methyl ethers or if they can be transformed into hemiacetals through, e.g., hydroxyl shift reactions. In the anaerobic degradation of ketones, the primary activation reaction is a carboxylation rather than an oxidation step.

Mononuclear aromatic compounds can be degraded anaerobically rather efficiently if they carry at least one carboxy, hydroxy, methoxy, amino, or methyl substituent, and four major degradation pathways have been elucidated in the recent past, which differ basically from the well known aerobic oxygenase-dependent pathways. The degradation kinetics differ considerably, depending on the sites of substitution.

Halogenated aliphatics and aromatics are reductively dehalogenated, more efficiently and better than by aerobes, the higher the degree of halogenation. Anaerobic degradation of sulfonates appears to be restricted to only a few compounds, whereas the majority of synthetic sulfonates (detergents) are degraded efficiently only in the presence of oxygen. Nitro-substituted compounds are preferentially attacked through reduction, and anaerobic processes therefore appear to be advantageous over aerobic ones. The same applies to azo compounds, which are not discussed here.

Several types of reactions were identified which activate or destabilize comparably inert substrates in the absence of oxygen. Among these are carboxylations, addition to fumarate, reductions and reductive eliminations, rearrangements of aliphatic carbon skeletons, cobalamin-dependent nucleophilic substitutions, and oxygen-independent hydroxylations. Numerous reactions proceed through radical mechanisms, and the diversity of radical chemistry in the absence of oxygen appears to be considerably greater than in its presence.

Transformation of polymeric compounds is restricted in the anaerobic world to extracellular hydrolysis reactions unless the polymer can be taken up into the cell, as occurs with polyethylene glycol. There is no equivalent in the anoxic world to the fungal lignin-degrading enzyme apparatus. Therefore, polynuclear aromatics (lignin, other polyphenols) remain comparably recalcitrant in anoxic environments and represent barriers to microbial attack in the absence of molecular oxygen.

9

Soil Remediation and Disposal

INTRODUCTION

For the treatment of contaminated sites, securing as well as remediation methods are applied. While remediation achieves decontamination or reduction of pollutants, securing sets up technical barriers for the protection of the environment. Since the source of contamination remains in place and the technical barriers are subject to aging and environmental influences, securing measures often represent only a time restricted solution and future remediation activities become necessary.

Remediation methods are classified according to their operation location as well as to processing aspects. Thus, ex situ and in situ processes are available on the one hand, and thermal, chemical, physical, and biological processes on the other. The ex situ processes require excavation of the contaminated soil and soil treatment either at the site (on-site remediation) or at an external soil treatment plant (off-site remediation). In contrast, in situ treatment takes place at the site in the contaminated soil itself, without any soil excavation.

Thermal processes are used for the treatment of highly concentrated organic pollutants, but they are suitable only to a small extent for the elimination of heavy metals. With soil scrubbing, the coarse-grain fraction >63 μm is purified, transferring the pollutants into the water phase and/or into the fine-grain fraction. This fine fraction is highly loaded with pollutants and thus has to be treated and disposed of afterwards. The biopile process is applied on a large scale as a state-of-the-art technology. It is an effective process for the treatment of biologically degradable pollutants such as mineral oil and its derivatives, aliphatic hydrocarbons, phenols, formaldehyde, and other soil contaminants.

In remediation practice, there is a trend toward actions with a minimum of requirements. Contaminated sites are remediated or secured, depending on the intended after-use, e.g., housing, development of commercial or industrial facilities, or as recreational areas. Depending on the kind of use, specific target values have to be met after treatment. If the contaminated site is not being used and so far no major dangerous contamination of the groundwater, surface water, etc. has occurred, one relies more and more on natural attenuation processes in soil and groundwater. Economical active (e.g., selective biostimulation) and passive in situ measures (reactive walls, funnel and gate systems) are developed and need to be investigated with regard to their long-term effectiveness.

For the ex situ remediation of soils that are nearly not amenable to treatment (sil-ty soils contaminated with chlorinated hydrocarbons, polycyclic aromatic hydrocarbons, or tar oil) combined processes with soil scrubbing as basic process are increasingly being considered. For the subsequent treatment of problematic polluted residues (fine-grain fraction, process waters, etc.), a variety of processes are available, e.g., suspension bioreactors, oxidation with ozone or H_2O_2, and thermal treatment.

Experiences in dealing with hazardous old sites have basically shown that balancing pre-investigations are of essential importance regarding the process evolution as well as the evaluation of remediation measures. Far-reaching investigations have been carried out in the field of microbiological (ex situ) treatment, and standardizations have been defined (Dechema, 1992; GDCh, 1996). In the future, emphasis should be placed on process evaluation for the in situ treatment so as to predict the processes of natural attenuation by balancing as far as possible the fate of pollutants.

THERMAL PROCESSES

Thermal soil purification is based mainly on transfer of the pollutants from the soil matrix into the gas phase by thermal energy input. The pollutants are released from the soil by vaporization and then burned. The polluted gas is purified further.

The different processing concepts for the thermal purification of contaminated soils are characterized by variations of the process parameters (e.g., temperature range, retention time for solids and waste gas in certain temperature zones, supply of oxygen, supply of reactive gases for gasification, supply of inert gas, kind of heat input, and optimum heat utilization, etc.). The large variability has led to a multitude of ex situ and in situ process combinations.

Thermal Ex Situ Processes

The basic principle of a thermal soil purification plant includes the following processing steps (Figure 9.1):

1. soil conditioning
2. thermal treatment
3. waste gas purification

In soil conditioning, the contaminated soil is freed of interfering foreign matter (e.g., scrap, plastics) broken, sieved, and homogenized by mechanical preparation processes to be of a particle size consistent with the technical requirements of the subsequent thermal treatment [<20 mm (fluidized bed) to 80 mm]. During thermal treatment the soil is heated so that volatile pollutants are stripped from it. In the gas phase above the soil, the combustion of pollutants takes place, but in this phase complete destruction of volatile pollutants cannot be achieved. For this reason the gases are burned in an afterburner chamber at high temperature (~1200 °C) for a certain retention time. Under these conditions dioxins are also destroyed. Two different technologies are mainly used in thermal soil treatment:

- processes with an exclusively thermal effect: directly and indirectly heated processes (pyrolysis) with subsequent gas treatment (afterburning, condensation) (rarely used)
- processes with a thermal effect and additional measures (common practice)

Processes having an exclusively thermal effect (directly and indirectly heated) are conventional processes available on a large scale, using, e.g., rotary kiln plants, fluid-ized-bed plants, and sintering strand plants, for which long-term experience in practice has been achieved. Most of the processes work in the low-temperature range of 100 to 550 °C (residence time of the soil in the furnace 10–20 min; throughput 20 to 30 Mg (megagramms) h^{-1} (VDI, 2002)) at which the structure of the soil is not fundamentally changed and humic components are only partly destroyed. In the early days of thermal soil treatment, high-temperature processes were practiced in which the soil was heated to temperatures of 800 to 1100 °C (residence time of the soil in the furnace 20–45 min; throughput 2 to 7 Mg h^{-1} (VDI, 2002)). Under these conditions, partial liquefying or sintering of the soil particles is possible. At the same time, the organic components and the clay minerals of the soil are destroyed to a large extent, hydroxides are changed into oxides, and primary minerals are crushed by gritting. Furthermore, the quantity of NO_x increases rapidly at temperatures >1000 °C, so that special equipment could be necessary for decreasing NO_x in the waste gas.

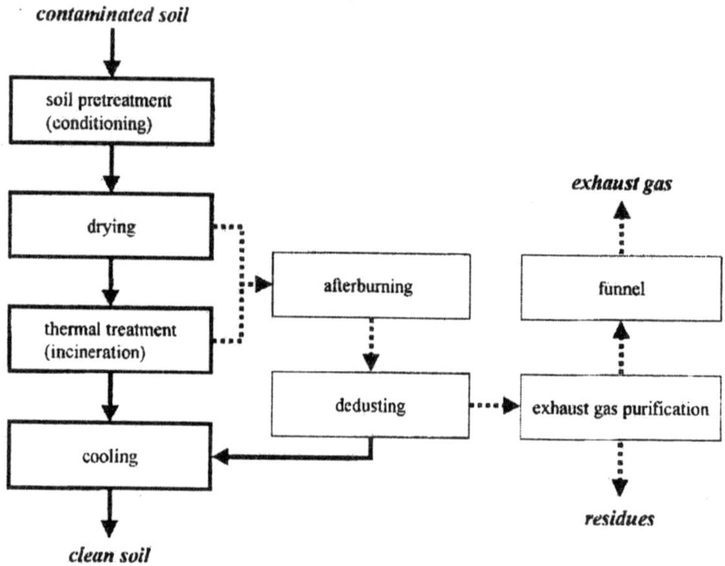

Fig. 9.1 The thermal ex situ treatment process.

Depending on the contents of pollutant, water, and fine soil particles, thermal treatment with indirect heating is carried out under reducing conditions (pyrolysis) in a temperature range between 400 and 600 °C (residence time of the soil in the furnace approx. 45 min; throughput 5 to 13 Mg h^{-1} (VDI, 2002)).

The processes using an exclusively thermal effect show significant differences regarding the waste gas purification systems used. The selection of the waste gas purification system used, is decisive influenced by the local regulations on air emissions. Usually, aggregates are used, which are normally used for flue gas purification in large-scale power plants and in waste incineration plants. The waste gas purification equipment in these processes mainly contains three partial units:

1. high-temperature afterburners
2. dedusters
3. flue gas purifiers

The separation of fine soil particles from the gas stream (dedusting) is done by means of cyclones, hot gas filters, or combinations of different filter techniques specifically adapted to the process. Although the organic pollutants (hydrocarbons) are completely oxidized during the afterburning step (high temperature afterburning) at 900–1300 °C, flue gas purification minimizes the amounts of inorganic pollutants such as hydrogen chloride, hydrogen fluoride, and sulfur dioxide and brings the levels of dust and heavy metal emissions down to target values. Fundamentally, flue gas purification processes can be divided into a dry sorption process, a wet cleaning process (wet scrubbers), and a combination of both (semidry process). If reduction of nitrogen oxides is required, special measures are necessary. The efficiency of the various processes increases from the dry sorption through the semidry up to the wet scrubber process – as do the total costs. But at the same time, the degree of pollutant separation effected by these processes increases so that – especially regarding the wet cleaning processes – high waste gas quality requirements can be met. To guarantee the target values of the waste gas, activated carbon filters are used as a final step in almost all processes. An operation without excess water can be achieved by treatment of the washing water (heavy metal precipitation and stabilization) and subsequent recirculation for semidry and wet cleansing processes (Fortmann and Jahns, 1996).

Processes involving thermal effects and additional measures include various designs that use a temperature range of 60–350 °C, at which the pollutants (especially low-boiling and medium-boiling hydrocarbons) are stripped from the soil by the influence of heat and additional measures (e.g., steam stripping, vacuum). The efficiency of the process depends not only on the effect of the temperature, but also on the physical properties of the pollutants.

For these processes, the waste gas treatment normally includes no high-temperature afterburning of the waste gas. The purification is carried out via condensation and/or absorption (Fortmann and Jahns, 1996; ITVA, 1997).

THERMAL IN SITU PROCESSES

The use of thermal in situ processes is still not state-of-the-art. Thermal in situ processes differ mainly in the kind of energy input for heating the soil matrix to transfer the pollutants into the gas phase. To capture and treat the gas phase, a combination of soil vapor extraction (SVE) and subsequent gas treatment is necessary. Compared with pure soil vapor extraction, the required treatment period can be reduced. In the steam-injection process, a hot steam–air mixture is passed into the unsatu-rated soil zone by steam–air injection (60–100 °C). In consequence, the volatile as well as the semivolatile compounds (NAPL) pass into the gas phase. The soil gas phase is extracted by means of gas extraction systems and is treated afterwards. Transport of the mobilized pollutants toward groundwater must be prevented by specific temperature control and by specific adjustment of the steam–air mixture. This process has limitations for soils with low permeability and for soils with very high inhomogeneities, because these soils require long periods of time for heating (Betz et al., 1998). As an alternative, the temperature within the unsaturated soil zone can be increased by imposing high-frequency electromagnetic fields by using electrodes (Jütterschenke, 1999).

APPLICATION OF THERMAL PROCESSES

In principle, all kinds of pollutants that can be stripped from the soil under the influence of thermal energy can be treated by means of thermal processes. The operation temperatures and retention times depend on the type and concentration of the pollutants as well as on the intended use of the treated soil material.

Thermal ex situ processes are preferably used when high initial concentrations of organic compounds are found and a high degree of purification is required. They can remove mainly petroleum hydrocarbons (TPH), polycyclic aromatic hydrocarbons (PAH), volatile organic hydrocarbons (benzene, toluene, ethylbenzene, xylenes (BTEX)), phenolic compounds, cyanides, and chlorinated compounds such as poly-chlorinated biphenyls (PCB), pentachlorophenol (PCP), volatile halogenated hydrocarbons, chlorinated pesticides, polychlorinated dibenzodioxins (PCDD), and poly-chlorinated dibenzofurans (PCDF). Furthermore, thermal ex situ processes can be used as a pre- or post-treatment step in conjunction with other ex situ processes.

Compared to thermal ex situ processes that also use additional measures, processes having an exclusively thermal effect are mainly used for soils characterized by single substance class contamination with volatile pollutants. Because of their comparatively low generation of heat, in situ processes are suitable only for pollutants that can be stripped in the lower temperature range (e.g., BTEX).

Basically, soil materials of all particle size distributions can be purified by thermal ex situ processes. A limitation on the proportion of silt (<30% to 50%) can become necessary for economic reasons. The use of thermal in situ processes can also be restricted because of inhomogeneities or unsuitable soil water content.

The efficiency of thermal treatment processes for removing organic pollutants from contaminated soils approaches almost 100% and is usually higher than the efficiency of biological or chemical/physical ex situ processes. However, to evaluate the application of various treatment processes, additional aspects, e.g., the necessary energy input, technical requirements, treatment costs, possibilities for reuse of the treated soils, and other aspects have to be considered. Usually, the costs of thermal soil treatment are higher than the costs of biological or chemical/physical processes.

CHEMICAL/PHYSICAL PROCESSES

Chemical/physical soil treatment processes are mainly extraction and/or wet classification processes. The principle of ex situ soil scrubbing technologies is to concentrate the contaminants in a small residual fraction by separation. In general, water (with or without additives) is used as an extracting agent. For the transfer of contaminants from the soil to the extracting agent, two mechanisms are of importance:

- strong shearing forces induced by pumping, mixing, vibration, high-pressure water jets (to break up agglomerates of polluted and nonpolluted particles and disperse contaminants into the extracting phase)
- dissolution of contaminants by extracting agents

In situ extraction basically consists of percolation of an aqueous extracting agent into the contaminated soil. Percolation can be achieved by means of surface trenches, horizontal drains, or vertical deep wells. Soluble contaminants present in the soil dissolve in the percolate, which is pumped up and treated on-site.

CHEMICAL/PHYSICAL EX SITU PROCESSES

During soil scrubbing, the pollutants are detached from the soil particles by means of mechanical energy and/or solubilizing effects, often supported by surfactants. In consequence, pollutants become concentrated in the liquid phase and in the solid fine fraction of the soil containing pollutants sorbed onto the surface. Water, optionally enhanced with additives, serves as a dissolving agent and as a medium for transport. In general, soil scrubbing consists of the following steps (Figure 9.2):

1. soil pretreatment
2. soil washing
3. separation by gravity (classification)
4. separation of dispersed particles
5. separation of process water and rinsing of the purified soil fraction
6. process water recirculation
7. wastewater purification
8. waste gas purification

First, the contaminated soil is mechanically prepared to separate coarse substances that might disturb subsequent process steps. The soil, which includes rubble, is granulated to < 30–100 mm in diameter by crushing and sieving. This also serves as a homogenization step. In the next step, the solids are dispersed in the liquid phase and strongly agitated, so as to detach the pollutants and to separate the fine particles from the coarse particles. Sometimes chemical additives are added to the water (acids, bases, surface-active substances/surfactants) to overcome the binding between pollutants and soil particles. The conventional equipment for wet separation is high-pressure water jet pipes, centrifugal impact equipment, washing drums, vibration screws, attrition cells, blade washers, and fluidized-bed reactors. Pollutants are frequently situated in and on light matter (e.g., charcoal, slag, wood). It is not possible to transfer this contamination into the washwater. Constituents are removed in suitable sorting equipment: sedimenting machines, up-current separators, helical separators, flotation equipment, etc. For successful sorting, classification by particle size must be provided upstream of the sorting equipment (VDI, 2002). Depending on the process, the forces necessary for the detachment of the contaminants are restricted to a certain range of particle size, for economical reasons. The fine particles have to be removed and disposed of or be treated by other processes. The separation of the fine particles from the soil takes place in three successive steps:

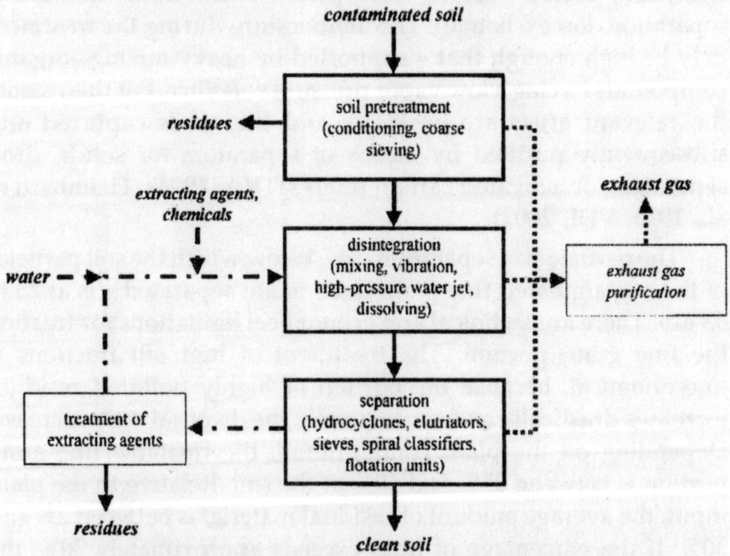

1. separation of the highly polluted fine particles from coarser components that are polluted at only a low level, using hydrocyclones (separation down to 0.1 to 0.01 mm)
2. separation of the fine particles from the process water by means of coagulation, flotation, and sedimentation
3. dewatering of the fine particles using screens and filter systems, e.g., filter presses

After separation of the polluted fine particles, the purified coarse fraction has to be separated from the process water. For this, drain screens or vacuum band filters are used, depending on the particle size. For the removal of the remaining process water, rinsing with uncontaminated water is done, followed by another dewatering step. To reduce the consumption of rinse water, the water is recirculated (process water recirculation). To keep the concentration of the pollutants in the process water at a certain level, some of the water - usually up to 10% - is separated and treated in a wastewater purification plant. This water is treated just enough so that the water can be reused as rinsing water instead of taking fresh water. Depending on the kind of pollution, various processes or process combinations of wastewater treatment technology are used (e.g., oxidation, reduction, neutralization, emulsion breaking, heavy metal precipitation, gravel/sand filtration, active carbon adsorption, extraction, membrane separation, ion exchange). The temperature during the treatment may be high enough that - supported by heavy mixing -organic compounds having a low vapor pressure volatilize. For this reason, the relevant areas are enclosed, and the air is captured and subsequently purified by means of separators for solids, drop separators, or activated carbon filters (ITVA, 1994a; Heimhard et al., 1996; VDI, 2002).

The particle size separation cut - below which the soil particles of the contaminated fine grain fraction are separated - is at 25 to 63 μm. There are technical and economical limitations for treating the fine grain portion. The treatment of high-silt fractions is uneconomical, because the portion of highly polluted residues increases drastically and consequently the disposal costs increase. Depending on the plant configuration, the treatable fine grain portion is between 25% and 40% of the soil. Relative to the plant input, the average amount of residual material is between 2% and 30%. If the percentage of fines exceeds approximately 30%, the disposal costs become the main cost factor for soil washing (Wilichowski, 2001).

CHEMICAL/PHYSICAL IN SITU PROCESSES

During pump-and-treat processes, water is supplied to the soil so as to leach out the contaminants. The contaminated water is pumped to the surface and treated. Surfactants that increase the solubility of the pollutants may be added to the water. The extracted washing water is treated with standard wastewater treatment technologies. The possible applications of chemical/physical in situ processes are especially limited by the permeability of the soil. For hydraulic in situ measures, the soil permeability needs to have a permeability factor k_f of at least 5×10^{-4} m s^{-1}. Side effects such as bioclogging can be responsible for further decreasing the natural permeability of the soil. The problem always remains that the entire amount of the injected water is not recaptured by pumping, so that there is a risk of pollutant transport into the groundwater. In addition, the added surfactants may be a source of secondary pollution.

Soil vapor extraction (SVE) is an effective and economical process for decreasing highly volatile pollutants (e.g., BTEX) in the unsaturated zone of permeable soils ($k_f < 10^{-3}$ m s^{-1}). Perforated pipes are placed in the contaminated soil area. The volatile pollutants are sucked out of the soil by using low vacuum blowers. The extracted pollutants and condensates are treated on-site using activated carbon filters, compost filters, etc. The kind of treatment system used depends on the amount of air to be treated as well as the kind of pollutants. The time needed for extraction of the pollutants to an acceptable degree lasts from months to years. Often, complete decontamination of the soil is not achieved (ITVA, 1997).

The efficiency of the soil vapor extraction process is influenced by the characteristics of the soil (permeability, moisture content, temperature, homogeneity) and the kind of pollutants (vapor pressure). Often, the pollutants are in the liquid phase in the soil, so that volatilization takes place at the border of the liquid plume, which prolongs the extraction process. Sometimes extraction can be enhanced by increasing the temperature in the soil (e.g., by adding steam).

APPLICATION OF CHEMICAL/PHYSICAL PROCESSES

There is no limit to the kind of pollutants that can be treated by soil washing processes, as long as they can be detached from soil particles and solubilized in the washing water. Therefore, all kinds of pollutant groups have been treated with the ex situ soil scrubbing process: BTEX, TPH, PAH, PCB, heavy metals, and PCDD/PCDF (VDI, 2002). A systematic approach to estimating the prospects of recycling contaminated soils by soil-washing processes was described by Feil et al. (1997). The actual purification of the polluted liquid phase and of the fine particle fraction can take place outside the soil washing plant, in separate treatment facilities. But the polluted fine fraction is usually dumped in a landfill, meaning that no actual treatment, but only separation, is achieved.

Biological Processes

During biological treatment soil microorganisms convert organic pollutants (e.g., hydrocarbons) into mainly CO_2, water, and biomass. Some of the pollutants can also be immobilized by binding to the humic substance fraction. Degradation may take place under aerobic as well as under anaerobic conditions. The aerobic process is predominantly used in soil remediation. For efficient biological treatment of contaminated soils, it is important to optimize the environmental conditions for the microorganisms (oxygen supply, water content, pH value, etc.). By appropriate adjustment of the conditions, the degradation processes are enhanced and the degree of degradation is improved, especially for high concentrations of readily degradable pollutants. To stimulate biological activity, soil homogenization, active aeration, moistening or drying, heating, addition of nutrients and substrates, or inoculation with microorganisms can be done. However, in comparison to thermal or chemical/physical treatment processes, less energy input but longer treatment periods are generally required.

Biological Ex Situ Processes

Biological ex situ processes usually follow the following treatment steps (Figure 9.3):

1. mechanical pre-treatment
2. addition of water, nutrients, substrates and microorganisms
3. biological treatment

After excavation, the contaminated soil is mechanically broken up and sieved to remove disruptive material, homogenize the soil material, and loosen the soil structure. In addition, oxygen supply to the soil particles is improved. Mineral components separated during the sieving process can be crushed and later added to the contaminated soil. To activate biological degradation of the contaminants, water, nu- trients, and substrates are added. Optionally, substances that improve the soil structure or, in very special situations, microorganisms are added. Organic additives like compost, bark, wood chips, or straw serve as cosubstrates or nutrient sources for the microorganisms and as structural material. Biological treatment of contaminated soils is done in thin soil layers (landfarming process), in biopiles, or in bioreactors (dry and slurry reactors).

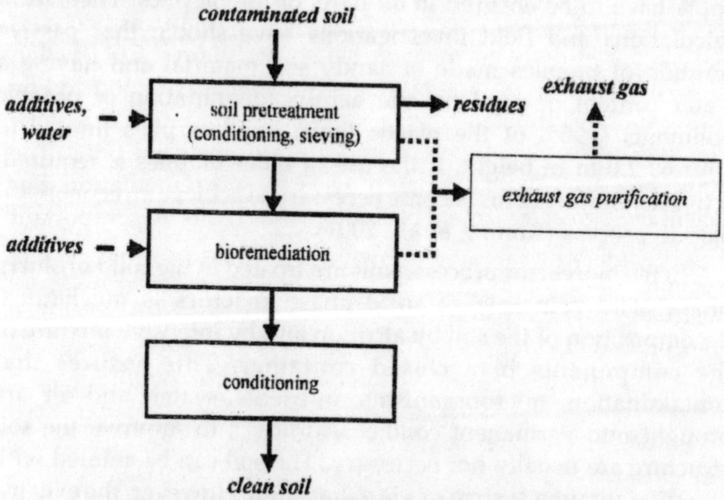

Fig. 9.3 The biological ex situ process.

In the landfarming process, the contaminated soil is treated in thin layers of up to 0.4 m thickness. Therefore, large treatment areas are required if large amounts of contaminated soil need to be treated. The pretreated soil is placed on foil, concrete, or a clay layer. Enhanced oxygen supply as well as mixing are done by plowing, harrowing, or milling at regular intervals (Cookson, 1995).

Biopiles for soil remediation are constructed similar to biopiles for composting organic wastes. Rectangular, oblong, or pyramidal forms are used. The height of the biopiles is usually between 0.8 and 3.0 m. The biopile process can be carried out at water contents below and above the maximum water holding capacity (dry and wet systems). Although dry systems can be operated with or without agitation (dynamic or static biopile process), wet systems are all static. In contrast to the static biopile process, the principle of the dynamic biopile process is decomposition of the soil by repeatedly plowing and turning the biopiles. If necessary, water and nutrients are added during the turning process. This increases the bioavailability of the pollutants, and the contamination is brought into close contact with microorganisms, nutrients, water, and air. Today, the biopile process is predominantly done dry and is used mainly for aerobic degradation processes. To achieve unrestricted aerobic degradation processes, oxygen contents >1 vol.% have to be ensured in all parts of the biopiles. Theoretical calculations and field investigations have shown that passive aeration of biopiles made of sandy soil material and having a water content optimal for the aerobic degradation of organic pollutants (~95% of the plastic limit) requires piles limited to approx. 2.0 m in height. If the use of taller biopiles is required, active aeration systems become necessary to achieve an economical biopile process (Koning et al., 2001).

In the bioreactor process, soils are treated in the solid or slurry phase. The principle of solid-phase reactors is mechanical decomposition of the soil by attrition and by intensive mixture of the components in a closed container. This ensures that contamination, microorganisms, nutrients, water, and air are brought into permanent contact. Additives to improve the soil structure are usually not necessary. The soil can be aerated with an active aeration system or via exhaustion. However, the exhaust air has to be purified, for example, by the use of activated carbon filters or bi-ofilters. Soils that are not suitable for solid bioreactors (clayey and silty soils) can be treated as a slurry in suspension bioreactors. Suspension bioreactors are also suitable for treating the residual fine-particle fractions from the soil scrubbing process, which are highly loaded with contaminants. After treatment, the slurry is dewatered, and the contaminated water fraction is purified. Usually much of the water is recirculated (ITVA, 1994b). In comparison to landfarming and biopile processes, bio-reactors offer better conditions for process control; therefore, usually shorter treatment periods are required. However, compared to the biopile process, only a few bioreactors are used, since the advantages gained often do not justify the relatively high technical effort.

BIOLOGICAL IN SITU PROCESSES

The ability of microorganisms to degrade organic pollutants under environmental conditions naturally present in the field is the basis for intrinsic bioremediation processes. As part of the natural attenuation processes, these biological degradation processes can contribute to decreasing the levels of organic pollutants in soil over long-term periods (Newman and Barr, 1997). However, although under suitable environmental conditions natural biodegradation processes can be used as a passive remedial measure, the natural biodegradation processes can come to a standstill under limiting environmental conditions and in the absence of additional biostimu-lating measures. Therefore, environmental conditions must be monitored in a natural attenuation program (ITVA, 2003).

In biological in situ treatment, the environmental conditions for the biological degradation of organic pollutants are optimized as far as possible. Oxygen usually has to be supplied, which can be done by artificial aeration or by addition of electron acceptors such as nitrate or oxygen-releasing compounds. Sometimes also H_2O_2 or O_3 dissolved in water is added. By these means the organic contaminants are degraded. If oxygen is supplied via the water phase, nutrients and, sometimes bacteria, are also added. However, usually the authochtonous microflora is adapted to the present contaminants and addition of cultured microorganisms is not necessary.

The supply of oxygen to the saturated respectively into the unsaturated soil zone is also the basis for active aeration processes like bioventing (pressure aeration of the unsaturated soil zone), air sparging (pressure aeration of the saturated soil zone), and bioslurping (combined soil atmosphere and groundwater exhaustion) (Gidara-kos and Schachtebeck, 1996).

APPLICATION OF BIOLOGICAL PROCESSES

The biological turnover of organic pollutants depends mainly on the bioavailability and biodegradability of the contaminants, as well as on the environmental conditions for the degrading microorganisms. Therefore, the degree of biological degradation achieved in a technical process is influenced by many factors (e.g., type, concentration, and physical state of the contaminants, soil type, content of organic substances, adjustment of the environmental conditions) and can be limited for biological, physicochemical, or technical reasons (Dechema, 1991).

Bioremediation methods are used for several different contaminants. Biological treatment of TPH-contaminated soils can be considered state-of-the-art technology. Biological degradation can also be expected for BTEX and phenols, although release of the volatile substances has to be taken into consideration. PAHs are biodegradable only to a certain extent (up to 4-ring PAHs) and the rate of degradation is relatively slow (Kästner, 2000). Furthermore, PAH can be located within coal particles and thus be not bioavailable (Weibenfels et al., 1992). Regarding soils contaminated by TNT, an irreversible fixing of the conversion product TAT (2,4,6-triaminotoluene) in the soil components can be achieved by means of anaerobic biological treatment with very low redox potentials (Reis and Held, 1996). PCBs are relatively inert. Nevertheless, their biological degradation by anaerobic dechlorination and aerobic oxidation is possible (Abramovicz, 1990). However, PCBs are in general not treated biologically due to their low biodegradation rates.

Statements in the literature about possible biodegradation endpoints vary for different types of contamination and treatment methods. Basically, remaining residues from the contamination are expected.

Disposal

Due to economical reasons, the excavation and disposal of contaminated soil at landfills became a frequent used option in redevelopment projects for contaminated sites. Although, the contaminated soil is removed from the original site, the contaminated soil remains usually untreated and therefore represents a potential source of environmental risk at the landfill site. The same applies to residues from ex situ soil treatment processes (e.g. sludges from wet soil scrubbing) which are disposed of at landfill sites. From a technical point of view, the landfilling of contaminated soil can be regarded as a securing measure with future remediation activities required. In order to save landfill capacity for other wastes and to promote the utilization of decontaminated soil, preference should be given to remediation measures.

UTILIZATION OF DECONTAMINATED SOIL

A major aspect in ex situ soil remediation is the reuse of decontaminated soil. During the various treatment processes, the soil materials change their chemical and physical properties in different ways. Residual concentrations of contaminants and of organic materials originating from organic additives (e.g., compost, bark, wood chips) can restrict the reuse of biologically treated soil. This soil is not normally suitable for reuse as filling material or in agriculture. Therefore, it is often used in landscaping. Thermally treated soil can be used as filling material (i.e., refill where excavated) but is not suitable for vegetation due to its inert nature. Soil from wet scrubbers can be used in a similar way. It is often not easy to find adequate possibilities for utilization of the treated soil.

A crucial factor for the reuse of decontaminated soils is toxicological/ecotoxicolog-ical assessment. For this purpose bioassays are conducted to measure the possible impacts of treated soils. Bioassays should be an appropriate tool if treated soils have to be tested with regard to their hazard potential. They integrate the effects of all relevant substances, including those not considered or recorded in chemical analyses (Dechema, 1995; Klein, 1999).

Conclusions

The selection of a suitable remediation process depends on the kind and concentration of pollutants, the soil type, the local availability of remediation processes, and economical aspects. Adequate treatment processes are available for all kinds of situations: biologically degradable pollutants should preferably be treated biologically. Soils contaminated with non-biodegradable organic pollutants can be treated by thermal processes. Heavy metals can be concentrated in the fine soil fraction by means of wet scrubbers (soil washing). Wet scrubbers can also be used on organically polluted soils as a concentration step; the fine fraction may subsequently be treated thermally or biologically (e.g., as a slurry) (Mann et al., 1995; Kleijntjens, 1999; Koning, 2002).

To treat soils under controlled conditions, ex situ treatment, in which the soil is excavated and treated in specialized plants, should be preferred. Of course, these processes are costly, since, in addition to the actual treatment costs, excavation, transport, and pre-treatment of the soil (sorting out bulky materials, homogeniza-tion, etc.) must be considered. Today the costs are very much influenced by strong competition and are often not real costs.

In situ treatment avoids excavation and is therefore less costly, but it is often less effective and less controllable due to ubiquitous soil inhomogeneities. Additionally, it has to be assured that during in situ remediation no secondary pollution takes place and uncontrolled movement of the pollutants into uncontaminated areas is prevented. Therefore, extensive monitoring and securing measures may be necessary. This is especially true when natural attenuation processes are taken into consideration (ITVA, 2003).

The excavation of significantly polluted soil and its disposal in landfills should be abolished. The possibilities for reuse of treated soils should be improved. It is essential that, as a first step in soil treatment, pre-investigations be performed to predict as far as possible the efficiency of the selected treatment process. This is especially true for biological soil treatment (Dechema, 1992; Hupe et al., 2001).

10

Bioremediation by the Heat Technique

INTRODUCTION

Although the potential of microorganisms to degrade contaminants like petroleum hydrocarbons has been known for more than 100 years, the technical application of this knowledge has a history of only about 15 years. During this time biological soil remediation has made strong development, marked by great efforts in research and development, manifold conceptual and technical innovations, as well as economical ups and downs.

Today biological treatment of contaminated soil is the most-used technology for large-scale soil remediation (Schmitz and Andel, 1997), with global proliferation and an expanding international market (Cookson, 1995). The heap technique has an especially high potential for widespread use, because this technology is easy to handle and needs only a low technical and monetary input.

A large number of investigations and case studies all over the world have shown the potentials and limits of soil remediation. Biological treatment of contaminated soil by the heap technique is considered to be the most effective and competitive technology for dealing with pollution by petroleum hydrocarbons (Schulz-Berendt, 1999).

Nevertheless, there is some need for further development, especially for technical solutions to enhance the height of soil heaps or to establish thermophilic conditions to use the high metabolic potential of extremophile microorganisms (Sorkoh et al., 1993; Feitkenhauer, 1998).

This chapter describes the principles of the heap technique and the different approaches and technological solutions. It also shows the advantages and limits of this technique and the research being done to overcome these problems. Additionally, it discusses some economical and legal considerations.

PRINCIPLES OF THE HEAP TECHNIQUE

The heap technique for biological soil treatment is an ex situ technology, that is, the contaminated soil is excavated and separated from the uncontaminated material. In contrast to so-called 'landfarming', where the contaminated material is spread over a large area in a comparably thin layer and mixed with the existing soil cover, in the heap technique the contaminated soil is prepared by homogenizing and mixing with additives and then piled up in heaps. Figure 10.1 shows the different steps of treatment, as implemented in the Terraferm system (Henke, 1989).

Before starting the treatment, samples of the excavated contaminated soil are tested for biological degradation of the pollutants by standardized laboratory procedures (Dechema, 1992). After a positive result is obtained in these tests, the first step in soil preparation is the separation of non-soil material like plastics, metals, etc., as well as stones having a particle size of more than 40–60 mm. Although non-soil material has to be disposed of or treated by other methods, the stones can be crushed and added back to the soil. Often the stones are not contaminated to the same extent as the fine particles, because the pollutants did not penetrate into them. If so, the separated stones can be reused directly. Therefore, separation is not only important for the degradation process but is also a way to reduce the volume of material that has to be treated.

The most important steps in pretreatment are homogenization of soil material and mixing with additives. Homogenization means that the normally inhomogeneous distribution of the pollutants is changed into an average concentration of contaminants in the total volume of soil. Statistical evaluation of 35 large-scale remediation projects using the heap technique (Krass et al., 1998) shows that the standard deviation of the hydrocarbon concentration is reduced significantly after homogen-ization and that the average level of concentration decreases to about 50% of that calculated for the original material. This second effect is due to overestimation by the analysis of the original material because samples are normally taken from more-contaminated parts of the soil.

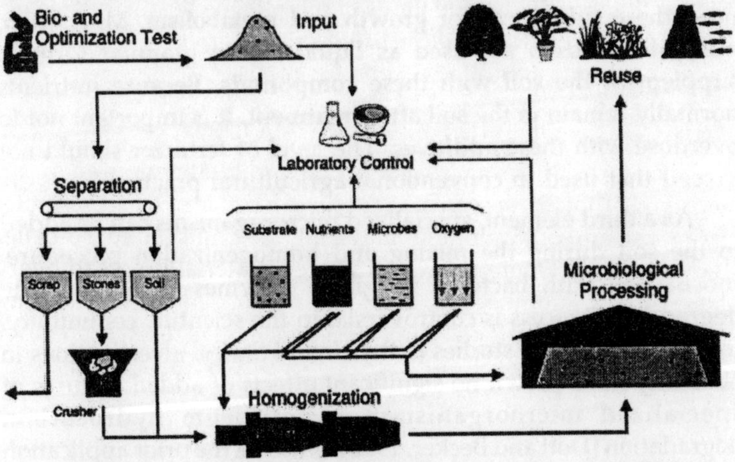

Fig. 10.1 Biological soil treatment by the Terraferm technology.

Determination of requirements for and addition of additives of suitable quality and quantity is another important step for successful soil treatment with the heap technique. As shown in Figure 10.1, additives can be divided into different categories. Here, 'substrate' indicates all additives that improve the physical and chemical soil structure. Depending on soil quality parameters like particle size, pH, organic matter, etc., and the results of laboratory testing, materials such as compost, bark, lime, tensides, etc. are added to create optimal environmental conditions for the degrading microflora. 'Substrate' can also be used to enhance the soil temperature by including a high amount of easily degradable organics, although with the risk of a high level of carbon sources that are competitive to the contaminant. Otherwise, the added carbon source can be used as cosubstrate for energy supply or an inducer for degrading enzymes; this use has been investigated for the degradation of chlorinated hydrocarbons like tetrachloroethylene and trichloroethylene (Ewers et al., 1990; Koziollek et al., 1999; Meyer et al., 1993).

The second class of additives are the nutrients for the degrading microflora. Because contaminated soil often comes from industrial sites and is often excavated from layers several meters deep, it usually has no significant content of nutrients like nitrogen, phosphorous, or potassium. Of course, degrading microorganisms need these substances for growth and metabolism. Most often, mineral fertilizers are used as liquids or in granular form to supplement the soil with these compounds. Because nutrients normally remain in the soil after treatment, it is important not to overdose with these additives. The level of fertilizer should not exceed that used in conventional agricultural practice.

As a third element, specialized microorganisms can be added to the soil during the mixing and homogenization procedure. Inoculation with bacteria, fungi, or enzymes to enhance the degradation process is controversial in the scientific community. In contrast to many studies in the United States, investigations in Germany have shown no significant effects of added cultures of specialized microorganisms on petroleum hydrocarbon degradation (Dott and Becker, 1995), which is the prior application of the heap technique. The potential of the autochthonous microflora is normally sufficient for effective degradation.

Good results have been obtained by adding complex mixtures of 'substrates', nutrients, and microorganisms, e.g., compost (Hupe et al., 1998) or activated sludge from wastewater treatment plants. The overall goal of the mixing and homogeniza-tion process is to obtain optimum conditions for aerobic metabolism of the contaminating substances.

For sufficient homogenization and mixing of contaminated soil, special machines and aggregates have been developed, which have to combine powerful homogeniza-tion and mixing units with controlled and sophisticated dosing of the various additives. Today, specialized equipment is available (Fig. 10.2) with capacities of 50 t h^{-1} or more and which have been adapted to different soil qualities from sand to clay. Crushing units can be integrated directly in this machinery.

After pretreatment, the soil is transferred to the degradation area and piled in heaps. According to the environmental regulations for treating hazardous wastes in Germany, the heaps must be located in a closed space. Depending on local climatic conditions, locating the process in a closed system is not only necessary for complying with environmental regulations but is also an important tool for controlling the degradation process, especially the water content and temperature.

The area must be prepared below the ground surface to prevent contaminated seepage water from penetrating into the subsoil. This can be done by compacting the soil or by installation of an area sealed with concrete or asphalt. Often, layers of 1.0–1.5-mm-thick high-density polyethylene (HDPE) are used to ensure safe and sustainable enclosure of the contaminated material.

To minimize emissions of volatile compounds to the air, the heaps are set up in structures such as tents or sheds or covered with plastic sheeting or membranes. With this measure it is also possible to protect the heaps from unsuitable weather conditions like rainfall or extreme temperature.

The design, construction, and material of the cover depend on the kind of heap technique that is used. In the past five years in Germany, soil treatment has changed from on-site to off-site installations. Therefore, the heap technique is used mainly in stationary treatment centers, which are permanent installations and normally equipped with a treatment shed or a similar building in which the heaps are set up.

During the process of degradation, the soil is monitored continually by analyzing samples from different parts of the heap. The main control parameters are:

- concentration of the contaminants
- water content
- concentration of available nutrients
- biological activity (soil respiration)

Depending on the monitoring results, the degradation conditions are optimized by aeration, addition of water or nutrients, and further homogenization. The treatment ends after reaching the target values, which are sufficient for reuse of the cleaned soil. The time of treatment differs greatly, depending on the kind and concentration of the contaminants, the target values that have to be reached, and the soil quality. The normal residence time is in the range of several months. For example, Krass et al. (1998) detected average halftimes of 85 d with a 95% confidence interval in a range from 75.4 to 94.6 d.

Fig. 10.2 Soil preparation unit type 'mole'.

After treatment by the heap technique, the soil quality is adequate for it to be used as topsoil for landscaping or as dumpsite cover. Because of the treatment procedure the soil is free of larger stones, very homogeneous, and enriched in nutrients and humic substances.

DIFFERENT HEAP TECHNIQUES

Besides the different technical solutions for below-surface preparation and heap cover, various treatment systems have been developed to establish and maintain suitable conditions for microbiological degradation of toxic compounds. Figure 10.3 shows several approaches concerning humidity, agitation, aeration, and temperature and their impact on the area needed for treatment.

The first technologies used for large-scale biological soil remediation were open-air heap installations with facilities for water recycling (Altmann et al., 1988). The moisture in the heaps is above the maximum water holding capacity (whc), and the seepage water is collected via a drainage system in a pond at one end of the heap (Fig. 10.4).

From the collecting pond, the water is pumped to the surface of the heap and spread over the heap. Nutrients and other soluble additives are mixed with the water, and the microorganisms are supplied with the added substances and oxygen via the water phase.

In contrast to these 'wet' systems, comparable 'dry' technologies have been developed and are mainly used today. The moisture in the dry heaps is below the maximum whc, so that water seepage is prevented and the soil pores are filled with water and air.

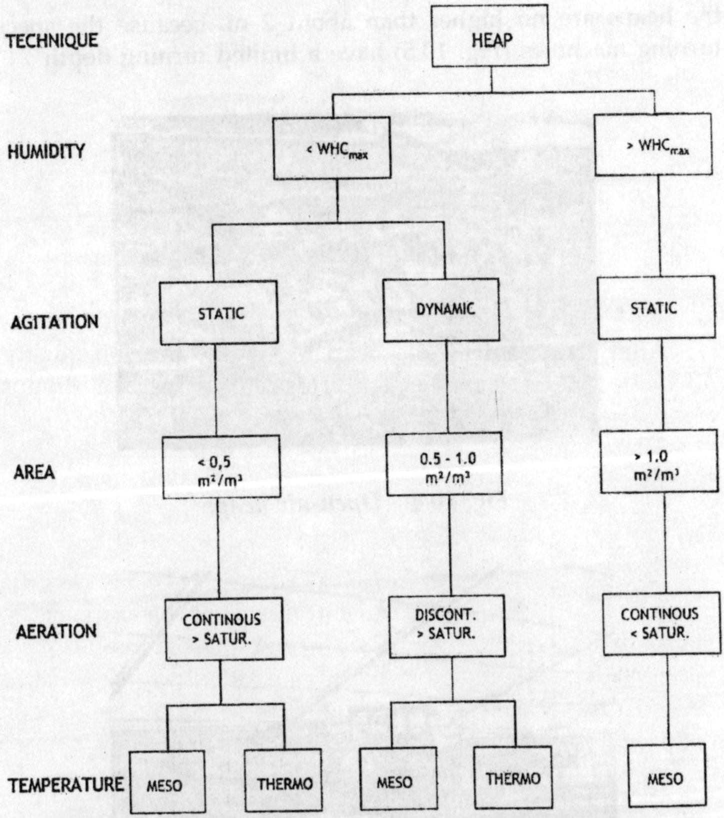

Fig. 10.3 Comparison of different heap techniques.

Systems with low water content can be operated with (dynamic) and without (static) agitation, but the wet systems are all static. By agitation, i.e., turning and mixing the soil at time intervals of days to weeks depending on the level of biological activity, the heap is aerated and the water or nutrient content can be readjusted.

With the static and dry systems, no additional supply of additives is possible, so all ingredients must be added during pretreatment. Therefore, special additives such as slow-release fertilizers must be used with these technologies. It is also necessary to install some kind of aeration system to supply the microorganisms with oxygen.

One advantage of the static and dry system is the height of heaps, which can be up to 3–5 m, whereas in dynamic systems the heaps are no higher than about 2 m, because the special turning machines (Fig. 10.5) have a limited turning depth.

Fig. 10.4 Open-air heap.

Fig. 10.5 Turning machine on the surface of a dynamic heap.

The 'wet' systems require the greatest area, because the limited capacity of water to transport oxygen leads to anaerobic layers if the height of the heaps is >0.5 m.

Supply with oxygen is the most critical factor in biological soil remediation by the heap technique. Because of the high oxygen consumption during aerobic degradation of hydrocarbons, an aeration system must be installed in all static heaps. The 'wet' technologies supply oxygen through the water phase. Therefore, the efficiency of oxygen transport to the different parts of the heap is limited by the concentration of dissolved oxygen and cannot exceed saturation. Investigations of changes in oxygen concentrations in different parts of the heaps show a rapid decrease during the first phase of degradation, with creation of anaerobic zones and methane production inside the heaps (Koning et al., 1999). Recent results of large-scale experiments show that high-pressure injection of air can solve this problem and may be an efficient alternative to dynamic treatment technologies.

If oxygen supply is sufficient, the temperature in the heaps increases by biological activity to a level of 30–35 °C. Especially in closed systems this temperature level can be maintained independent of outside conditions, so that optimum mesophilic conditions can be established by the heap technique. Research on extremophile microorganisms and their practical biotechnological application indicates a high potential of thermophilic bacteria for hydrocarbon degradation (Sorkoh et al., 1993). The establishment of thermophilic conditions in heaps is one approach to increasing degradation efficiency. Besides using the existing climatic conditions, in some regions of the world, such as Arabia, Africa, and South America, it is possible to increase the temperature by adding easily degradable organic matter. This leads to enhanced oxygen consumption, which must also be ensured by the technical design.

Today the dry and dynamic solution is the common technology for treating petroleum hydrocarbons by the heap technique. 'Wet' solutions have failed because of their long degradation times of (1–2 years) and the large demand for space. If the dry and static approach could overcome problems with limited oxygen supply, it may be the technology of the future because of the small area needed for the installation and the possibility of thermophilic process design, which together can enhance the efficiency of the heap technique.

Efficiency and Economy

As mentioned in Sections 10.1–10.3, the heap technique has been used in large-scale bioremediation for more than 10 years and is a standard technology for cleanup of soil contaminated with petroleum hydrocarbons. Depending on their origin, petroleum hydrocarbons can differ greatly. Successful bioremediation with the heap technology has been described for contamination with gasoline, light and heavy heating oil, and crude oil from different drilling areas. For successful bioremediation, not only the quality of the pollutant is important, but also its concentration and the target value that has to be reached. With the heap technique it is possible to achieve degradation rates of about 80%–90% in a reasonable time depending on the quality of the pollutant. This means that starting concentrations should not exceed 10000–20000 mg kg^{-1} to reach end concentrations of 1000–2000 mg kg^{-1}, which is sufficient for reuse on industrial sites. As mentioned in Section 10.2, the average concentration in the heap is significantly lower than that calculated from the average value from single soil samples; therefore, concentrations of up to 100000 mg kg^{-1} can be treated after homogenization.

In addition to petroleum hydrocarbons, the following classes of pollutants can be treated by the heap technique:

- BTEX aromatics
- phenols
- polycyclic aromatic hydrocarbons (PAH) having up to four aromatic rings
- explosives (TNT, RDX)

Each of the different compounds requires some modifications to the basic technique. Especially if volatile substances have to be treated, emissions must be controlled and waste air has to be treated. An example of how to manage this problem is shown in Figure 10.6 for the remediation of a soil contaminated with phenols and aromatics.

For efficient extraction of volatiles from the soil, extraction pipes are installed in the heap for soil air extraction. During setup of the heap and the turning procedure in the dynamic system, the air of the tent is exhausted and treated, instead of extracting the soil air. The treatment system consists of four biofilter units and two activated-carbon filters. In addition to the usual tent material, another plastic cover having a thin layer of aluminum is installed inside the tent as an effective barrier to the volatile compounds. This example demonstrates that the heap technique is very flexible and can be modified from a very simple installation to a high-performance technology.

Another modification has been used for the bioconversion of explosives, especially TNT and its derivates. For biological detoxification, TNT (trinitrotoluene) is converted to TAT (triaminotoluene) under anaerobic conditions (Lenke et al., 1997). Under aerobic conditions TAT is fixed to the soil matrix. To establish strictly anaerobic conditions in the heap, organic material is added to the soil to a high extent. During degradation of the organic material, all oxygen is consumed and the temperature reaches levels of about 60 °C. By turning the soil, aerobic conditions appear for a short time so that TAT is bound to the soil matrix and cannot be detected after treatment. With this technology, the treatment time can be reduced to less than four weeks to achieve target values (Fig. 10.7). The concentration of PAH is also reduced in the heaps. This example shows that the heap technology can be used for thermo-philic degradation processes and that, under thermophilic conditions, degradation times can be reduced significantly.

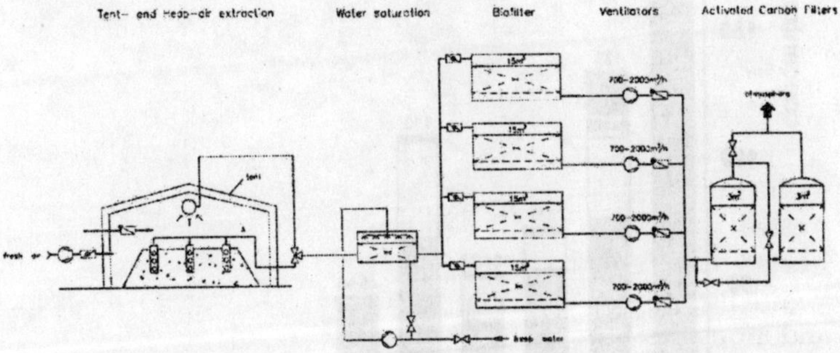

Fig. 10.6 Schematic representation of soil air extraction from heaps.

Efficiency has to be discussed in relation to the economics of the process. Because of the low investment costs for installation and the simple operation procedures, the heap technique is of course a low-cost technology compared with other biological technologies like bioreactors or soil washing and incineration. Therefore, about 80% of the soil treatment plants installed in Germany are biological treatment plants (Schmitz and Andel, 1997), most of them working with the heap technique. However, because of the high number of treatment plants in Germany, with an annual capacity of about 2500000 t the competition is extremely strong. During the last decade prices for soil remediation have decreased from nearly 100 US$ per ton to 30–50 US$ per ton. Even for the simple heap technique, this is the absolutely lowest limit for any reliable operation.

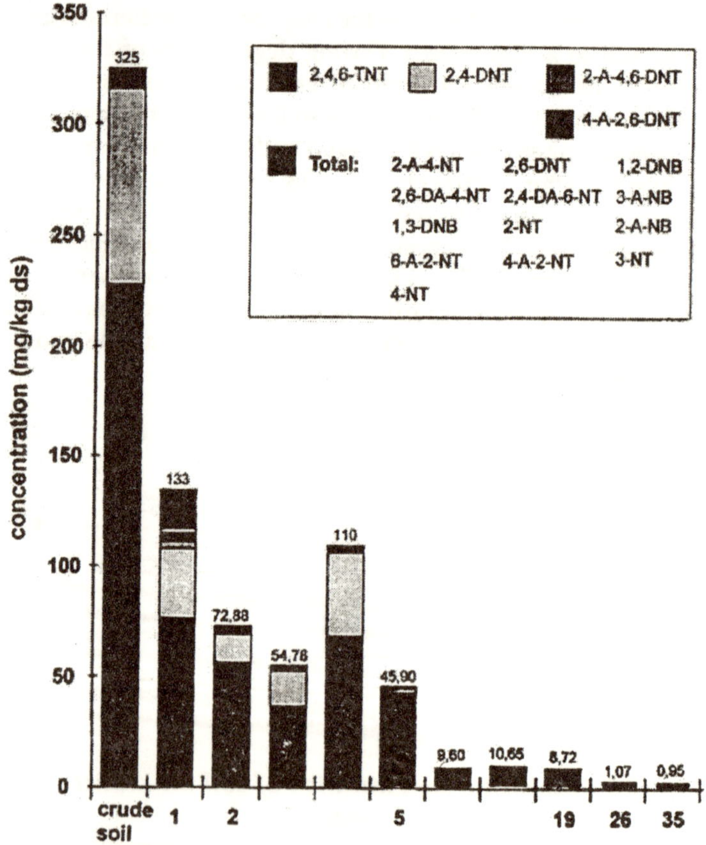

Fig. 10.7 Time course of TNT degradation.

On the other hand, legislative regulations regarding soil handling and plant operation have become stricter, so that nearly half the costs for soil bioremediation by the heap technique are due to measures set by the authorities. In contrast to this high level of environmental-safety and health-care concerns regarding treatment plants that destroy contaminants and lead to recycling of soil for different uses, dumping contaminated soil and leaving the problem for the next generation is still allowed.

Nevertheless, soil treatment by the heap technique is suitable for many different situations involving contaminants, soil quality, or climatic conditions. It is adjustable by technical modifications to meet any requirement of the degradation process. Therefore, although it was the first large-scale remediation technique, it still needs further development to become the biological treatment technology of the future.

11

Bioreactors

INTRODUCTION

Contaminated Solid Waste Streams (Soils, Sediments, and Sludges)

Waste recycling plays a key role in the development of a sustainable economy (Suzuki, 1992). The classical approach, remediation without the production of recycled materials, does not contribute to durable material flows. Moreover, the production of reusable materials is a necessity to make waste treatment an attractive economic solution. Recycling, however, cannot be done without regard to the effort and costs needed. The overall environmental benefits should be positive and fit within the local economic and legal framework.

A practical way to qualify these benefits is found in three issues:

- the quality of the recycled products
- the amount of energy required per ton
- the cost per ton

Solid waste streams (contaminated soils, sediments, and sludges) can be recycled. The solids have to be transformed into usable products while the contaminants are removed or destroyed. If the contaminants are organic (such as mineral oil, PAH, solvents, BTEX, PCB), the use of bioreactors can result in environmental benefits (Riser-Roberts, 1998). In bioreactors populations of soil organisms degrade the contaminants to yield carbon dioxide, water, and harmless byproducts (Schlegel, 1986). A prerequisite for the implementation of new technologies such as bioprocessing is the definition of the goals of recycling and treatment. In the Netherlands legal targets for recycled materials were set in the Dutch building materials law (Building Material Act, 1995). Depending on the content and the leaching of components, two different ways for using recycled materials in plants are defined:

- category 1 products, needing no further isolation
- category 2 products, needing further isolation and monitoring

In the Dutch practice, treatment processes are aimed at the production of category 1 recycled products. Although each country still has its own standards, and standardization is far away (Northcliff et al., 1998), it is clear that practical recycling standards accelerate the development needed to create sustainable technologies.

CHARACTERISTICS OF CONTAMINATED SOLIDS

In soils the solid matrix is frequently dominated by sand, while the water content may be <25%; various levels of debris can be found depending on the history of the site, but rarely exceed 10%.

River, harbor, and canal sediments contain mostly water (frequently >60% to 70%), while the fine fraction (<63 μm) dominates the solids if dredging takes place in the upper sediment layers.

Industrial and municipal sludges are mostly very moist (>95% water) and have a large content of organics (>60%) (INES, 1997). Industrial sludges mostly originate directly from corrosion and wear from equipment or water treatment units on the site.

Disregarding the heterogeneous nature of the waste, the contaminant behavior is largely determined by the fines (Werther and Wilichowski, 1990), because submi-cron particles such as humic-clay structures and clay agglomerates have an extremely high adsorption capacity (Brady, 1984). The solid waste, therefore, basically contains a contaminated fine fraction, a less contaminated sand-gravel fraction, cleaner debris, and a contaminated water phase.

In Figure 11.1 the line shows a typical particle size distribution for soils having a dominant fraction of fines (the step between 10 and 20 μm) and a dominant sand fraction (the step between 150 and 250 μm).

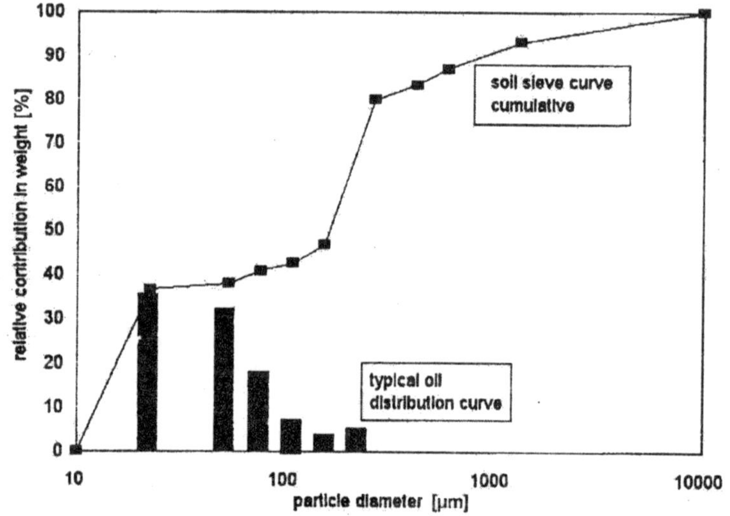

Fig. 11.1 Distribution of contaminants over the solids fractions (in percentage of the total amount of oil present) and particle size distribution (cumulative).

The bars show the measured mineral oil concentration as distributed over the fractions. For efficient processing of this waste, only the fractions <150–200 μm should be treated.

In general one can state that, to develop an appropriate recycling technology, the particle features of the solids have to match the type of process operation. For bio-processing this implies integration of the separation technology and bioreactors in a sequence of operation in which the clean fractions are removed from the feed before entering the reactor (Kleijntjens et al., 1999).

BIOREACTORS

Reactor Configurations

The aerated bioreactor for solids processing is a three-phase (solid–liquid–gas) multiphase system. The solid phase contains the adsorbed contaminants, the liquid phase (process water) provides the medium for microbial growth, and aeration complicates the system. Nutrients and adapted biomass may be added to enhance breakdown. Furthermore, processing conditions (temperature, pH, O_2 level, etc.) can be monitored and to some extent controlled. Regarding the bioreactor configuration there are two major topics:

- physical state of the multiphase system – bioreactors with a restricted solids holdup: slurry reactors (typical solids holdup <40 wt%) – bioreactor with restricted humidity: solid-state fermentation (solids content >50 wt%)
- operation mode – batch operation: no fresh material is introduced to the bioreactor during processing; the composition of the content changes continuously – continuous operation (plug flow): fresh material is introduced and treated material removed during processing, the composition in the reactor remains unchanged with time (Levenspiel, 1972); in practice, semicontinuous operation is often used (batch-wise feeding and removal giving small fluctuations in the reactor)

Three basic reactor configurations exist:

- slurry bioreactors
- solid-state fixed-bed bioreactors
- rotating-drum dry solid bioreactors
- Characteristic of all types of slurry bioreactors (Fig. 11.2) is the need for energy input to sustain a three-phase system in which the solid particles are suspended; the force of gravity acting on the solids has to be compensated for by the drag forces executed by the liquid motion (Hinze, 1959). In a properly designed slurry system, the energy input is used to establish three phenomena:
- suspension
- aeration
- mixing

A slurry bioreactor can work properly only if these three measures are balanced. For each reactor configuration, the appropriate processing conditions depend on parameters such as the reactor scale, particle size distribution, slurry density, slurry viscosity, oxygen demand of the biomass, and the solids holdup (Kleijntjens, 1991).

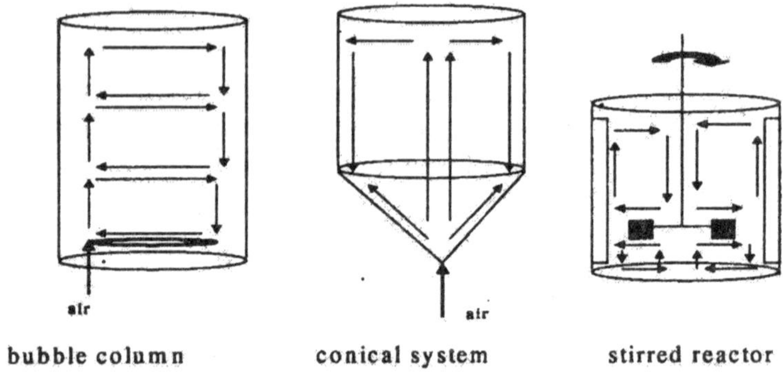

Fig. 11.2 Common configurations for slurry bioreactors.

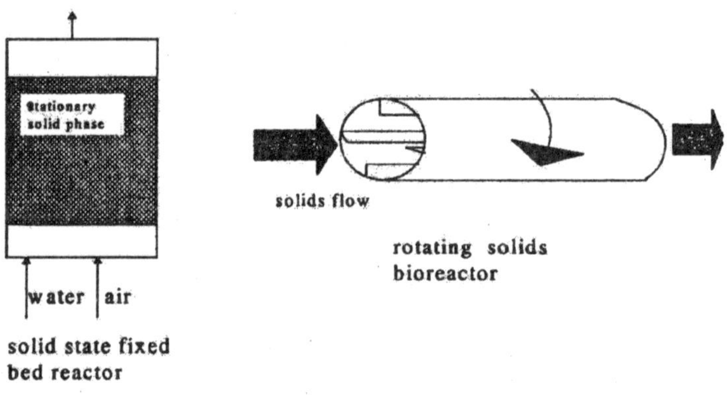

Fig. 11.3 Bioreactors for solid-state processing: (a) fixed-bed reactor, (b) rotating-drum reactor.

For solid-state fermentations there is no need to maintain a solids–liquid suspension; a compact, moist, solid phase determines the system. Both the fixed-bed reactor and the rotating-drum bioreactor are suited to solid-state fermentation (Fig. 11.3). In the fixed-bed reactor the contaminated solids rest on a drained bottom as a stationary phase. Forced aeration and the supply of water are mostly applied as a continuous phase (Riser-Roberts, 1998). Fixed-bed reactors are mostly batch operated. Although landfarming might be considered a form of solid-state batch treatment under fixed-bed conditions (Harmsen, 1991), this technique offers limited control options (in comparison to other solid-state treatment) and is therefore not considered to be a bioreactor within the present context.

Continuous solid-state processing is possible in the rotating system. Here, the solid phase (as a compact moist material) is 'screwed and pushed' through the reactor. In line with slurry processing, energy is required to transport the solids through the system.

DIFFUSION OF CONTAMINANTS OUT OF SOLID PARTICLES

Regardless of the bioreactor type, the presence of sufficient water is crucial. Not only is a water activity around 100% a necessity for microbial action (van Balen, 1991), but biodegradation fully depends on the availability of the components in the water phase. On the microlevel, diffusion of the adsorbed contaminants into the bulk phase is the rate-determining step (Fig. 11.4). Mathematical models focus on capturing of the different physical processes into single diffusion parameters (Wu and Geschwend, 1988). The overall diffusion process depends also on the flow conditions around the particles (Crank, 1975).

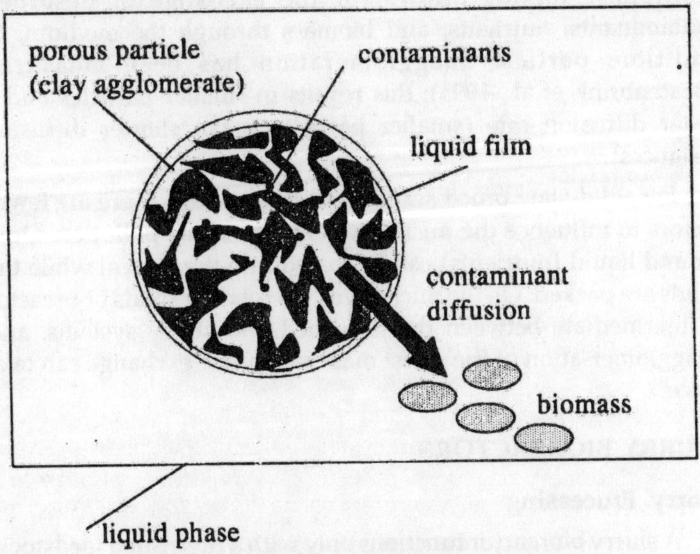

Fig. 11.4 Diffusion of contaminants.

An illustration of the importance of the flow around the particles was given by Koning et al. (1998), who analyzed microbial breakdown of a petroleum-contaminated soil. A conversion level of 80% was reached within about 10 d in a slurry reactor, but under fixed-bed conditions some 150 d were required to reach the same conversion level. They concluded that "the enhanced breakdown is based on an increasing bioavailability of the contaminant due to suspending of and the mechanical strain on the soil material in the slurry reactors". In another slurry experiment, it was shown that manipulation of reactor parameters such as the energy input result in faster breakdown (Reynaarts et al., 1990). The reactor type, scale, energy input, and aeration rate each have an impact on the diffusion. The better these parameters can be optimized, the faster the breakdown proceeds.

Having established proper diffusion conditions, the presence of adapted biomass capable of degrading the desorbed contaminants is essential. Organisms that are already present in the waste are almost always the most practical source of adapted bi-omass.

Of the three different bioreactors, the slurry system offers the best features to substantially influence the diffusion rate. Intense multiphase mixing allows for the exchange of desorbed contaminants, nutrients, and biomass through the medium. In addition, particle deagglomeration has been measured (Oostenbrink et al., 1995); this results in smaller particles and a faster diffusion rate (smaller particles mean shorter diffusion distances).

For solid-state processes in fixed-bed reactors there are fewer factors to influence the microenvironment of the pollution. Only air and liquid (nutrients) can be forced into the system while the solids are packed. On the microlevel, the rotating solids bi-oreactor is intermediate between the fixed-bed and slurry systems, and deagglomer-ation of the moist mass and phase exchange can take place.

SLURRY BIOREACTORS

Slurry Processing

A slurry bioreactor functions only with a pretreated feedstock; therefore, the bioreac-tor is necessarily integrated with washing–

separation operations and includes a de-watering operation at the end of the process (Kleijntjens, 1991; Robra et al., 1998).

A typical setup of an integrated (slurry) bioprocess is shown in Figure 11.5.

First, the feedstock is screened using a wet vibrating screen to remove the debris (typical size >2–6 mm).

Second, sand fractions are removed by one or more separation techniques such as sieves, hydrocyclones, Humphrey spirals, flotation cells, jigs, and up-flow columns; a typical separation diameter (the so-called cutpoint) for the hydrocy-clone depicted is 63 μm (Cullinane et al., 1990).

In the cyclone the slurry flow is split into a sand fraction (particle size >63 μm) at the bottom and a fine fraction at the top (<63 μm).

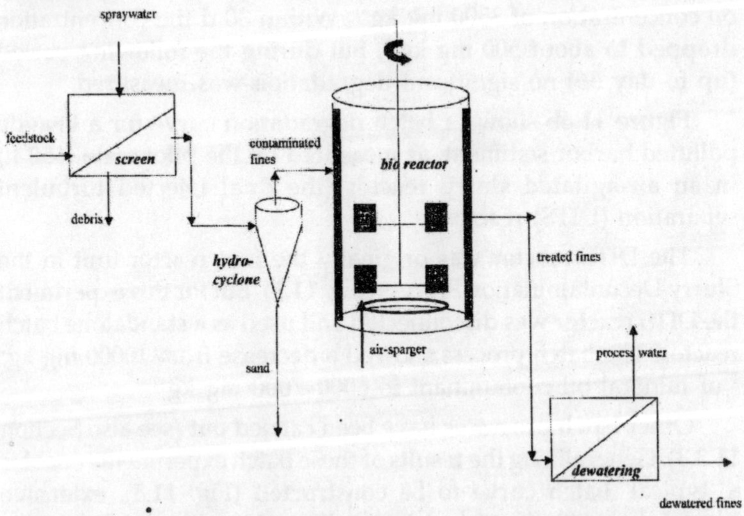

Fig. 11.5 Typical setup for a slurry bioprocess using a batch-operated aerated stirred-tank reactor (typical solids holdup is 20 wt%).

The top flow of the cyclone, containing the contaminated fines, is fed to the bio-reactor (a stirred tank is shown, but any of the three types in Figure 11.2 can be chosen). The final operation results in a dewatered product containing the fines and a flow of process water.

BATCH OPERATION

A slurry bioreactor is often designed as a standard continuously stirred tank reactor (CSTR) having a mechanical stirrer, baffles, and a sparger at the bottom (Fig. 11.5). In the system a three-phase suspension of contaminated solids, water, and air is maintained. Batch degradation experiments in aerated, stirred, slurry bioreactors have been carried out frequently.

Figure 11.6a shows the experimental results from a batch experiment on a 4-L scale. Using a conventional stirred bioreactor with baffles (stirrer speed 600 rpm, aeration rate 1.5–3 L min^{-1}, temperature kept at 30 °C), adapted biomass and nutrients were added (ammonium, phosphate, and potassium) while the pH was kept at 7–8.

The soil was an oil-contaminated sandy soil having an initial oil concentration of 3500 mg kg^{-1}. Within 30 d the concentration dropped to about 500 mg kg^{-1}, but during the following period (up to day 56) no significant degradation was measured.

Figure 11.6b shows a batch degradation curve for a heavily polluted harbor sediment, as measured on the pilot scale (650 L) in an air-agitated slurry reactor (the dual injected turbulent separation (DITS) reactor).

The DITS reactor was originally the first reactor unit in the Slurry Decontamination Process (Fig. 11.7). But for this experiment the DITS reactor was disconnected and used as a standalone batch reactor. The batch process showed a decrease from 10000 mg kg^{-1} of mineral oil contaminant to 6000–7000 mg kg^{-1}.

Other batch processes have been carried out (see also Section 11.3.3). Generalizing the results of these batch experiments enables a 'typical' batch curve to be constructed (Fig. 11.8): extensive breakdown in the first few days is followed by slower degradation during the second stage.

In this stage only a small percentage of the contaminant is degraded over a relatively long time period.

The exact shape of the curve and the conversion level at which breakdown stops vary with the composition and age of the solids and the type of contaminant.

To understand the typical batch curve, three major phenomena have to be considered:

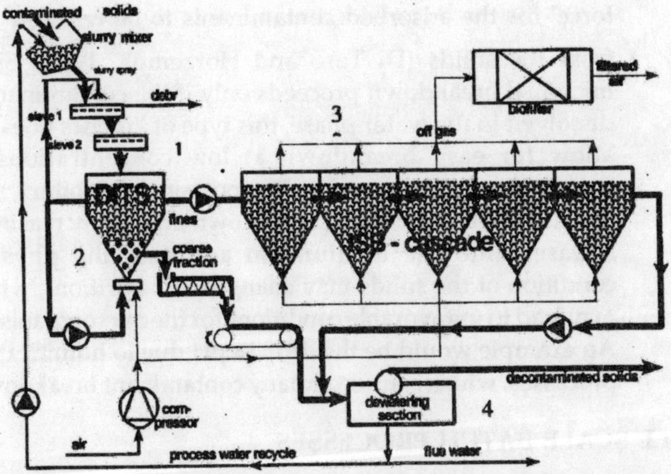

Fig. 11.7 Slurry decontamination process (SDP), including dual injected turbulent separation reactor (DITS) and a cascade of interconnected suspension bioreactors (ISB cascade).

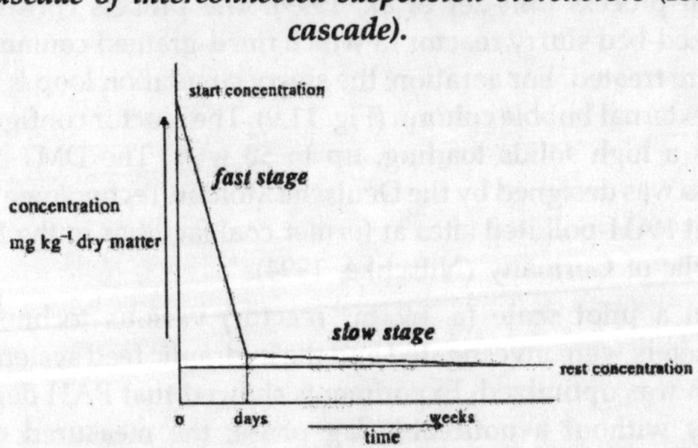

Fig. 11.8 Generalized curve for decontamination during batch operation.

- In batch processing the biomass, growing on a complex substrate, has to adapt continuously to different components, since the 'easy' parts are degraded first (Teschner and Wehner, 1985). This pattern inevitably leads to increasing difficulties for the resident microbial population. The adaptation rate of the population to the available contaminants is insufficient.

- The contaminant desorption kinetics are of such an order that at lower concentrations there is a limited 'driving force' for the adsorbed contaminants to be released
- from the solids (Di Toro and Horzempa, 1982). Since microbial breakdown proceeds only if the contaminant is dissolved in the water phase, this type of kinetics does not allow for easy breakdown at low concentrations of contaminant. • During batch processing. inhibitory side products of the microbial breakdown may be increasingly released into the medium; in addition, the physical condition of the solids may change (e.g., attrition), which may lead to unfavorable conditions for the microorganisms. An example would be the drop in pH due to humification processes, which can accompany contaminant breakdown.

FULL SCALE BATCH PROCESSES

The DMT–Biodyn Process

A full scale batch process has been implemented as the DMT–Biodyn process (Sin-der et al., 1999). The process consists of a fluidized-bed slurry reactor in which fined-grained contaminated soils are treated. For aeration, the slurry circulation loop is treated in an external bubble column (Fig. 11.9). The reactor configuration allows a high solids loading, up to 50 wt%. The DMT–Biodyn process was designed by the Deutsche Montan Technologie GmbH to treat PAH-polluted sites at former coal facilities in the Federal Republic of Germany (Nitschke, 1994).

On a pilot scale (a 1.2 m^3 reactor) various technological parameters were investigated and the hydraulic feed system at the bottom was optimized. Experiments showed that PAH degraded rapidly without a noticeable lag phase; the measured oxygen consumption rate correlated with the PAH degradation rate. For this specific soil (starting concentration of PAH about 250 mg kg^{-1}), the target levels were reached after 6 d. Comparison of the pilot results with results on a laboratory scale using a respirometer showed that the degradation of this test soil in each of these systems was similar. With a higher level of PAH contamination (starting at 1100 mg kg^{-1}), the target levels could not be reached (treatment time, 30 d). The researchers concluded that, for this specific soil, "adsorption of the PAH to the organic matrix results in a reduced bioavailability". Later experiments on this contaminated soil, in which bioprocessing and soil washing was combined, resulted in final contaminant levels below target values.

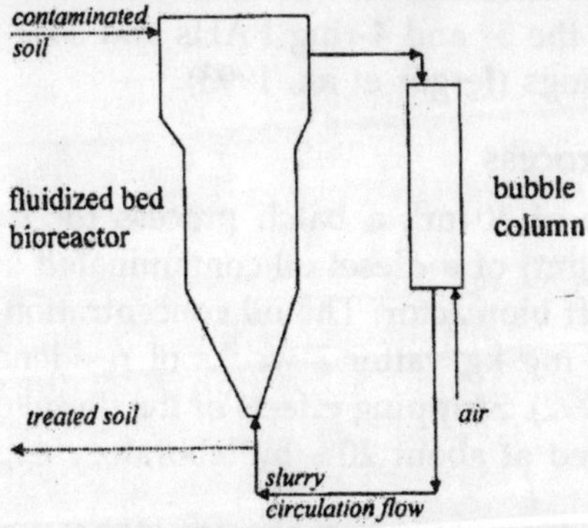

Fig. 11.9 DMT–Biodyn process configuration.

In Sweden a full scale (55 m^3) DMT–Biodyn processor was installed to treat a contaminated gas plant area. The first trials on this scale have been successfully completed (Sinder et al., 1999).

The FORTEC Process

In the Netherlands the FORTEC process (fast organic removal technology) for treating contaminated sediments combines several separation technologies with bioreac-tor treatment (ten Brummelen et al., 1997). The first step in the process is the use of hydrocyclones to remove the sand fractions. The efficiency of the separation step is optimized by a multistage hydrocyclone configuration, and separation down to a particle size of 20 μm is achieved. After the sand separation, the contaminated fine fraction is fed to the bioreactor section. Based on initial experiments with aerated stirred-tank bioreactors, a full scale bioreactor section with a total volume of 300 m^3 (several reactors) was constructed (RIZA, 1997). A heavily contaminated harbor sediment (port of Amsterdam) was treated with the FORTEC process. After sand removal, the fine fraction (<20 μm) was treated batchwise in full scale bioreactors. On this scale 85% of the PAH and 78% of the mineral oil were removed after 15 d of batch processing (ten Brummelen et al., 1997).

The OMH Process

In the United States a large scale slurry bioreactor (750 m^3) was used to treat creosote-contaminated lagoon solids stabilized with fly ash (total PAH was 11 g kg^{-1}). An extensive pretreatment to classify the material was combined with an aerated and stirred (900 rpm) bioreactor (20% solids load). Remediation with respect to the PAH contaminants was determined to be 82%–99% conversion for the 3- and 4-ring PAHs and 34%–78% for PAHs having more rings (Jerger et al., 1993).

The Huber Process

On a scale of 30 m^3, a batch process for treating the fine fraction (<200 μm) of a diesel oil-contaminated soil was carried out in an air-lift bioreactor. The oil concentration dropped from 12 000 to 2000 mg kg^{-1} after 2 weeks of residence time (Blank-Huber et al., 1992). Stripping effects of the diesel oil contaminant were determined at about 20% by laboratory experiments.

SEQUENTIAL BATCH OPERATION (SEMICONTINUOUS)

To overcome some of the limitations of batch processing, continuous operation in a plug-flow system is considered.

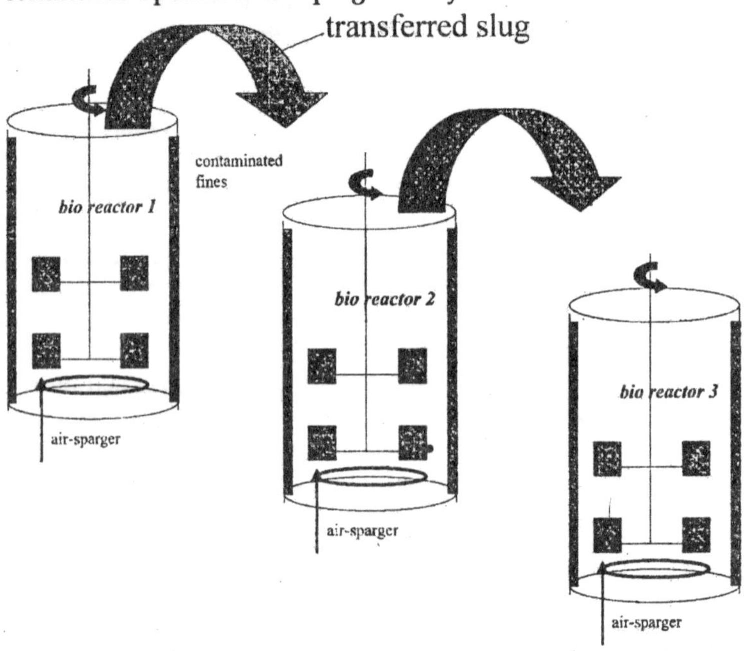

Fig. 11.10 Cascade of three batch reactors in sequence.

As the contaminated solids travel through the system, specific conditions in the successive reactors develop. A practical way of achieving a plug flow system is to use a sequence of batch reactors (Fig. 11.10). In an experimental cascade of three stirred-batch slurry reactors, the contaminated solids (oil contamination) are periodically transferred to the next step (only part of the reactor slurry content is transferred, the so-called 'slug') (Apitz et al., 1994).

Figure 11.11 shows the breakdown pattern in the transferred slug during its residence in each individual reactor. The authors explained "that each successive stage of the cascade maintains a microbial consortium that is optimized to consume organic compounds of increasing complexity. When compared to the batch process the biocascade was shown to be more effective, both in terms of the rate and degree of degradation" (Apitz et al., 1994).

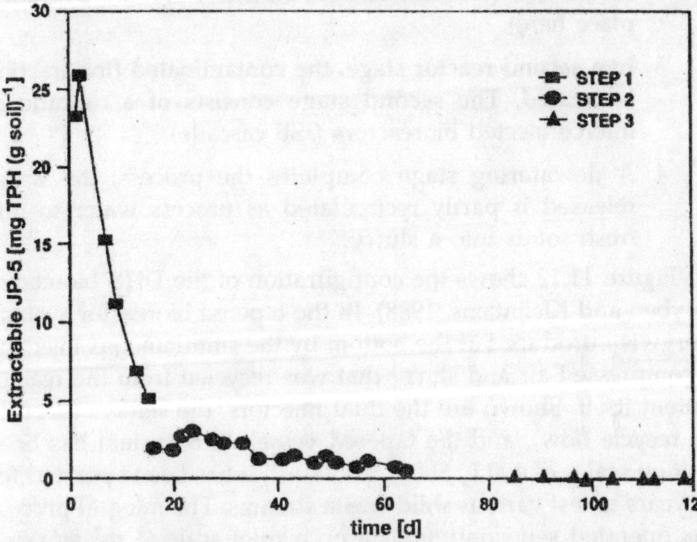

Fig. 11.11 Level of contamination in one slug of material traveling through the sequenced batch process (three-step biocascade). Successive steps reflect the degradation of more recalcitrant components (Apistz et al., 1994; with permission).

Continuous Operation

In the Netherlands a continuous plug-flow system has been achieved with the Slurry Decontamination Process (SDP) (Fig.

11.7). This process contains four major unit operations (Kleijntjens, 1991).

1. The contaminated solids are mixed with (process) water to form a slurry and are sized by passage over a vibrating screen. In this wet sieving step, debris is removed and a slurry having the proper density (about 30 w/w%) is prepared.
2. In the first reactor/separator (a tapered air-lifted bioreactor: the DITS reactor), the sand fractions are removed by means of a fluidized bed. Extensive organic material is removed by fine screening of the light material. In addition, agglomerates of contaminated fines are demolished owing to the power input and are thereby opened to biological breakdown (inoculation with the active biomass also takes place here).
3. In a second reactor stage, the contaminated fine fraction is treated. The second stage consists of a cascade of interconnected bioreactors (ISB cascade).
4. A dewatering stage completes the process; the water released is partly recirculated as process water to mix fresh solids into a slurry.

Figure 11.12 shows the configuration of the DITS bioreactor (Luyben and Kleijntjens, 1988). In the tapered bioreactor system, energy is introduced at the bottom by the simultaneous injection of compressed air and slurry that was recycled from the reactor content itself. Shown are the dual injectors, the settlers (used in the recycle flow), and the tapered vessel. This system has been built on scales of 400 L, 800 L, and 4 m^3. It has been operated for 2.5 years to test various solid waste streams. The integral process was operated semicontinuously on a pilot scale (3 m^3 working reactor volume).

Figure 11.13 shows the experimental results for a heavily polluted harbor sediment during a steady-state period of six weeks. Nutrients (nitrogen, phosphorous, and potassium) were added and the temperature was kept at 30 °C. The steady-state PAH concentration in the solids is shown as a function of time. The upper symbols show the feed concentrations in the slurry mill, which have an average of about 350 mg kg^{-1} (the input data are scattered because of the heterogeneous feedstock). In the DITS reactor the steady-state concentration dropped to around 100 mg kg^{-1} (first part of the microbial breakdown).

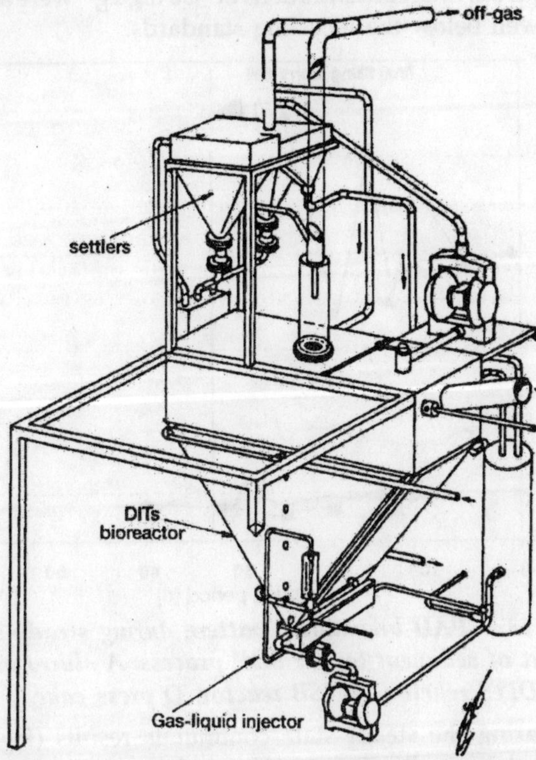

Fig. 11.12 Technical schema of the DITS bioreactor.

In the ISB cascade the average concentration dropped to 30–40 mg kg^{-1}. After de-watering, the final concentration increased somewhat in the filter cake. The overall PAH degradation level was about 92% for an overall residence time of 16 d. No significant evaporation was measured in the off-gas. In this sediment, the degradation of mineral oil showed a similar pattern (Fig. 11.14); however, an overall degradation level of only 65% was achieved. Final concentrations after dewatering were around 3000 mg kg^{-1}. In this sediment, mineral oil seems to be less available for microbial breakdown than the PAH. Recycling standards for PAH could be achieved, but levels of oil contamination remained too high.

A contaminated soil treated by the slurry process showed a steady-state breakdown pattern (Fig. 11.15).

Starting at moderate contamination levels of 1200–1300 mg kg^{-1} mineral oil, final concentrations of <50 mg kg^{-1} were achieved, which is well below the recycling standards.

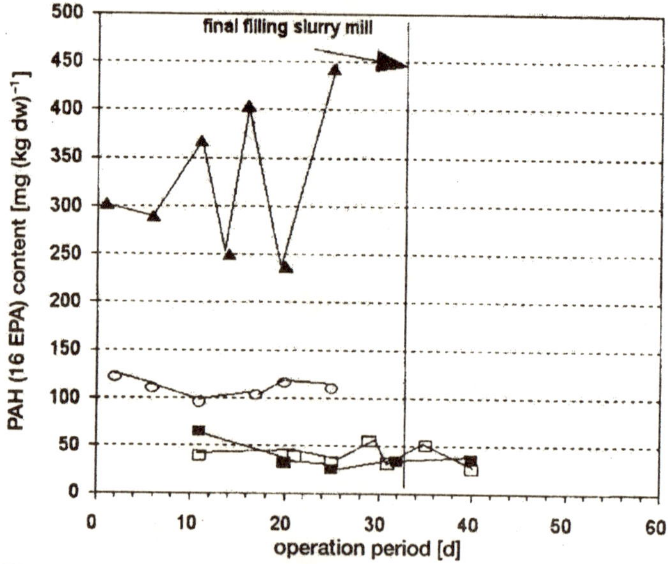

Fig. 11.13 PAH breakdown pattern during steady-state treatment of sediment by the SDP process: A slurry mill, O DITS reactor, % ISB reactor, Q press cake.

Comparing the steady-state continuous results (Fig. 11.14) with the batch results (Fig. 11.6b) for the same sediment and contaminant, we can clearly see that the continuous mode results in much better conversion (final concentration in continuous mode is ±3000 mg kg^{-1} vs. 7000 mg kg^{-1} in batch mode).

This improvement due to continuity is in accordance with observations on cascade breakdown (Apitz et al., 1994). However, despite the improvement shown in Figure 11.14, the Dutch recycling standard (mineral oil = 500 mg kg^{-1}) for this specific sediment was not met.

For a less contaminated solid waste (Fig. 11.15), the recycling standard was met without difficulty: a mineral oil starting concentration of 900 mg kg^{-1} was decreased to an output concentration <50 mg kg^{-1}. If this oil conversion is compared with the results in Figure 11.14 (8000 mg kg^{-1} of mineral oil input was decreased to 3000 mg kg^{-1} output), we can see that, at higher concentrations, limited bioavailabil-ity seriously hinders microbial breakdown.

As a consequence, it is often difficult to achieve complete conversion and achieve low end concentrations when starting with high input concentrations.

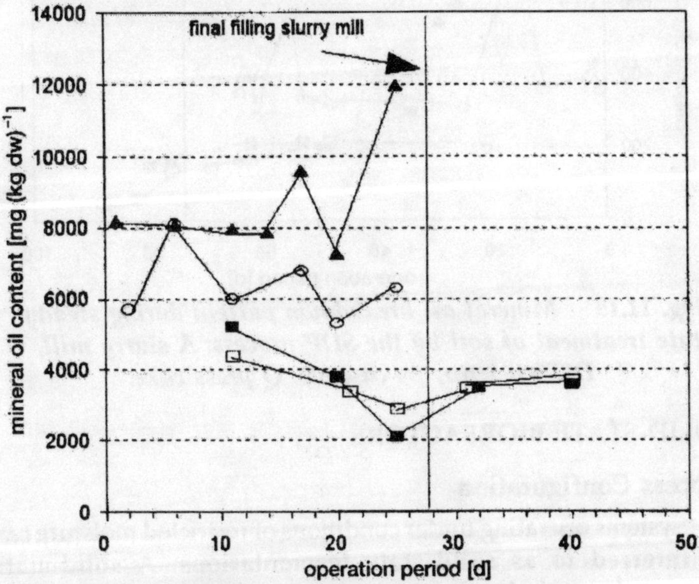

Fig. 11.14 Mineral oil breakdown pattern during steady-state treatment of sediment by the SDP process: A slurry mill, O DITS reactor, % ISB reactor, Q press cake.

We should note that analytical difficulties (especially for oil) in the handling of wet samples can easily lead to incorrect data. For example, in addition to a standard deviation of 20% within one laboratory, sample-exchange assays between various laboratories led to results that had a variation of more than 75% (Warbout and Oubot-er, 1988).

Bearing in mind these variations, analytical results should be regarded with care. This holds even more when samples of processed solids are compared to recycling standards.

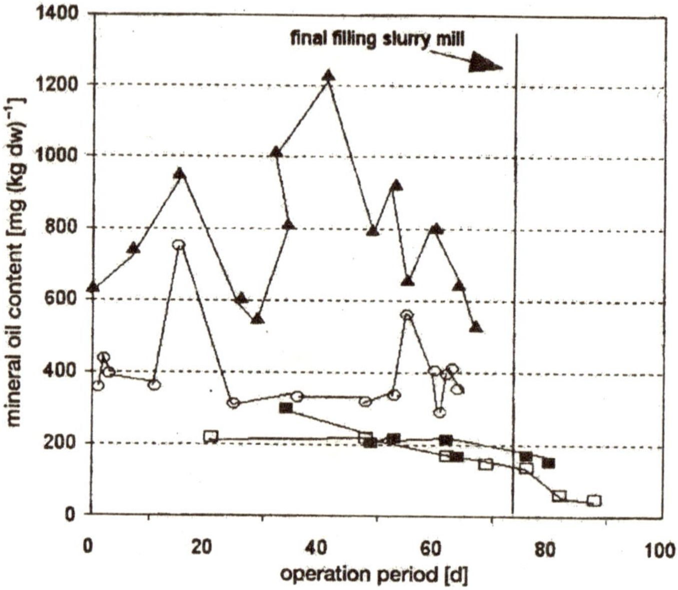

Fig. 11.15 Mineral oil breakdown pattern during steady-state treatment of soil by the SDP process: A slurry mill, O DITS reactor, % cascade, Q press cake.

SOLID-STATE BIOREACTORS

Process Configuration

Systems operating under conditions of restricted moisture can be referred to as solid-state fermentations. A solid-state fermentation includes the growth of microorganisms, both fungi and bacteria, on a moist solid. In contrast to the slurry systems, solid-state systems operate with:

- limited pretreatment
- restricted energy input (no intense multiphase mixing)
- a limited amount of unit operations (the solids remain as a 'solid phase')

In a solid-state fermenter, process conditions are maintained by controlling the temperature, humidity, and aeration. In contrast to slurry systems, a compact, moist, solid phase dominates the reactor physics. Because handling the moist mass is tedious, solid-state fermentation typically takes place as a batch operation.

Continuous operation depends on the possibility of practical and smooth loading and unloading procedures.

Batch Operation: Composting

In line with its traditional role as a soil fertilizer, compost has been used as an additive in soil remediation. Composting mostly takes place in fixed-bed reactors (Fig. 11.3a). Basically, the compost is added to stimulate microbial breakdown. In experiments, soil contaminated with hydrocarbons has been mixed with compost in various ratios (soil–compost ratios of 2:1, 3:1, and 4:1). In 3-L test batch reactors, the hydrocarbon degradation was >90% after a period of 44 d. Compared with the results in the absence of added compost, soil–compost systems had a much faster degradation rate and a lower end concentration (Lotter et al., 1990). In addition to composting, experiments focusing on the use of white-rot fungi have also been carried out (Schaeffer et al., 1995).

Another example of composting contaminated soil (in a column) was presented by Gorostiza et al. (1998). In a soil column the degradation of pentachlorophenol with and without added compost was tested; compost addition significantly enhanced the degradation rate (residence time about 60 d).

On a larger scale (in Finland), composting systems have been implemented by mixing contaminated soil with spruce bark chips as a bulking agent, lime, and nutrients beforehand. The bed is constructed as a biopile and can be turned by a tractor-drawn screw mixer. Degradation temperature rose during composting to as high as 44 °C. During five months the mineral oil concentration dropped from 2400 to 700 mg kg^{-1} (Puustinen et al., 1995).

In another experiment, four biopiles of 10 m^3 each were created to treat chloro-phenol-contaminated soil. Chalk, commercial fertilizer (NPK), and bark chips (as a bulk aeration agent) were added. After two months 80% of the contaminant was removed (Laine and Jorgensen, 1995).

Comparison of Bioreactors

Experiments show that during batch processing, the microbial breakdown slows down at low concentrations and full conversion is not reached. Continuous processing significantly improves the results.

The economic feasibility of bioprocessing depends largely on the nature of the waste streams to be treated. Basically, waste streams having a large water content and a considerable fine fraction (which is predominantly contaminated with organic components) are suitable for bioprocessing.

From the economic point of view, continuous slurry processing in an off-site installation can be beneficial only on a large scale. Capacities >40000–60000 t a^{-1} (depending on the local conditions) are needed to benefit from the economy of scale and thus to perform at acceptable cost levels. For batch-operated composting processes, smaller volumes, handled close to or on the site, may offer solutions if sufficient area is available and time is not limited. Rotating-drum systems in which solid-state processing is achieved are considered to perform well for smaller volumes (up to 3000 t) in a mobile plant used on-site.

Bibliography

Ausubel, F.M.: *Current Protocols in Molecular Biology,* New York, John Wiley and Sons, 1989.

Barnum, Susan R.: *Biotechnology: An Introduction,* Belmont, Thomson/Brooks/Cole, 2005.

Brandwein, P.F.: *Sourcebook for the Biological Sciences,* San Diego, Harcourt Brace JOvanovich, 1986.

Chrispeels, Maarten : *Plants, Genes and Crop Biotechnology,* Sudbury MA, Jones and Barlett Publishers, 2003.

Cox, Earl D. : *Beyond Humanity: Cyber Evolution and Future Minds,* Roackland, Charles River Media, 1996.

Fransman M, Junne G, Roobeek A: *The Biotechnology Revolution?,* Oxford, Blackwell, 1995.

Fumento, Michael: *Bioevolution: How Biotechnology is Changing Our World,* San Francisco, Encounter Books, 2003.

Goodman, D.C.: *From Farming to Biotechnology: A Theory of Agro-industrial Development,* Oxford, Blackwell, 1987.

Morholt, E. : *Sourcebook for the Biological Sciences,* San Diego, Harcourt Brace JOvanovich, 1986.

Retzer, W.J.: *Biotechnology Workbook,* Englewood Cliffs, Prentice Hall, 1991.

Shetty, Kalidas: *Food Biotechnology,* New York, Dekker/CRC Press, 2005.

Towle, Albert: *Modern Biology,* Austin, Holt, Rinehart and Winston, 1988.

Walden, Richard: *Genetic Transformation in Plants,* England, Open University Press, 1988.

Winston, Mark L.: *Travels in the Genetically Modified Zone,* Cambridge, Harvard University, 2004.

Index

□□□